L. Baikal
TRANS-SIBERIAN R.R.
R
Hulun
Lungkiang
MANCHURIA
Harbin
REP.
CHAHAR
MONGOLIA
SUIYUAN
Changchun
Vladivostok
Mukden
SEA OF JAPAN
Kweihsui
Kalgan
Peiping
Peitaiho
Tientsin
Darien
Pt. Arthur
Tengchow
KOREA
38°
Seoul
HOPEH
Taiyuan
GREAT WALL
SHANSI
Yellow
Chefoo
Weihsien
Tsinan
Tsingtao
Yenan
SHANTUNG
YELLOW SEA
Hiroshima
Kaifeng
Hsuchow
Yencheng
Sian
HONAN
KIANGSU
Nagasaki
JAPAN
Nanking
HUPEH
Soochow
Woosung
Shanghai
Hankow
ANHWEI
Yangtze
Hangchow
Ningpo
EAST CHINA SEA
CHEKIANG
Changsha
Nanchang
Wenchow
HUNAN
KIANGSI
FUKIEN
N
Foochow
Taipeh
KWANGSI
KWANGTUNG
Canton
FORMOSA
Nanning
Hong Kong
Pacific Ocean
CHINA SEA
HAINAN
PHILIPPINE ISLANDS

Fifty Years in China

Fifty Years in China

THE MEMOIRS OF

John Leighton Stuart

MISSIONARY AND AMBASSADOR

RANDOM HOUSE · NEW YORK

Ambassador Stuart visiting Ming Ling,
the Imperial Tomb of Ming Dynasty, 1946.

Lovingly dedicated to the memory of
My Father, John Linton Stuart,
My Mother, Mary Horton Stuart, and
My Wife, Aline Rodd Stuart

Contents

Illustrations

A Prefatory Note
on John Leighton Stuart

It is a great pleasure for me and a compliment to be permitted to introduce Dr. John Leighton Stuart.

I met Dr. Stuart for the first time at Nanking, China, in the late Spring, as I recall, of 1946. He was returning from a lengthy visit to the United States, recuperating from his years of imprisonment by the Japanese.

We talked over the current situation, and I was so impressed by his reactions that, later on, I proposed to the Department of State that he be appointed Ambassador to China—I was only an Ambassadorial Representative of the President. I took this action because of Dr. Stuart's fifty-odd years' experience in China, and his character, his personality and his temperament. With Dr. Stuart beside me, I had more than fifty years of vast experience unprejudiced by personal involvements in Chinese partisanship. On his appointment, I found his advice and leading assistance of invaluable help to me.

I doubt if there is anyone whose understanding of Chinese character, history, and political complications equals that of Dr. Stuart. His high standard of integrity made his opinions all the more important.

It is the man, the character and the general range of his experience which appealed to me.

GEORGE CATLETT MARSHALL

Introduction

John Leighton Stuart, who was born and brought up in Hang-chow, China, where both his father and mother were leading missionaries, tells us that in his boyhood he always had "an aversion for missionary life." Even after his graduation from Hampden-Sydney College, he still confessed his "lack of enthusiasm for missionary service."

It is difficult to exaggerate the aversion I had developed against going to China as a missionary, . . . haranguing crowds of idle, curious people in street chapels or temple fairs, selling tracts for almost nothing, being regarded with amused or angry contempt by the native population, physical discomforts or hardships, etc., no chance for intellectual or studious interests, a sort of living death or modern equivalent for retirement from the world.

But, after prolonged inner struggle, Dr. Stuart finally decided "to put my religious belief to what was for me then the ultimate test." He became a missionary to China and, as such, lived and worked in China for nearly half a century!

It was his good fortune that he did not have to remain an evangelistic missionary for more than two years. He was called to teach in the newly founded Theological Seminary at Nanking where he soon distinguished himself as a teacher of the New Testament and of New Testament Greek. After eleven years in Nanking, he was invited to Peking to undertake the great work of organizing a group of "little missionary colleges"—the Huei Wen University, the North China Union College, and later the North China Union Women's College—into a great union university.

Thus for nearly forty years he worked as a successful "educational missionary." And he confesses to us: "Whether or not I could have spent my life happily and successfully as a typical evangelistic missionary is a question about which I have more than once whimsically speculated."

In these memoirs he pays a hearty tribute to "the earnestness, high purpose, untiring efforts and unselfish devotion . . . of missionaries as a class." But, as a Chinese reader, I do hope that Dr. Stuart's frank records of his early impressions of the evangelistic missionary, of his long years of strong aversion against such life and work, of his mature judgment of the crude methods of the evangelistic missions in seeking, however unconsciously, numerical increase of converts and church membership—these records, I do hope, will not be lightly ignored by future leaders of Christian churches and mission boards when they have occasion to rethink the question of foreign missions.

Historically, the influence of the educational missionary— whether he be an astronomer or mathematician from the Society of Jesus in the sixteenth or seventeenth century, or a learned scientist, scholar or physician from a Protestant Mission in the nineteenth century—has always been greater and more lasting and far-reaching than that of the evangelistic missionary of whatever church or denomination. It was said of Robert Morrison, the first Protestant missionary in China, that after twenty-seven years in the East he had baptized only ten Chinese converts. But what a lasting influence Morrison's scholarly work—his Chinese translation of the Bible, his Chinese dictionary, and his first Chinese printing press with modern metal movable type—left on the entire Protestant missionary world in the East! Indeed, Robert Morrison inaugurated in China that one great century of illustrious Protestant missionary educators—the century of Alexander Wylie, Joseph Edkins, Alexander Williamson, S. Wells Williams, Young J. Allen, Calvin W. Mateer, W. A. P. Martin, John Fryer, Timothy Richard and a host of others equally deserving to be remembered. It was that galaxy of scholarly missionaries who, overcoming tremendous difficulties of language and culture, translated into Chinese the best works of contemporary Western science, technology, law and international law, and the geography and history of the modern world, as well as the religious literature of the Christian faith; and who, by preaching against such native customs as foot-binding and neglect of women's education, by advocating social, educational, and even political reforms, and by founding new schools and colleges, did so much in bringing about a gradual awakening in China.

Dr. Stuart will undoubtedly be remembered as one of the great representatives of that historic line of educational missionaries in China.

He came back to China in 1904, six years after the Reform Movement of 1898 and eight years before the founding of the Chinese Republic. China was at long last being aroused from her medieval slumbers. When he was called to Peking in 1919, it was already the eve of the Chinese intellectual renaissance and nationalistic revolution. The National Peking University was becoming, in the words of Dr. Stuart, "the intellectual dynamo of the nation." The Tsing Hua College, next-door neighbor to the future Yenching University, was soon to develop into one of the best and most influential national universities. The Peking Union Medical College was already being planned by the Rockefeller Foundation and was soon to rise up in that ancient capital as the most modern and best-equipped medical school and hospital in the entire Orient.

It was, therefore, not easy for the Christian missionary groups relying solely on the limited financial support of their home boards to hope to build up a real university at that late date and in Peking, the intellectual center of the nation.

Dr. Stuart's great achievement as the founder and builder of Yenching University must be judged against that background. "Dreams cost money," as he tells us. And his vivid descriptions of the successes and failures of the fund-raising campaign which he and Dr. Henry Winters Luce carried on for many years throughout the United States not only are valuable records but also often make the most interesting and most thrilling reading in this autobiography.

At last Yenching University became a dream that came true. As a friend and neighbor of Yenching who watched its growth with keen interest, I would like to say that Dr. Stuart's great success as a university builder lay chiefly in two directions. First, he and his colleagues planned and built up, literally *from scratch,* a full-sized university—the greatest of all the thirteen Christian colleges in China—with one of the most beautiful university campuses in the world. And, secondly, this university of his dreams became in the course of time more and more a Chinese university, which, with the help of the Harvard-Yenching Institute of Chinese Studies, was the first of all the Protestant missionary colleges to develop an excellent department of Chinese studies.

"Among many other advantages to Yenching," says Dr. Stuart, "the Harvard-Yenching Institute of Chinese Studies has enabled us—and through us several other Christian colleges in China— to develop Chinese studies fully up to the best standards of any purely Chinese institution."

I would like to pay a tribute to the Chinese scholars of Yenching, notably to Dr. William Hung (Hung Yeh), who deserves special credit for building up a very good Chinese library at Yenching, for editing and publishing the excellent *Yenching Journal of Chinese Studies* and that most useful series—the *Harvard-Yenching Sinological Index Series.*

Dr. Stuart's seventieth birthday was celebrated on June 24, 1946. Ten days later, he was urged by General George C. Marshall, Special Representative of President Truman in China, to serve as the American Ambassador to the Republic of China and to assist him in the work of the Marshall Mission. On July 10, President Truman sent his name to the United States Senate where it was unanimously approved. Dr. Stuart's ambassadorship lasted six and a half years (July, 1946—December, 1952). In August, 1949, three months after the fall of Nanking to the Communists, he returned to the United States. In December, he had a severe stroke, and on December 11, 1952, President Truman accepted his resignation.

Dr. Stuart's memoirs of these years occupy nearly one half of the book and fall into two main parts: part one (Chapters 9-12) records the political and military events of the years 1946-49 and his own impressions and comments about those events; part two (Chapters 13-15) contains the thoughts and reflections on the Department of State's "White Paper" on *United States Relations with China,* on the tragedy of the loss of the Chinese mainland to World Communism, on his own life and life ideals, and finally on "what policy the United States should pursue in regard to China."

I must confess that I have found the chapters of part one (Chapters 9-12) rather oversimplified and often difficult to follow as a summary report of the enormously complex events from the early months of General Marshall's Mission to China down to the fall of the Nanking-Shanghai area to the Communists. For instance, here is what he says about the early months of the work of the Marshall Mission:

I shall attempt in the light of subsequent events to reconstruct what happened in Chungking during and following the Political Consultative Conference called by the Chinese Government after General Marshall's arrival early in January. His personality and prestige and the lofty yet reasonable ideals which had brought the delegates together created an atmosphere of good feeling and high endeavor which made possible the five resolutions which, if put into effect, would have ended the controversy, formed a coalition government on a democratic basis and led to a reorganization and training of troops on both sides under American advice. . . .

What was the nature and object of the Marshall Mission? What was the Political Consultative Conference? What were the "five resolutions?" What was "the controversy" that would have ended if those resolutions had been put into effect? What was the form of the proposed "coalition government on a democratic basis?" What was the proposed "reorganization and training of the troops on both sides under American advice?"

Dr. Stuart has given no full explanation for any one of these questions in the body of the text. However, to make the record more understandable for the reader, there is a selection of documents in the Appendix. These include:

The Directives of the Marshall Mission (December, 1945).
The Five Resolutions of the Political Consultative Conference (January 31, 1946).
The Statement by President Truman on U.S. Policy (December, 1946).
General Marshall's Personal Statement (January 7, 1947).

With the help of these documents, we can hope to understand the objectives of the Marshall Mission and, at least in part, of the ambassadorship of Dr. Stuart. In the light of subsequent events, we can also understand how difficult, and how inherently impossible, those objectives were. Such an understanding is necessary to a sympathetic appreciation of Dr. Stuart's personal reporting of the earnest endeavors and the heart-rending failures of the Marshall Mission and his own ambassadorship.

The objectives of the Marshall Mission were summed up in these directives as "the unification of China by peaceful, democratic methods . . . as soon as possible." Specifically, they were twofold:

First, "the United States is cognizant that the present National Government of China is a 'one-party government' and believes that peace, unity and democratic reform in China will be furthered if the basis of this Government is broadened to include other political elements in the country. Hence, the United States strongly advocates that the national conference of representatives of major political elements in the country agree upon arrangements which will give those elements a fair and effective representation in the Chinese National Government."

And secondly, "the existence of autonomous armies such as that of the Communist army is inconsistent with, and actually makes impossible, political unity in China. With the institution of a broadly representative government, autonomous armies should be eliminated as such and all armed forces in China integrated effectively into the Chinese National Army."

The first objective was to cause the Chinese to form a coalition government with the Chinese Communists fairly and effectively represented; the second was to cause them to "eliminate" the autonomous armies of the Chinese Communist Party and "integrate" them into the National Army.

As Secretary of State Byrnes states in one of the directives:

This problem is not an easy one. . . . *It will not be solved by the Chinese themselves.* To the extent that our influence is a factor, success will depend upon our capacity to exercise that influence in the light of shifting conditions in such a way as to encourage concessions by the Central Government, by the so-called Communists, and by the other factions. The President has asked General Marshall to go to China as his Special Representative for the purpose of bringing to bear in an appropriate and practicable manner the influence of the United States for the achievement of the ends set forth above. (*Italics mine.*)

Such was the inherently impossible dual task of the Marshall Mission. The Chinese Communists wanted to get into a coalition government: that was the Yalta formula deviously devised by Stalin for Poland and for all "Liberated Europe"; that was what Mao Tse-tung openly demanded on April 24, 1945, in his fifty-thousand-word report to the Seventh Congress of the Chinese Communist Party held in Yenan—a report entitled "On Coalition Government." But they had absolutely no intention of having their autonomous armies "eliminated" or "integrated" into the National Army: on the contrary, the Communist Army, which Mao Tse-tung on April 24, 1945, claimed to number 910,000 men in regular units and 2,200,000 men in the "people's militia force," was expanding during the first six months of General Marshall's stay in China into 1,200,000 men in its regular formations.

And what were to be the ways and means by which the Marshall Mission was to "bring to bear the influence of the United States for the achievement of the ends set forth above"? President Truman directed General Marshall:

> In your conversations with Chiang Kai-shek and other Chinese leaders you are authorized to speak with the utmost frankness. Particularly, you may state, in connection with the Chinese desire for credits, technical assistance in the economic field, and military assistance, . . . that a China disunited and torn by civil strife could not be considered realistically as a proper place for American assistance.

In plain language, the weapon was to be not military pressure or intervention, but the withholding of American aid to China.

But this weapon could only checkmate the Chinese Government and had no effect whatever on the Chinese Communists, whose armies had been racing by land and by sea to Manchuria where they could obtain unlimited aid from the Soviet Occupation Forces and from the Soviet Union, now the contiguous, strongest base of revolution for the Chinese Communists. So, during the entire period of the Marshall Mission, the Chinese Communist delegation was constantly and successfully pressing General Marshall to stop or suspend American aid to China! And General Marshall and the United States Government did many times stop and suspend all American aid to China because of the loud protests of the Chinese Communists.

So the Marshall Mission failed because of its inherently impossible objectives, which neither Secretary Byrnes, nor President Truman, nor General Marshall, nor Mr. John Carter Vincent (who more than anyone else was largely responsible for drafting the Marshall directives) ever fully understood.

And the ambassadorship of Dr. Stuart failed too, because, in his own words, he was "a tyro in diplomacy"; and because, again in his own words:

General Marshall had originally brought me into his efforts to form a coalition government because of my reputation as a liberal American, friendly to the Chinese people as a whole, and with no pronounced sympathy for any one faction or school of thought. This included the Communists, several of whose leaders I had known fairly well.

All these seemingly harsh words I have said without the slightest intention of ridiculing the naïveté of those idealistic statesmen of an idealistic age. In fact I, too, was just as naïve a tyro in national and international politics in those days of expansive idealism. So naïve, indeed, was I that shortly after V-J Day I sent a lengthy radiogram to Chungking to be forwarded to my former student Mao Tse-tung, solemnly and earnestly pleading with him that, now that Japan had surrendered, there was no more justification for the Chinese Communists to continue to maintain a huge private army, and that his Party should now emulate the good example of the British Labor Party which, without a single soldier of its own, had just won an overwhelming victory at the recent election and acquired undisputed political power for the next five years. On August 28, 1945, Mao Tse-tung arrived at Chungking accompanied by the American Ambassador, General Patrick Hurley, another tyro in diplomacy, and my Chungking friend radioed me that my message had been duly forwarded to Mr. Mao in person. Of course, to this day I have never received a reply.

In conclusion, I want sincerely to voice my hearty agreement with the reflections of my old friend Dr. Stuart on the China "White Paper" and on what policy his great country should pursue in regard to China. And, since this is an introduction written by an unreconstructed, heathen Chinese to a book of memoirs by a great Christian leader, I would like to conclude with a quotation from his beloved New Testament. When in

1949 I read Secretary Dean Acheson's Letter of Transmittal of the China "White Paper" and came to these sentences: ". . . the ominous result of the civil war in China was beyond the control of the government of the United States. Nothing that this country did or could have done within the reasonable limits of its capabilities could have changed that result; nothing that was left undone by this country has contributed to it." —when I read those sentences, I wrote on the margin: "Matthew 27:24." This is the text:

When Pilate saw that he could prevail nothing, but that a tumult was made, he took water, and washed his hands before the multitude, saying, I am innocent of the blood of this just man: see ye to it.

Because of the betrayal of China at Yalta, because of its withholding of effective aid to China at crucial times, and, above all, because of its great power and undisputed world leadership, the United States was not "innocent of the blood" of fallen China.

And I agree with Dr. Stuart that the least the United States can do to redeem itself is to continue in its refusal to recognize the Communist Government and continue to oppose admission of that government to China's place in the United Nations. That is at least in line with the great tradition of the historic Doctrine of Non-recognition upheld by Henry L. Stimson and Herbert Hoover and written into the Atlantic Charter by President Roosevelt and Prime Minister Churchill.

Hu Shih

Hu Shih, professor of Chinese philosophy and later of Chinese literature at the National Peking University, 1917-1937; Dean of College of Letters at the same University, 1931-37; President of the same University, 1946-49. Chinese Ambassador to the United States, 1938-1942. He is usually known as the founder of the Chinese literary renaissance which has brought about the recognition and general adoption of the living spoken tongue (pai hua) as the tool of literature and education in place of the dead classical Chinese.

Fifty Years in China

Foreword

I have felt acutely the irony of my having been my country's Ambassador to China at a time when all that I had previously accomplished in the country to which I was accredited was apparently being destroyed. But my sense of frustration, my disappointments and anxieties have been only mental, whereas I know of many of my countrymen and other "foreigners" who, trapped in China when this happened—most of them voluntarily—have been roughly treated, some insulted, some imprisoned, some tortured in mind or body or both, some denied contact with their Chinese or other friends, and nearly all subjected to loss of all their property. A few died under this treatment. The treatment accorded to many millions of Chinese has been far more distressing. Many have been executed and many starved to death. I have recently been informed that no less than forty million have been condemned to forced labor. Many have preferred to leave their homes and go into exile despite the hardships involved. Many others have wished that they might take that course but have been unable to make their escape.

There was in China before the Communists came to power much that was good and much that was not good. There is, since they took over, less of the former and more of the latter. My lifetime effort and that of my missionary and educational co-laborers was devoted to making better that which was good and making less that which was not good. The visible evidence of that effort has been in considerable part liquidated: plants and equipment, churches, schools, buildings and hospitals have in some cases been destroyed and in more cases appropriated by the Communists for their own purposes. I feel, however, that the major part of the investment made by the patrons of missionary and educational and medical enterprises in China and by those who had devoted their lives to those enterprises—the investment in influence—has not been and cannot be destroyed.

There live on, in the minds and hearts of those who gave and of those who received, the benefits of the giving and the receiving. There live on in China both seeds and fruits of Christian teaching and practice. There live on in China—on the mainland and on Formosa—millions of men, women and children who are better in mind and in body in consequence of the efforts for and among them of Christian evangelists, Christian teachers, Christian physicians and surgeons, Christian scientists and Christian social workers. Were all else lost, which is not the case, the torch of Christian education in China, carried by the United Board of China Christian Colleges, still lights the way—on Formosa and among the overseas Chinese. Surely my life's work, and the work of my fellow missionaries and of our Chinese colleagues and of those who preceded us have not been in vain!

Nor do I feel that China, mainland China, is irrevocably "lost." The Communists have consolidated their position on the mainland, and it does indeed look now as though they are very firmly in control there. But who can say that any political regime in China is permanent? Who, if he thinks of the changes that have taken place in China and throughout the Far East since the days of Sun Yat-sen, can say that the Communist regime is in China to stay? The Communist ideology is alien to China's political philosophies. The Communist practices are violent, indifferent to human rights, and oppressive. The Communist importation and use of hordes of Russian advisers and technicians is bound to create friction both internal and external. The Communists show no regard for China's international obligations, are contemptuous of the rights and interests of other nations, and they have gone so far as to invade a neighboring state and make war on the United Nations.

I cannot believe that such a regime in China will last. I have faith that somehow and within a not very long time this monstrous evil will have run its course, and, having been weighed and found wanting, will be forced to relax its grip and be gone. I further have faith that the Chinese, a people who are fundamentally democratic in their social behavior and their political aspirations, will, when they have been "liberated" from the tyranny of this spurious "People's Government," resume the march which, begun in 1911 and interrupted and resumed repeatedly since then, leads toward the goal of national unity, national democracy, national security, peace, progress, and worthy performance as a good neighbor in their international relations.

In this book I have tried to tell the story of my life. I began many years ago the task of putting on paper the chronicle which I now bequeath to those who may care to concern themselves with such an account. The book thus has not been written all in one piece and all in the period immediately preceding its publication. Its chapters have been written one by one at intervals, after the manner, more or less, of a diarist's lengthy entries or an author's producing, over a long period, a series of articles or essays. Some chapters are retrospective. Some were written while the events and developments with which they deal were occurring. Some, the last three, have been written since my return in 1949 to the United States.

For the text of these three last-written and concluding chapters I am indebted to the collaboration of Dr. Stanley K. Hornbeck, a friend of long standing, whom I first met in China and who like myself was an educator before being inducted into diplomacy, and with whom I have over the years had many agreeable contacts and profitable exchanges of views. Of those chapters one deals with my activities—and inactivity—since I left China, with political developments which have been of concern to me, and with conclusions to which I have come in consequence of changes in my perspective, changes in myself and changes in the political scene, especially the changes which have taken place in China and in the relations between China and the United States; the second is a recording of my reflections as I look back over the years, meditate upon the present, peer into the future, and reaffirm the faith and hope that still are mine and that sustain me; and the third is a product of my effort to answer questions over and over put to me and constantly in my thoughts regarding relations between the United States and China. In these chapters the narrative still is mine, but, because I have not been able physically to do all of the actual writing involved, much of that work has been done by Dr. Hornbeck—on the basis of my notes and our many conversations. The text thus produced, referred back to me repeatedly, gone over by me many times and approved by me in its entirety, accurately reflects my recollections, my thoughts and my views. For these chapters, then, as for all others, the responsibility of authorship is mine, wholly mine.

I am indebted also to other friends for assistance. Dr. Frank W. Price, who is widely and favorably known in missionary and other circles, whom I have long known as a friend, whose father, Philip Francis Price, before him was a friend of my father and a revered senior among my friends—Frank Price has kindly and helpfully given the whole of my manuscript the benefit of physical and editorial attention. Mr. David McDowell, of the editorial staff of Random House, has concerned himself with editorial and publishing problems in a manner and to an extent which have been encouraging, reassuring and more than helpful.

That I am indebted to General George C. Marshall for his generous contribution of a prefatory note testifying to the good will which prevails between us and to his interest in my story needs no saying. He knows, I know, and all who read will know that such is the fact. Likewise, I am indebted to Dr. Hu Shih for the introduction in which he has generously given of his time, his vast knowledge, and his extraordinary talent, in analysis of and comment upon the story I have tried to tell.

Finally, Mr. Philip Fugh. I am indebted to Philip for the fact that this book has been written and is being published. Philip is not responsible for the contents of the book; there are even some matters of substance regarding which his views and mine do not entirely coincide. But without him I never would have been able to carry through to the completion of the manuscript; I would not have been able to carry on the contacts, the conversations and the correspondence which have been essential to that completion and necessarily antecedent to the publishing. In and toward the producing of this book, while it is obvious that I am the performer, full credit should go to Philip as the *impresario*.

To all of these friends I am deeply grateful for the assistance acknowledged above and for the sustaining encouragement given me by these and by other, not here mentioned, expressions of their good will.

JOHN LEIGHTON STUART

May 25, 1954
Washington, D.C.

1 Ancestry
and Early Years

China has been my home for the greater part of my life. I am
bound to that great country and people by ineluctable ties of the
spirit, not only because of my birth there, but also because of
long residence and countless friendships. It was my privilege to
grow up as an American boy in China, to return there later as
a missionary and student of Chinese culture, to serve as evangelist, theological professor and then as university president. In
1946, I was catapulted by strange circumstances into the United
States ambassadorship at Nanking, and it was in that capacity
that I finally and unhappily left that now unhappy land in 1949.

I have seen China under many governments—the old decay-
ing Manchu empire, the early Republic under the idealistic Sun
Yat-sen, the later Republic that struggled feebly against warlords
and venal officials, the National Government that began the task
of national unification and modernization, the arrogant but
short-lived Japanese rule over a part of the country, a China torn
by bitter civil war after V-J Day, and most recently mainland
China under the Communist regime. Through all these varying
periods of modern history I have observed the growing pains of
an old yet new civilization, striving to adapt itself to the twentieth century and destined to take its place some day among the
materially and morally strong nations of the world.

Looking back over nearly four score years, I am vividly aware
of a Divine Providence that has guided my life, and I realize too
how many of my significant choices have been made in the face
of outer restraints and inner reluctance. It seems that once and
again a force not my own has urged me forward to experiences

and adventures that I did not seek or anticipate. Whatever next, I am profoundly grateful to have had a small part in a great half-century of Sino-American cultural and spiritual relations, relations which though now apparently broken will, I am confident, be restored as a strong and colorful strand in the emerging pattern of world democracy and international community.

I

Both my parents came from long lines of intrepid pioneers. Our Stuart progenitor upon the American continent was Archibald Stuart, an Ulster Scotsman from Londonderry, Ireland. He is said to have been a noble descendant of Lord Ochiltree, subsequently Earl of Castle Stewart. After becoming involved in a rebellious movement growing out of religious persecution, he fled to western Pennsylvania. With him came two brothers, David and John, and seven years later his own family was able to join him. Archibald then settled on a farm near Waynesboro, Virginia. His four children had large families which scattered over the southern and eastern states. One direct descendant was Alexander H. H. Stuart, Secretary of the Interior in President Fillmore's cabinet, and later rector of the University of Virginia. Another was General J. E. B. Stuart, the dashing cavalry commander of the Confederate Army. The story is told that as he was carried wounded off the battlefield and his troops were wavering "Jeb" called out to them, "Go back! Go back! and do your duty as I have done mine."

John Stuart lived on Walker's Creek in Augusta County, Virginia, and later in Staunton. His grandson, Robert Stuart, was a Presbyterian minister who pioneered in a covered wagon from the valley of Virginia to the wilds of Kentucky (then part of Virginia) and helped to build up Transylvania College, at Lexington, Kentucky. There he taught Latin and Greek and was for a time president.

Robert Stuart married Hannah Todd, an aunt of Mary Todd

who became the wife of Abraham Lincoln. Robert's son David, my grandfather, was therefore a first cousin of Mrs. Lincoln. Another son, John T. Stuart, graduated from Centre College, moved to Springfield, Illinois, and later became Lincoln's law partner. I did not know of this relationship of the Stuart family to the Lincoln family until I came to America as an eleven-year-old boy, and then it was a great shock to my brothers and me living in Mobile, Alabama. We felt that on top of coming from China this would be the last straw as far as our southern friends were concerned: our lives might even be in danger!

David Todd Stuart pioneered in education for women. He was the founder and first President of Stuart Female College, at Shelbyville, Kentucky. His son John Linton, my father, was born in Shelbyville on December 2, 1840. He received his college training at Washington and Jefferson College in Pennsylvania and at Centre College, Kentucky, from which he graduated in 1861. After teaching for four years, he entered Princeton Theological Seminary and was graduated in 1868. It was at Princeton that a stirring message by Dr. John L. Nevius of China turned his thoughts to foreign missionary service. He became one of the first missionaries to be sent out by the Executive Committee of Foreign Missions of the new Southern Presbyterian Church, going to China with two associates in 1868. Their journey was by way of New York, the Isthmus of Panama and San Francisco, thence to Shanghai, and it occupied two months.

John Linton Stuart began his work at Hangchow, about 120 miles southwest of Shanghai, and he continued to live and serve there during his missionary career of forty-six years.

2

When my father went as a bachelor to Hangchow in 1868 he found that his immediate predecessor, Reverend E. B. Inslee, believed in learning the Chinese language by living "à la Chinese." So my father rented a place over an opium den and

and when this man's son became ill, the physicians and geomancers attributed the illness to the sinister influences emanating from the presence of foreigners higher up on the hillside. With elaborate excuses the local authorities therefore entreated the missionaries to exchange this location for a considerably larger property in the other end of the city. This was agreed to. The new location was in the heart of the area that had been devastated by the Taiping rebels and was one of the poorest parts of the city. Here a church, a school and some missionary homes were built. The side street upon which the missionary "compound" was located became known as "Jesus Lane."

In addition to their evangelistic work among the poor classes and rural people, both of my parents were interested in starting schools. My father's school for boys was later closed by the mission because its members felt that preaching rather than secular instruction was his proper function. Even so, a few choice spirits among his pupils were salvaged and given further opportunity for study, and were for many years the best Chinese workers in the mission. My mother was even more successful. She helped to start the second girls' school in China, a school which grew steadily in numbers and influence. She was principal of it for many years. It later became a part of the fine Christian Union Girls' School of Hangchow.

4

Four sons were born in the Stuart home at Hangchow: John Leighton (June 24, 1876), David Todd, Warren Horton and Robert Kirkland.

My brothers and I were for much of the time the only foreign children in the mission. As such we were petted. Our parents were remembered in our later years with admiring affection. They were wise and kind in their treatment of us and we have no recollections other than happy ones.

I remember excursions to the scenic spots of Hangchow, picnic lunches, hunting for wild strawberries, the hills ablaze with azaleas in the spring, summering in a dank old temple on a hilltop (the beginning in primitive camping out, of which grew the later missionary summer resorts) which for us little boys was surrounded with glamorous adventure. Another summer we went to Cheefoo, Shantung Province, where we stayed on a bluff at the seaside. Our ride on a mule litter to Tengchow to see Dr. A. W. Mateer, a famous missionary scholar and friend of my father, made a strong impression on us.

We had a few carefully selected Chinese playmates with whom we talked Chinese and of whom we were fond. For the most part, however, we were left to play by ourselves—out of school hours—in the large mission compound where my father and others had planted a number of trees. These grounds seemed to have shrunk into something small and commonplace when I returned there as an adult, in contrast with the expanse and mystery of boyhood associations. We enjoyed immensely Chinese food, candies, fruits, and most of all the elaborate feasts and ceremonial of the weddings as then celebrated. We studied no Chinese books, which is my only regret of those years, though my brother Warren went to a Chinese school after returning to China from a family furlough in the United States. On his subsequent return to China as a missionary, he remembered enough of both the spoken and the written Chinese to give him a good start in the language. Despite our seclusion, I have fairly vivid and colorful memories of New Year dainties and shows, the Feast of Lanterns and other holiday celebrations, riding in sedan chairs of pleasure boats on the West Lake, and similarly characteristic phases of Chinese life as then unspoiled by modern contacts.

Until I left China at the age of eleven, my only teacher was my mother. Her teaching must have been good, for my brother David and I were entered in the Mobile public schools without handicaps and were able to keep up in our classes. Besides our

daily school in the Hangchow home, we had Sunday School
and regular family prayers. Sometimes I went with my father on
his evangelistic trips to the streets and temple fairs. I remember some of the curious questions of "listeners" regarding my
father's clothes and appearance while he was preaching, and I
wondered whether it was all worth-while. Later in America I
was to experience something of a revulsion against this kind of
missionary effort, a revulsion that had to be overcome before
I made my own decision for missionary service.

In 1887 Reverend and Mrs. John Linton Stuart, after a missionary term of thirteen years, sailed from China for a furlough
year in America, taking with them four sons—ages eleven, nine,
seven and four.

5

Certain indelible memories of our journey to the United States
remain in my mind. It was a new and rather terrifying adventure for us. The stewardess on the ocean steamer said that we
were the "greenest children" she had ever seen—we knew so
little about many things that other children took for granted.
Having heard our parents tell of the higher standard of living
in America, we were surprised at the dock in San Francisco to
see roughly dressed newsboys—how could there be poor "foreign
children?" Locomotives and trains were a novelty to us; at that
time only one railway had been built in China, between Shanghai and Woosung, and that was torn up by Chinese farmers
for fear it would disturb the spirits of the graves.

On our arrival in Alabama the clash of emotions became
acute for me. My younger brothers and I were utilized by my
parents—such was the accepted procedure—as part of the
stock-in-trade for arousing popular interest in China as a mission
field. They had brought with them literally trunk-loads of
"curios," chiefly articles of daily use in dress, eating, worship
and such by the Chinese. We little boys were made to dress in

costume, eat with chopsticks, sing hymns in Chinese—especially "Jesus loves me, this I know"—and otherwise furnish an exhibit. When, later on, the two older of us were left in Mobile this aggravated our unpleasant notoriety. Our clothes were relics of the British styles in the Shanghai of earlier and very simple beginnings. Our speech was that of serious-minded elders who almost alone had been our acquaintances. We were unbelievably ignorant of the language, habits, standards and juvenile meannesses of our American contemporaries. Our cousins were in part ashamed of such queer relatives, in part amused or flattered by being connected with us. In this little provincial town of the deep South, from which my mother had committed the unheard folly or sacrifice of going as a missionary, we were the objects of verbal torture by schoolmates, or of even more resented questioning by her old friends or former pupils. The questions so kindly meant were such as, which country did we like best, did Chinese really eat rats, would we talk in Chinese, etc., a catechism which we came to detest. Callers would make such tactless remarks as, "Oh, they do look like Chinese, don't they?"

When our parents turned their faces back toward China in the autumn of 1888, my brother David and I were left in Mobile with my mother's sister and her husband who had a son and daughter about our ages. These foster-parents were as kind and solicitous as possible, and they treated us as their own children. But theirs was the strictest Scotch Presbyterian regimen which my uncle had inherited, accentuated by their conception of what the children of missionaries ought to be. They could not themselves go to China, but they helped maintain a home mission church in a part of the city a long way off and away from all our natural associations. In order to be worthy of "our saintly parents who were making such a sacrifice in a heathen land," we were taken across town every Sunday to this mission church. It was wrong to go there by streetcar or other conveyance on Sunday, so we had to walk in the mornings to Sunday School and worship service, and in the evenings to Christian Endeavor and still another religious service. On Sunday afternoons we memorized Bible verses and hymns. Dancing and the theatre were forbidden, which was more of a grievance because most of our cousins were permitted these worldly pleasures denied to us because our parents were missionaries. Two other aunts, one a socialite and the other out in the country, sympathized with the youngsters versus the aunt in control.

One great privilege that we enjoyed was staying every summer at one aunt's home across Mobile Bay. Her husband had been a lieutenant in the Civil War. There through the hot months we fished, crabbed, swam and sailed in the waters of the Bay. I remember vividly an episode involving a Negro playmate about our age, son of the cook. My cousin and I would tease him about not being able to row, and one day he said, "I'll row the boat back." My cousin and I dove into the water, intending to swim around a bit and then get back into the boat. The little Negro boy, thinking that we were testing him and with his racial pride hurt, started to row to the shore. We called to him to stop but he thought we were still teasing and he kept on until he finally maneuvered the boat home. We were frightened, and as we tried to swim back were increasingly exhausted. The mile, more or less, was a long, hard pull. I visualized the drifting in of our dead bodies, the sad funeral, the cemetery with its family plot, the accounts in the papers, the letters to my parents in China which would be more than a month on the way, the sadness and the tears! But we finally made it to shore, or I would not be writing this story. Another Negro in my boyhood experience was "Aunt Georgia," a colored mammy whom we loved and obeyed—otherwise we were spanked. But in that place and time, social lines between the races were strictly drawn, and we took them for granted.

The idealization of foreign missionaries and the awful responsibility of our upbringing in Alabama I have since learned to understand. Our devoted guardians lived long enough for the natural affection they merited to be purified from all child- ish complaints. Our two cousins in the family were then, and they remain, all but brother and sister in affection. The whole Mobile experience, however, against the background of the normal enjoyment of our companions, including a large circle of cousins, created an aversion for missionary life which lingered long. My earlier training, and the genuineness of motive appar- ent even to us little victims, together with uniform kindness and healthy summer sports at the seashore, served to carry me through what otherwise might have been a disastrous revulsion against all religion.

6

When sixteen years old, in September, 1892, I was sent to what was at that time regarded as one of the best private acad- emies in the South, Pantops Academy at Charlottesville, Vir- ginia. This was a preparatory school for "The University" (University of Virginia), and it was located on an eminence, originally part of Thomas Jefferson's estate, named by him "All-seeing" because of its lovely view in all directions across the Rapidan River from Monticello.

In Mobile I had been like other boys in looking upon school as a necessary evil to be endured with as little exertion as possible. In classes of forty or fifty boys, I was usually on the lower bor- ders of the first ten percent, never at the head of the class. Private schools for boys were thought of as for the very rich and for those expelled from the public schools. Instruction was uninspiring and unavoidably regimented, and I did the mini- mum of home study. Partly because of sensitiveness over not having grown up knowing boys' games, partly through lack of aptitude or interest, I often spent my leisure in reading through Walter Scott, Bulwer-Lytton, Charles Dickens and other stand- ard novelists, rather than in playing with others.

When the removal to Pantops came the effect was striking. At last I was a normal American boy. The fifty other boys came from all over the South, and I from Alabama. The awful brand of being from China had vanished and, when it gradually became known, had only casual historical interest for my schoolmates. Other causes of change in my attitude were the glorious climate and scenery, the small but carefully selected school enrollment, and above all the quality of the teachers and their individual interest in the students. The Principal, W. J. R. Sampson, was a man of the finest personal qualities, admirably suited to the task, and his wife (three of whose brothers, Reverend Henry M. Woods and Drs. Edgar and James B. Woods were missionaries in China) was an influence for good long after I had grown to manhood. They were both especially kind to me, and later on to my brothers, both of whom followed me there. It was also a home for us in the summer months whenever we had need of one.

Partly due to the climate, but chiefly, perhaps, to two greatly admired teachers, who had just been graduated from Hampden-Sydney College, I discovered that I could study well and enjoy the effort. One of my teachers, George H. Denny (afterward President of Washington and Lee University, later of the University of Alabama) made Latin and Greek fascinating subjects for me. Another stimulating teacher was James L. Bell, in English literature. I easily won the highest honors that year and the Gold Medal for the best average.

Pantops had a somewhat severe religious discipline, but after my five years in Mobile this seemed natural, and far less exacting. The healthy life, the personality of the Principal, the delight of being released from the notoriety of my missionary origin, pleasant companionships, and the wisdom with which on the whole the strict religious standards were enforced, combined to stabilize my religious habits. My attitude was perhaps rather negative but free from strain. It was a very happy year.

2 College
and Theological Seminary

Through the introduction of my favorite teacher, George H. Denny, I was admitted from Pantops Academy to the Sophomore class of Hampden-Sydney College in the fall of 1893. I also joined his fraternity, Sigma Chi, and his literary society. This was all that a young hero-worshipper could ask.

Hampden-Sydney College was founded in 1776, the year of the Declaration of Independence by the Continental Congress, and it was named after two English liberal patriots, John Hampden and Algernon Sydney. Patrick Henry and James Madison were among its incorporators. Among its alumni have been one President of the United States, thirty members of Congress, eight governors of states and twenty college and university presidents. Now it has nearly 400 students; then the enrollment was less than 150. However, a study made in 1931 of American college alumni listed in *Who's Who* resulted in Hampden-Sydney heading the list with 7.45 percent of its alumni in the book of notables. Amherst College came second with 7.40 per cent and Harvard third with 6.60 per cent. This fact drew wide editorial comment. The Knoxville *Journal* remarked, "Hampden-Sydney is venerable beyond the most and of incontestable accomplishment. In history and atmosphere it holds an affection all its own and a place unique in the history of Southern education."

The best features of college life for me were personal friendships, especially among my fraternity mates, the high tradition of the institution and its pleasant atmosphere. But Hampden-Sydney at that time was in a period of decline, and its enrollment was falling. Its location was in a region of Virginia where tobacco had exhausted the soil, and the more virile of the better families were leaving for the North or West. The brilliant professor of English literature who had been one of the chief attractions to me left the year I entered and was succeeded by one who was insufferably dull. The outstanding man taught the physical sciences in which I took only what was required, and did little more than pass. Altogether I was not sorry when the time for graduation came, and although I was offered the fellowship which led to the Master's degree after one more year, the idea of staying there another year did not appeal to me.

My best college friend, E. Lee Trinkle, and I had seemed to take turns in leading the class in alternate years. This friendship is one of the happiest memories of my years at Hampden-Sydney. Lee and I were the same age, fraternity mates and roommates, and as neither of us went in for organized athletics we usually took a walk together in the afternoon. We even called on our girl friends together, though never competing. We met at his home in Wytheville, southwest Virginia, to start for college and returned there before separating for the summer. I usually spent Christmas at his home. After graduation he studied law at the University of Virginia while I was teaching at Pantops Academy, so that we kept up our friendship. He became President of the Shenandoah Life Insurance Company, and President of the State Board of Education. In 1921 he was elected Governor of Virginia for a four-year term by the largest majority ever given a governor up to that time. For many years he was an active elder in the Second Presbyterian Church of Roanoke, Virginia. Until his death in 1939 we maintained our correspondence with each other, and one of my pleasures on trips to the States was always a brief visit with him.

It happened that our class had more honors men than usual. The fellow of the previous year was valedictorian. Trinkle and I came close together for second honor. In order to bring us all in on Commencement Day an old custom, long since lapsed, of a Greek oration was revived and was assigned to me. My kindly and scholarly old Professor Brock helped in its composition and I had the satisfaction of knowing that there would be no other critics among the perspiring audience. I received my B.A. and B.Litt. diploma on the day before my twentieth birthday.

Hampden-Sydney in my day was very strongly denominational in conduct and control. In the same neighborhood was Union Theological Seminary (soon to be removed to Richmond) which was almost like a graduate school to the college. There were many college students preparing for the ministry. Again the religious requirements seemed to me to be expected, and in the main the spiritual atmosphere was earnest and sincere. We students did not admire the scholarship or social origin of most of the ministerial students, nor in all cases their moral behavior. The compulsory Bible courses were deadly dull, the chapel and Sunday services none too inspiring. But this was not thought of with impatience or protest.

Spontaneous religious life expressed itself chiefly in the Y.M.C.A. which both in the college and in Virginia and other connections supplied vital and vigorous leadership. During my three years of college life I was more or less actively a member, and was president in my Senior year. The fact that the authorities somewhat frowned upon the Y.M.C.A. as an innovation from the North may have aided its popularity among the students. The Student Volunteer Movement for Foreign Missions was beginning to reach the flood tide of its influence in recruiting college students for missionary service and in arousing interest in a world-wide Christian movement. When its secretaries visited Hampden-Sydney, I was of course their obvious victim. My parentage, active Christian position, health, lack of any insurmountable obstacles to volunteering, combined to single me out.

In later life these secretaries—Willard Lyon, Fletcher Brockman, Harry Luce—became my closest friends. But at the time they crystallized my most acute religious problem—my lack of enthusiasm for missionary service. My father's experiences seen through a little boy's impressions, the childish sorrows all blamed upon this origin, the increasing attractiveness of life in Virginia and of the teaching profession had all developed in me a violent reaction against foreign missions as a career. The Student Volunteer Movement slogans, on the other hand, regarded it as almost axiomatic that any sincerely Christian young man or woman must show why he should not be a foreign missionary. This was my dilemma and it was agonizing. I was able to resist the pressure to sign the pledge for missionary service, but not able to evade the haunting issue. My personal choice of a life-work lay between teaching the classics or perhaps entering the ministry, hoping that either would keep me in Virginia. My reluctance to enter the ministry was mainly because I felt this would lead logically to China. I had visions of graduate study in the University of Virginia (where my brothers were studying), Johns Hopkins University or Germany. But I did not want really to commit myself to a career by going on with either classical or theological study, chiefly no doubt because of the vexatious missionary issue.

A whimsical speculation grows out of my hesitation over further graduate study. If I could have foreseen that I was to be occupied with higher education in China, I would most certainly have worked at least for a Master's degree in some university that would be known in China. On the other hand, had I done so there is a fair probability that this would have deflected me from the Christian ministry as a profession and hence from going to China at all. I have always found that when I have submitted to the dictates of my conscience, I have never had cause for regret.

2

At this juncture my admired Mr. Denny accepted a position on the Washington and Lee faculty, and I was invited to take his place and teach Latin and Greek at Pantops Academy. I had every reason for accepting and did so eagerly. For three years I taught these subjects and found great satisfaction in the life. The charm of Virginia deepened steadily. I was near my two brothers, and I had so many other contacts at the University that I have ever since felt almost as though it were mine. After the first year I was urged to stay a second, and then a third, and did so largely to postpone a difficult decision. The second year at Pantops I had as a colleague a college classmate, A. D. P. Gilmour, who during that session decided for the ministry and began his theological studies the year following. We often talked together on this subject and his decision undoubtedly influenced mine. When I entered the Seminary a year later we roomed together until his graduation.

I was an "old boy" at Pantops, and this gave me a sentimental advantage, helping me to understand the peculiar features of that school. I was very young, scarcely older than some of my pupils, which exposed me to danger. What saved me was a certain friendliness which seemed to form naturally between the boys and me. Out of classes I mingled with them, sometimes went with them to other schools as manager for their athletic teams. In class, remembering the transforming experience I had there under my teacher George Denny, I tried to make the work interesting. It was an instance of the old question, "Are you teaching Latin or are you teaching boys?" For me it was very much a matter of teaching boys, and this kept even these elementary classes from seeming dull. For instance, instead of the traditional Caesar's *Commentaries,* the jottings of a military commander about his campaigns and, of course, never intended for successive generations of bored students in other lands and centuries, I introduced the short biographies of famous men by Cornelius Nepos, written especially for Roman boys; it was full of interesting anecdotes, and fully capable of supplying practice in Latin grammar.

This almost instinctive relationship with students showed

itself subsequently with the widely divergent types I had in
Nanking Theological Seminary, and again at Yenching University where the students were almost as different from the
simple theological students in Nanking as they were from American boys.

During the summers of this teaching period I attended two
summer conferences held at Northfield, Massachusetts, under
Y.M.C.A. and Student Volunteer Movement leadership. I
found immense religious encouragement from the vital, practical,
winsome concepts of religion there presented and inspiration
from the noble personalities who promoted, addressed or attended these very successful meetings. They were wholly different from the rather stereotyped, jejune beliefs and practices
with which I had been most familiar. Jesus Christ became an
adored Master and ideal object of a young man's enthusiastic
devotion, instead of being primarily a theological doctrine about
whose mysteriously sublime nature and attributes it was heret-
ical to have any doubts. Like many other youth of the time, I
owed most perhaps to Robert E. Speer for this fresh and fascinating appreciation of Jesus. This became then and still is the
essence of my religious faith. It has remained undimmed and
free from all disillusionment after all the experiences and altered
theological views of these intervening years.

3

In the autumn of 1899 I entered Union Theological Seminary
which had been removed from Hampden-Sydney to a delightful
location on the outskirts of Richmond. Under the capable
administration of President Walter W. Moore, it was in a
condition of wholesome growth, stimulated by its new plant and
environment. Again I had a pleasant three-year period and developed not only to the Seminary but also to the city of Richmond a sentimental attachment which still lingers.

Of problems, in addition to the missionary question, there was the slowly forming one of theological beliefs, or more accurately perhaps, of attitude to progressive and fearlessly unbiased biblical scholarship. Although thus far my religious interests had been chiefly practical, yet by visits in the North, by reading, as well as by some inner urge, I was increasingly aware of the conflicting standpoints of Southern Presbyterian orthodoxy and the current trends under free inquiry, and I found my sympathy with the latter.

On the other hand the Seminary professors without exception, and notably the President, were men of unquestionable sincerity, piety, scholarship and broad human sympathies. They had been chosen largely as having been successful pastors, and were interested in training useful preachers rather than in polemical theology. I had come to realize that with them, as was almost universally true in the South, loyalty to the past and its heritage was a primary virtue. This was no less true in social and political life than in religion. I determined therefore to appreciate their characters and instruction but to think and study independently. The preparation for classes did not require very much time, and I tried to keep the evenings free for reading from the excellent library, selecting chiefly the newer books on religious, scientific and related issues. This helped me to reconcile even the form in which the doctrines were taught with what seemed to me the essential truth in their sometimes unconvincing or even repellent statements and proofs. There was thus a minimum of tension within myself and in my ecclesiastical relations, which still holds true. It is because I have always felt that, in the beliefs and purposes that both they and I care about most, I am at one with my Southern Presbyterian colleagues, I have seen no necessity for severing my connection with the Church of my fathers, and have been conscious that this sentiment of affection and confidence has been reciprocated.

During my first session in the Seminary, Lacy Irving Moffett came there from Louisville Presbyterian Theological Seminary on a missionary errand. We were attracted to each other at once, and partly for this reason he transferred the following year to Richmond. He had already decided to be a missionary. After Pollock Gilmour's graduation he became my roommate. Thus began an intimacy which still continues, strengthened as it is by our having married sisters, and by lifelong associations before and since our going to China together.

The crisis in my missionary problem came in the second session. The occasion was as usual the visit of a traveling secretary of the Student Volunteer Movement, in this case Reverend Arthur Ewing, a missionary to India home on furlough. It happened that I was president of the student organization so that it was my duty to entertain him, arrange interviews, and preside at his public addresses. As he was about to leave he asked, "Now, what about yourself, Stuart?" I told him that I knew the question would have to be answered, but that neither he nor any other person could help me, that I was aware of all the considerations he might urge. He had the tact and good sense to give my hand a hearty grip and leave it at that. But I knew that my indecision must end; the momentous issue could no longer be evaded.

That night I lay awake and heard the clock in the tower strike the hours until after five o'clock the next morning. It is difficult to exaggerate the aversion I had developed against going to China as a missionary. It was not the country so much as what I conceived to be the nature of the life and work—haranguing crowds of idle, curious people in street chapels or temple fairs, selling tracts for almost nothing, being regarded with amused or angry contempt by the native population, physical discomforts or hardships, etc., no chance for intellectual or studious interests, a sort of living death or modern equivalent for retirement from the world. This had all been accentuated by the boyhood trials due to the peculiar missionary background which in varying forms had followed me ever since. In contrast was the delight of life in Virginia which presumably would hold true more or less anywhere in the southern states. It was of course an abnormally subjective state of mind or emotion. It would be interesting to speculate as to how I might have felt if I could have foreseen my life in China as it developed.

Fortunately my parents never raised the question of my being a missionary, and they attempted no persuasion. I knew of course that nothing could make them happier than to have their sons follow them in this form of service. My second brother David, then a medical student, was perfectly certain he would never succumb, though eventually he did. He was a missionary surgeon for two years at Elizabeth Blake Hospital, Soochow, until his death by accident in 1909. My third brother Warren (who had remained in China till his fifteenth year) escaped the childish griefs and the resulting tensions that affected David and me, and he seemed always easily predestined for a missionary career. He served as a professor in a Chinese college and then theological seminary for nineteen years until the revolution of 1927.

To return to that fateful night, this was the antipathy I felt to being a missionary, but the undisputed opinion of the time was that if one were really a follower of Jesus in the fullest sense he would be a foreign missionary unless prevented by external causes. Or at least he should be willing to be one if "called." I quite definitely was not willing. Did I then have any message here in America of sacrificing everything for the sake of Christ, of the supreme value of spiritual as against material issues? Was Christian faith really the most real, the biggest element in my life? If not, could I enter Christian work in a pleasant environment, or even honestly call myself a Christian at all? Restlessly I tossed in bed as I went over these familiar questions.

Finally, I decided to put my religious belief to what was for me then the ultimate test. I would decide to be a missionary and have the satisfaction of proving to myself that Christianity was for me the supreme value. If God had work for me in my home country or knew that I could not meet the demands of life in China, I must trust Him to lead me. Exhausted, I fell asleep. On arising I told Pollock Gilmour, my roommate, and Lacy Moffett. They were not surprised. Instead of a feeling of renunciation, I felt contented, relieved, even enthusiastic. Nor have I for a single moment regretted that decision. It did give me the assurance of religious reality, and of the wisdom of doing what at the time seemed right. The career upon which I thus entered has probably enabled me to contribute far more to the Christian cause and to find much more enjoyment in my life than would otherwise have been possible.

4

The effectiveness of the Student Volunteer Movement crusade had led to volunteering for foreign mission service in excess of the ability of the leading ecclesiastical organizations to accept these enthusiastic young recruits. This in turn led to vigorous efforts to increase missionary support. Notably in the Northern Presbyterian and Congregational bodies a "Forward Movement" was started on the basis of getting churches to support individual missionaries by what later developed into the "every member canvass" for the entire budget of the local churches. This situation had affected the Southern Presbyterian Church also, where the foreign missions receipts had remained virtually stationary for several years and practically no volunteers could be added to the existing force. Moffett and I together with J. Fairman Preston, graduating the same year from Princeton Seminary, conceived the wildly visionary idea of launching a similar "Forward Movement" in our own Church, borrowing the whole technique of presentation from and benefiting by the tutelage of one of the most successful promoters of the scheme in the North, Dr. Louis A. Wishard.

The Church authorities gave permission, the necessary information, and their private blessing, but quite properly protected themselves from any official responsibility. A few businessmen supplied our expenses, which were absurdly small. We took no salary. Hotels were thought of as only an emergency measure. We traveled with maps and pledge cards and set up local committees to collect the pledges. We began our work in limited areas, each where he had a natural start. For Preston this was North Carolina, for Moffett Kentucky, for me the valley of Virginia. My first trial was the Sunday after my Seminary graduation in Washington, D.C. when an aged minister, Reverend A. W. Pitzer of Central Presbyterian Church, whom I had consulted, allowed me to make an experiment on his people. After listening to the plan while lying down on a couch he sat up and slapped his knee. "Why, of course, I've been wondering for years why some church hadn't tried it." "But it's a pretty radical idea," I said. "That's all right, young man, you go right ahead. If you can get some more money out of the Church—God bless you." I spoke in this church, and when the congregation came to select their "foreign pastor" they argued that they had allowed me to practice on them and so had a right to claim me. This led to a relationship that continued happily for many years. Woodrow Wilson was during his presidency a member of Central Presbyterian Church, and I had the privilege of speaking there once on a furlough from China when he was among the worshippers.

The thoroughness and novelty of this method and the glamour of young men and women offering themselves for missionary service but unable to go because of lack of money, which in turn was explained as due primarily to lack of general awareness of the need as well as of systematic organization, made it easy to secure surprising results. To laymen it put foreign missions on a business basis, to others there was romance in the idea, and instead of contributing to a vague abstraction the relationship was localized in a particular "foreign field" and personalized. The success of the plan was almost automatic. Money poured into headquarters. By the next spring the General Assembly, the highest ecclesiastical body, had approved the plan—unanimously as I recall; we three had been made secretaries for it with salary, expenses and official status. It seemed best for one of us to prove good faith by going that summer to the field of appointment. Preston was chosen. He had meanwhile become engaged, as a by-product of his travels, and after a wedding in which we all took part, he and his bride went to Korea. Moffett and I were to stay for one more year by which time we argued that a permanent organization would be perfected. We were offered the position for an indefinite period but were convinced that there would be a greater gain to the whole enterprise if we ourselves lived up to our claim of being among those ready to go as missionaries if only money could be secured. We had achieved our original purpose and had the satisfaction of seeing our extremely conservative Church officially endorse the method and appoint a permanent secretary to maintain it.

Looking back upon the religious value of this experience to me personally, it gave me an immediately practical outlet for my new purpose while becoming committed to it on other grounds than fancied self-immolation. On graduation from the Seminary I had been offered a fellowship for graduate study, as at college, but declined it for somewhat analogous reasons. For one thing, I had wrongly assumed that scholarship was of no importance on the mission field. And I was perhaps correct in thinking that the additional year for study in the same institution would not be of much benefit. The positive consideration was, however, the lure of being actively occupied in as adventurous and potentially useful a project as our little "Forward Movement." In consistently advocating the missionary enterprise and answering objections to it, I was able to appreciate its significance and to develop an enthusiasm for it which stood me in good stead when finally I was on the mission field. I was so absorbed in these promotional and administrative affairs that intellectual or theological issues were quiescent. I had occasion to travel all over the southern states and felt an extension of the sentimental attachment which had become so pronounced in reference to Virginia. My religion for the time was concentrated on a task in which I was at one with the pastors and church leaders with whom I was continuously associated, whatever differences there were in doctrinal beliefs, and alike among them and the members of the local churches, many pleasant friendships were formed. I was able more than ever to feel an inner harmony with my Church in what have always been to me—and I am convinced this is true of most of the Churches—the real fundamentals of Christianity.

5

Lacy Moffett and I had been ordained by our presbyteries soon after our Seminary graduation, and after two years of experience in the "Forward Movement" we were ready to start for China as missionaries. Should we go as bachelors? We decided not to marry unless both did! While visiting in New Orleans, Moffett and I met some distant cousins of mine, the daughters of Mr. and Mrs. John Edwin Rodd. We gradually realized that something was happening and the awful thought entered our minds, "Is it the same girl? What about our agreement?" We were to attend a conference at Lookout Mountain, Chattanooga, in July, 1904. I suggested that we invite the two sisters that Moffett and I had been interested in. When they came we found, to our great relief, that each was most interested in a different sister. We decided to propose at the same time, and did. We were both accepted, and a double wedding took place at New Orleans on November 17 of the same year. My bride was Aline and Moffett's bride Kate. Another sister Florence later went as a missionary to China and a fourth to Africa. Aline had not thought previously of being a missionary, but her other three sisters helped her to decide affirmatively.

Our life together was a continued romance for twenty-two years until Aline's death at Peking in 1926.

3
Back to China

My parents met us in Shanghai toward the end of December, 1904, and we went with them to Hangchow where we arrived on New Year's Eve. The Moffetts had been assigned to Soochow, greatly to our mutual disappointment.

Now there began for me the revival of my old aversion as I realized the feeble results of my father's life-long labors, the small church membership of very humble people. There was also the reaction from the somewhat idealized advocacy of Foreign Missions during my promotion of the "Forward Movement." Fortunately, my immediate task was the mastery of the Chinese language. My natural taste for language study strengthened the fascination that Chinese seems to have for all students. What little I had learned as a child seemed to have been completely forgotten during the eighteen years that had elapsed, but there was undoubtedly an advantage in hearing and perhaps enunciating Chinese sounds, as well as in learning the idiom. There were then no language schools or language-study classes supervised by older people proficient in its use.

A young man was engaged to be my "teacher," but he had no idea how to perform this function. He had had no previous contact with foreigners and was afraid to sip our tea because we were supposed to put medicine pellets into it that turned the drinker into a Christian. (He became a devout believer later.) But we soon learned to work together, and I profited greatly by his alert attention once he came to appreciate the problem. I was able with his help to master many proverbs and local idioms of everyday use, and had I continued to live in Hangchow might have become fairly fluent as westerners go. This dialect is unique in all China, having existed from the time when Hangchow was the capital of the Southern Sung Dynasty, a blend of the Court Speech (Mandarin) and the so-called Wu dialects (southern Kiangsu and northern Chekiang). It seems to me to have a musical lilt and expressiveness lacking in all others, but I am prejudiced. Many Hangchow residents are from Ningpo, including those who came with the first missionaries, and because of this fact, and my assignment to my father's large rural field between Hangchow and Huchow, I became somewhat familiar with various Wu dialects including the places mentioned, and also Shanghai and Soochow. They are all basically alike but each has its peculiar variations especially in pronouns. The years spent in and near Hangchow were invaluable to me in that I lived intimately with the people and spoke and heard their vernacular almost constantly except when in the family and in the comparatively rare intercourse with other missionaries in the city.

Another curious benefit of having been born in China was that the Chinese preachers, teachers and other employees assumed that this enabled me to understand their point of view, with the result that they were soon taking me into their confidence as they had never done my seniors in the mission. As my father's son they also treated me as a sort of younger brother or apprentice. I was not slow to realize the privilege of gaining insight into their ways of thinking, presuppositions, grievances, and misunderstandings of mission policy. With that start—for which I deserve not the slightest personal credit—I have always sought the confidence of Chinese associates, and have profited from their generous acceptance of me as one who understood them. Incidentally, this helps to explain away the myth that being born in China gives any peculiar intuition as to the Chinese habits of thought, or for that matter any ability to learn the language.

After a year or so of language study, I began to work in a large rural district north of Hangchow where my parents had spent

many years. A native houseboat was at once the means of loco-
motion along the numerous canals and also the place of abode
on arrival at towns. Under my parents' tutelage I learned the
procedure for managing a group of churches which were then
growing rapidly, for conducting evangelistic meetings and for
getting acquainted with the people in their homes. These trips
to the country and similar contacts with people in the city gave me
a close association with Chinese life which stood me in good
stead in later years when institutional responsibilities absorbed
my time.

I also began to evaluate missionary methods. Acceptance for
baptism was chiefly a matter of doctrinal beliefs in simplified
form, attendance on Sunday services and the rigid keeping of
that day, more than in the moral and social implications of the
Gospel. Repudiation of ancestor-worship seemed to be a need-
lessly harsh aggravation of the difficulties for the Chinese convert.
Worship was chiefly preaching, with no sensuous appeal through
the pageantry of ritual, artistic adornment and such, all of which
are instinctive among Chinese. In general the tendency was
toward a somewhat severe, repressive, formalized conception of
religion, which was a natural fruition of accepted standards in
the parent Church. In other missions, and latterly in most of
them, there have been notable changes in all these matters.

A far more serious problem, then at its worst, was the abuse
of the secular power represented by the governments supposedly
behind the missionaries. Roman Catholics, through the Con-
cordat with the French Government claimed official status for
their hierarchy and protected their members in lawsuits and
other political issues. To join a Church meant political and
economic security. This statement is made without impugning
the motives of the Catholic priests. Still less is there criticism of
their piety and devotion for which I have the greatest admiration.
But it led to false reasons for joining the Church and to constant
legal injustices due to the fear Chinese officials had of complica-

tions with the Great Powers which were too often made the
pretext for additional territorial or commercial concessions.
Chinese workers in Protestant missions were appealed to to help
relatives or neighbors in difficulties and also had the temptation
to supplement their meager salaries by assisting in such negotiations. Missionaries were misled into thinking that there was
awakening eagerness for salvation from sin in a given locality
only to discover later that there were much more sordid motives
behind the desire to join the church, and that more often than
not their trusted local preacher was in the racket. Missionaries,
especially Americans with our commercialized habits of thought,
practical emphasis and salesmanship, tended not unnaturally to
seek for growth in statistics of church membership and of newly
formed congregations, and of similar direct results of organized
propaganda. These would be easily calculated and were understood by the supporting constituency. Chinese, on the other hand,
being skilled in evaluating human motives and behavior as one
of their notable characteristics, did not fail to recognize this and
attempted to give satisfaction. The livelihood of Chinese helpers
depended on it. There was but little conscious insincerity or
hypocrisy on either side, the missionaries as a rule not even being
aware of their own artificial emphasis on tangible ecclesiastical
gains in contrast with revealing a new way of life, but the mis-
conceptions both within and without the little Christian communities were regrettable.

Having, however, recorded those early impressions of mine,
I should like to take this occasion to testify also to conclusions
begun then and strengthened by all subsequent experience in
China as to the earnestness, high purpose, untiring efforts and
unselfish devotion to their purely religious objectives, of missionaries as a class. I write thus after having become in my later
life more detached in attitude and with old prejudices relegated
to the background. The intellectual average and general fitness
for their work is also much higher among missionaries than is

generally recognized. I soon learned to be proud of my association with so fine a personnel. I also began to find a real interest in the details of my own assigned duties, as well as in the more general matters of policy, administration and union projects which were slowly gaining ground. Whether or not I could have spent my life happily and successfully as a typical "evangelistic missionary" is a question about which I have more than once whimsically speculated.

What I have said about the high standard of the majority of missionaries is true also of many early Christians in China. Some did seek church membership from unworthy motives yet the martyrdom of thousands in the Boxer uprising of 1900, and the faithfulness of many times that number in spite of an unfavorable environment and social as well as family hostility cannot but evoke our deep respect. From Christian families of the nineteenth century have come a number of outstanding leaders in the Chinese Christian movement of today.

2

One of the union enterprises which was inaugurated soon after my arrival in China was a Theological Seminary in Nanking under the Northern and Southern Presbyterian (or Presbyterian U.S.A. and U.S.) Missions. That forty years after the ending of the Civil War, across the Pacific Ocean, these two still separate branches of the same denomination were at last able to unite to this limited extent suggests the difficulties in the way of all ecclesiastical union as well as the hope that with patience, tact, and a deeper insight into the true nature of our religion there can be progress even in church union, this paradoxically most obstructed of all efforts for enlarged human fellowship.

One senior missionary from each of these Churches and a younger Chinese were on the faculty when I was invited to join their number. After refusing the call two or three times, I left the decision to my mission which with one exception voted in favor of my accepting. That exception was the Reverend P. Frank Price who objected to young missionaries being drafted from evangelistic work to educational work. I had the delight of welcoming him to this same faculty a few years later, where until his retirement in 1941 he was an honored teacher and a beloved *pastor pastorum*. Very soon after my removal to Nanking, the union was extended to include Northern and later Southern Methodists (U.S.A.) and the Disciples of Christ. We might have secured the Northern Baptists (U.S.A.) also had it not been more desirable to retain denominational unity than to force the secession of the Southern Baptists—even more rigid theologically than Southern Presbyterians—from their own union college and seminary in Shanghai.

It was agreed that I should have the Department of New Testament Literature and Exegesis, and I thus had occasion to study these books as I never had before. The Presbyterian creedal standards stress the supreme authority of the Bible, yet curiously in the Seminary curriculum there was in my time only a modicum of the teaching of the Bible itself. There was much emphasis on Hebrew, Greek, Theology, Church history etc., but it was probably assumed that students were sufficiently familiar already with the Book itself. At any rate, I soon discovered not only how little I knew, but how fascinating was the subject. I therefore secured all the best aids to its study which were available and found an almost exploratory zest in acquainting myself with the textual, historical, philosophical, devotional and other aspects of New Testament scholarship. There was also the challenging problem of how to teach in a way that stimulated the same desire to learn more in the students, while at the same time keeping within their range of understanding and not disturbing their previous beliefs. There were no college graduates, the higher grade being more or less equipped with a modern high school education, the lower being only of ordinary attainments in traditional Chinese study. Mencius offers a bit of advice about giving instruction according to the students' capacity, and I tried to plan instruction that would prepare for meeting modern knowledge and at the same time make it elementary, constructive and practically useful.

My days at Nanking Seminary were very full, with usually four hours a day of classroom work, other duties shared in by my colleagues, the necessary preparations for teaching and constant study of Chinese. The move to Nanking required a mastery of that dialect, a southern corruption of Mandarin and one of the ugliest dialects in all China. It is on the fringe of the Wu dialects and is not so much a blending as a coarsening of Mandarin. My life here was much more removed from the common people, but my teaching was all in Chinese. I also preached, and had other occasions for public speaking or social relationships, almost always in Chinese.

In time I began attempts at literary work, devotional articles in a Presbyterian weekly paper widely read both inside and outside that denomination, articles in Hasting's *Bible Dictionary* which was being translated into Chinese with adaptations, commentaries, etc. I also wrote articles in English in the *International Review of Missions, Chinese Recorder* (interdenominational organ of missionary activities published monthly), and other periodicals. We were located close to the University of Nanking where I frequently preached, taught Bible classes and met with religious study groups. I formed the conviction that Chinese preachers, especially those who did not read English (the knowledge of which had come to be the badge of modern education) would be much helped by being able to read their New Testaments in the original Greek. This would enable them to appreciate better the difficulties of translation into Chinese (no two languages could be more unlike), would give them a sense of intimacy and reality in their reading of the original text, would have a general cultural value in accord with Macaulay's *dictum* that no one can understand his own language properly until he knows at least one other, and would give them "face" or prestige in having this professional attainment in lieu of the coveted mastery of English. For these reasons I published a primer of New Testament Greek and then a Greek-English-Chinese dictionary. It was interesting to discover how many Greek forms, needed for reading classical Greek, were not used in the New Testament and could be eliminated. I was fortunate also in preparing the dictionary at a time which synchronized with the new archaeological finds in Egypt and elsewhere that illustrated how completely and naturally the New Testament was written in the current form of Greek in use then all over the Mediterranean world. This explained the divergences from classical standards in a way that did not reflect upon the learning of its writers and made more natural the translation of the Bible into the spoken style of the Chinese people. It also enriched and vitalized the definitions of words in a way that added freshness and vivid meaning to many terms and phrases.

Soon after joining the Seminary faculty, I became seriously concerned over the lack of college graduates in the Christian ministry and tried to ascertain causes and remedies. It was a great joy after several years of unsatisfied inquiry to welcome the first college graduate as a regular student, Handel Lee from the University of Nanking who fifteen years later was elected the first Chinese president of the Seminary. Before this event the Student Volunteer Movement for the ministry had been organized on the analogy of the American-Student Volunteer Movement for Foreign Missions, and I was one of its enthusiastic supporters. A Chinese evangelist from Shantung (Reverend Tin Li-mei) was made secretary and traveled widely over the country organizing local bands of students. This Movement broadened out into dedication to Christian service and then lost all vocational emphasis which led to its decadence. But for a while it attracted not a few choice spirits to the ministry and called attention to the importance of the problem of church leadership.

3

Another influence upon me during my three-and-a-half years in Hangchow and the following eleven years in Nanking was the Y.M.C.A. Under the wise leadership of Willard R. Lyon, Fletcher Brockman and others, free from ecclesiastical, doctrinal or organizational restrictions, and meeting a timely need among young intellectuals eager for western learning or progressive ideas, it opened up to me an aspect of missionary effort very different from the prevailing evangelistic methods, including the training of Chinese workers. The Y.M.C.A. was able to secure college graduates, including some who had studied abroad. These were treated in every way as colleagues who shared equally with the foreign secretaries in all matters of policy and finance, instead of as employees who took orders from the foreign group meeting separately. The applications of Christian faith to political, social, intellectual and economic problems were stressed and frankly discussed. The Y.M.C.A. promoted games, scientific lectures, social friendship, together with Bible classes and religious meetings. It happened that I was frequently called upon to take part in summer conferences held usually in some secluded and attractive spot in the hills, and this experience affected further my outlook.

Incidentally, it was at one of these conferences that I first met Bishop Logan Roots. On several of these occasions we were the only western "outsiders" present, which threw us the closer together and began for me one of the most delightful friendships of my missionary career. I remember how startled I was when I saw Bishop Roots for the first time in full episcopal robes after knowing him only in the informal costume of a summer camp.

During the early years of our residence in Nanking, I came to know Randolph T. Shields who was teaching in the Union Medical College, which was later moved to Tsinan and called the Cheeloo Medical School. Acquaintance ripened into friendship, the third great friendship in my life. We lived later in the same house; our wives were like sisters; his daughter and my son, born only one day apart, played and studied together. "Ran" later became an outstanding leader and scholar in the field of medical education in China.

4

Professional duties in a theological seminary inevitably led to thought on the issues which may be loosely described as conservative or liberal, orthodox or modernistic. All my training and official connections had been with those of the former type; all of my instinctive sympathies and critical studies led me to the latter. As in my student days in Virginia and while traveling for the Foreign Missions cause before leaving for China, the tension was greatly eased by my respect for the beliefs and behavior of my elder colleagues among missionaries and by a prevailingly genuine mutual friendship and understanding. I have always tried to distinguish between sincere religious convictions and those which are matters of human opinion or intellectual study. These latter are influenced, more perhaps than is generally recognized, by adventitious circumstances of locality, traditional heritage, temperament, reading and study. Most of the controversies which force into one or the other of these antagonistic groups those who would naturally work together in harmony seem to me to belong to this latter category, although confused with what are thought of as religious doctrines further exacerbated by emotion.

Nanking Theological Seminary, although founded on a conservative acceptance of Protestant evangelical doctrines, was never entirely free from criticism and suspicion on the part of those even more insistent on what they regarded as "sound" or conservative theology. This was most pronounced in the so-called North Kiangsu Mission of our Southern Presbyterian Church. We had two missions, one north and one south of the Yangtze River, of which this was the former. I belonged to the Mid-China Mission, the members of which though of essentially the same theological position were far less disputatious and intolerant. In my whole experience I have never met with *odium theologicum* as implacably virulent and polemical as it was among members of that northern mission. It was strange because as individuals and in personal relationships they were not unlike the rest of us. It may be that the harsh conditions of their life in a poverty-stricken, ill-governed, inaccessible part of the country tended to embitter or at least harden them, for among themselves in matters of internal mission business they showed a somewhat similar spirit. Pearl Buck grew up in that environment and knew little of other missionaries until after her marriage. Her father, the "Fighting Angel" of her stories, had been in our mission but was later transferred to North Kiangsu. This largely perhaps explains her reactions to missions.

Members of the northern mission were always investigating the orthodoxy of one or another of us on the faculty—I being especially suspect—or criticizing those whose own theology was irreproachable but who were too tolerant of the views of others with more questionable opinions. Fortunately our own faculty harmony and mutual confidence were undisturbed by these attacks. When I finally resigned to move to Peking there was absolutely no thought of escaping from this sort of inquiry, but in reviewing these tendencies, it is quite possible that with the growth of aggressive fundamentalism among China missionaries, I might have become a target and involved the Seminary in a theological controversy than which none can be more obnoxious.

As a matter of fact, I did become the object of such attack about the time of my leaving Nanking, and, although I knew nothing about it until several years later, it may well be recorded here as my first and last theological arraignment. It happened that the Y.W.C.A. had asked me to give a series of lectures at their Secretarial Conference on basic Christian beliefs—God, Christ, the Holy Spirit, the Bible—explaining these in modern language and with their capable young Chinese secretaries especially in view. These lectures were delivered without having been written out and were taken down in shorthand. Later on the Y.W.C.A. asked whether these could be printed for their own use but not published. This was at the very time when I was most preoccupied with the problem of my call to Peking, and I agreed without even looking over the proof. Whether it would have made any difference if I had not is doubtful.

Later on that year two visitors came from the United States, ostensibly to conduct inspirational meetings for missionaries at their summer resorts, but with the additional commission to search out evidences of modernism among China missionaries. The notes on my Y.W.C.A. lectures had somehow been secured by zealous fundamentalists and a copy supplied to these men. Later on a flaming article by Dr. Griffith Thomas on "Modernism in China" appeared in the *Princeton Theological Review*. These notes on my lectures were extensively drawn upon, together with quotations from book reviews and other printed articles. When next in the States on a financial campaign for Yenching University, I had a letter from our aged Secretary for Foreign Missions asking me to take some action which would help them in view of questions and complaints coming to their office over this article. I had been ordained in and was a member of East Hanover Presbytery centering in Richmond, but in accord with the practice then beginning of transferring to a presbytery in China I had severed connection with it. I asked, however, to be allowed to appear before East Hanover Presbytery at its spring meeting, making a special trip from Detroit for the purpose.

There was no practical concern to me in any judgment the presbytery might render. I was supported by Yenching University. My prestige among its constituency in the northern states and in China would not be in the slightest degree prejudiced against me if the Virginia presbytery voted unfavorably against my creedal "soundness." But I was anxious to reassure myself that these conservative southerners—all of whom knew me as a

fellow student or younger colleague from earlier associations—
were more interested in vital religious belief than in matters of
intellectual opinion or interpretation. While voluntarily putting
myself on trial before them I was also in a sense trying them out
in my own mind.

When they asked how I should like the trial to proceed, I replied that I would be willing to have a detailed investigation by
a special committee based on those disturbing Y.W.C.A. lecture
notes (copies of which had been plentifully supplied by the
fundamentalist zealots) or any other procedure that would satisfy
them, but that I personally preferred to make a statement to the
whole body as to what those four basic beliefs I had discussed
meant to me. This I then did, using phraseology with which
they were familiar. They also had a committee to interrogate me.
The result was a unanimous rising vote endorsing me. One tall,
lanky brother proposed a vote of disapproval for the secret methods
used by those northern people who had denounced me as being
contrary to the code of gentlemen, to say nothing of being un-
christian, but this was not pressed.

The originators of the attack (in Philadelphia and Princeton)
were, however, unwilling to accept this decision and instigated
like-minded people in the South to carry the issue up to the Synod
of Virginia and even to the General Assembly. Technically the
Synod could only deal with its presbytery, not with me, but,
having full confidence in the presbytery they refused to discuss
the matter. So the case was concluded. But on my next trip to
the United States I made another visit to Richmond and asked to
have my presbytery membership transferred back from China so
that if similar charges were brought against me in the future,
they would have official jurisdiction over me. This was unanimously approved and I am still a member of East Hanover Presbytery "in good and regular standing."

The Presbyterian of the South said in an editorial on September 29, 1926, "No man has ever had his views of theology more

carefully gone into by a Presbytery than has been the case with Dr. Stuart, and no man ever more fully convinced a Presbytery of his holding the faith held by the Southern Presbyterian Church. The Presbytery feels that the attacks on Dr. Stuart were entirely uncalled for and entirely groundless. He has shown his high Christian character by not entering into a public controversy on this matter, but leaving it entirely in the hands of the Presbytery, while he went quietly on with his great work in far away China."

The point of this narrative to me is that Christian workers of differing theological interpretations can work together happily and harmoniously if there is mutual confidence in one another's religious faith and a common purpose to reveal the spirit of Christ in all human relationships.

4 Yenching University—
a Dream that Came True

Late in 1918 when the call came to me to leave Nanking Seminary and undertake the building up of a new union university in Peking, my whole inclination was to refuse. I was perfectly happy in my Seminary work, had reached a stage in teaching and study when I could think of my subject as really mine, and had several literary projects under way.

Two little missionary colleges in the capital, *Huei Wen* or, as it was called in English, Peking University (Methodist) and North China Union College at Tungchow near Peking (Presbyterian and Congregational), had been trying to unite ever since the disasters of the Boxer uprising in 1900. They had at last agreed to do so and were occupying improvised premises in the southeast corner of the city, to the rear of the old Methodist university. But some points were still at issue, particularly the name of the union institution, and feelings ran high. On the other hand, there seemed no hope for a strong Christian university in Peking unless these differences were reconciled and a new start made.

A member of the Board of Trustees of Peking University, a retired clergyman living then in Seattle, visited Nanking on his return from Peking and stayed in our home. He inquired whether I would consider the presidency of the new institution. I replied that I was ready to serve the Christian cause in China in whatever way seemed most useful, but went on to say that I had no administrative experience fitting me for such a task, that I found my present work in every way congenial and that he should therefore not consider me as available. I soon learned that his trip to Peking had been to end the seeming deadlock between the two small colleges, and that he was now looking for some one to consolidate the union and give leadership in an advance effort.

A few weeks later I received an official invitation to be President of Peking University. All my friends advised me to keep out of what they felt to be a hopeless mess, with the exception of Dr. Harry W. Luce, who warned me, however, to look very carefully into the financial aspects before accepting. Many others had refused the invitation now extended to me. It was generally agreed that the President must be some one outside of the local personnel and entirely unrelated to the issues involved. I could at least meet that specification. I remembered my experience in facing the decision to become a missionary, and determined to put this question to a similar test. As the weeks passed, both parties urged me to make a decision, but I felt no clear leaning. I had meanwhile reluctantly promised to make a trip to Peking to look over the situation, and despite my attempts to be released was compelled to carry out this promise.

I arrived in Peking on January 31, 1919, and took a rickshaw in the face of a violent, cold, northwest wind to the Presbyterian Mission in the north city. Immediately I began to realize how much more intense were the divergencies between the two groups than I had expected. A delegation of *Huei Wen* graduates told me in effect that, whatever English name was used for the union institution, unless it continued to be *Huei Wen* in Chinese they would repudiate it as their *alma mater*. This looked sufficiently serious for me to ask to meet with a similar delegation from the other side. They would approve any name chosen except *Huei Wen*, but if that was decided on they would dramatically pile their diplomas on the Tungchow campus and let the bonfire symbolize the destruction for all of them of their *alma mater*. In each case the men with whom I met were the leading graduates, many of them prominent in Christian work. Their attitude revealed the strong feeling against the union, as well as of the Chinese sense of "face." Dr. H. H. Lowry of the existing Peking University was unyielding in his insistence that the old name of the institution be retained and that the new site be adjoining. Yet the Chinese name *Huei Wen* was unacceptable to the other group.

What attracted my attention at once was that with the downfall of the Manchu Dynasty and while missionaries were wrangling over their own institution names, a government university, known in Chinese and English alike as "Peking University" had been founded and was rapidly becoming famous all over the country and abroad. Chancellor Ts'ai Yuan-p'ei, a scholar with the highest literary degree of the ancient system and some European education, was drawing to his faculty a brilliant galaxy of young western-educated scholars, most notable among them even then being Dr. Hu Shih. They were publishing books and periodicals on progressive reforms which were eagerly read by educated youth. It was, as the title of one of the best of these indicated, a *renaissance*. In Nanking I had been following this awakening with enthusiastic interest. What had begun as a purely internal controversy between two missionary groups had made their obscure little college ridiculous in arrogating to itself a name that rightfully belonged to the Chinese who were making it the intellectual dynamo of their nation.

When I met with the Board of Managers—all foreigners—I said that it would be impossible for me to decide my question until these controversial issues had been settled among themselves. They saw the logic of this and named ten men to represent each party, five foreigners and five Chinese, to reach an agreement. I was asked to be chairman as the only neutral person. They argued vigorously for three long days, over the name and other disputed items. Once they went long past the lunch hour, again until after midnight. As I listened it was transparently clear that they all desperately wanted to find a solution but had become so entangled in promises and contradictions and institutional rivalries that they could not extricate themselves. Also, that if I declined after all this agitation they would not have the heart to try again. There was also forming in my mind the potentialities of a Christian university, broadly conceived and free to experiment with new policies, in this fascinating old city, once the cultural as well as the political capital of the nation.

On the fourth morning I awoke with what a Hebrew prophet might have described as a vision from Jehovah. I knew then that it was my duty to accept the call chiefly because I was their only hope, their last resource; because they were in a fix where left alone they could go neither forward nor backward, although the issues were trivial in themselves and by no means insoluble; because in Peking of all places there ought to be a university worthy of the missionary enterprise. My prayers for guidance had been answered. So when they assembled again I ventured to make a suggestion and said that if they cared to act on it I was prepared to accept their invitation. I proposed that they name an impartial commission of foreigners and Chinese to make a categorical decision on each of the points at issue, this to be regarded by all concerned as final. They responded with alacrity. The whole atmosphere changed and they became at once among themselves the friends and colleagues which they had all been at heart.

But the commission yielded to the Chinese penchant for compromise. They proposed that one side make certain concessions, the other side some more, until they were all back again in the old morass. I had returned to Nanking to await the outcome and received telegrams from members of the Board and also friends outside the institution urging me to make another trip to Peking without delay. It was now March and I had my first taste of the gritty dust storms of early spring which enable the residents of Peking to appreciate what a gorgeous climate they have except when the Gobi Desert blows down upon them.

Again I met with the dejected Board of Managers, and indicated that they had as far as I could see three solutions: 1) to refer the matter again to the commission with a reminder that it confine itself to the original instructions; 2) to abandon the whole effort to get together; 3) to sacrifice all that they had severally been insisting on and think only of what would be best for the new institution. I added that unless at this meeting they could settle the problem I would feel that I had exhausted my efforts to help them. Dear old Dr. Lowry then arose and with tears streaming down his face said that he had had enough of commissions, that to scrap the idea of union was unthinkable and that as perhaps the one who had been most obdurate he would begin by throwing all of his cards on the table.

This provided the needed catalyst and the disagreements that had hitherto seemed so insuperable were rapidly disposed of. It was agreed that the Chinese name would be used for the remainder of that session and that a new one would be virtually left to me. Dr. Ch'eng Chin-yi, probably the outstanding Chinese Christian leader of this century, suggested "Yenching," a glamorous word meaning capital of the ancient state of Yen and regarded by all Chinese as a poetic allusion to Peking. This soon became the title in both languages to the satisfaction of everyone. The whole experience illustrated the difficulty in effecting a union enterprise and the benefits that immediately accrue when this has been achieved.

The old issues having been happily settled, I announced my formal acceptance but on two conditions. One was that the question of location should be reconsidered without any reference to the past. The other one was that I should not have the financial responsibility. I thought this quite clever and original only to learn in time that it is standard practice with the incoming president of a private American institution and invariably a fatuous idea. I had asked Dr. Harry W. Luce to accompany me on this second trip and proposed that he be recommended to the Board of Trustees as Vice-President with the financial task in view. He had pioneered in securing funds for the new plant of Cheeloo University in Shantung with notable success and shared my hopes of what might be done in this instance.

2

This vision of possibilities was the only attractive feature. There was certainly nothing in the existing assets. The four constituent Mission Boards had each obligated itself to us $50,000 for capital outlay and this had already been more than used up in purchasing and reconditioning the scattered plots of the intended site. I was from the beginning dismayed at the thought of so objectionable a location. The budget for current expenses, small as it was, was twice the income. There were less than a hundred students, and most of these not the sort one would have thought of as promising college material. Most of them were on scholarship aid. Only two Chinese teachers had remained after the merger, Dr. J. F. Li and Dr. Ch'en Tsai-hsin. Many of the foreign members of the faculty had few qualifications for university teaching. Everyone had been so absorbed, both in Peking and in New York City, with the disputed issues that no plans had been formed—or even thought of—for securing additional funds or for other progressive efforts. Added to all this, I knew myself to be a tyro in educational administration, and unfamiliar with north China and my prospective associates. I thought of the security of my Nanking job with no administrative worries, nothing to do but teach congenial subjects and pursue no less congenial studies. As a missionary I seemed to be going from bad to worse —first I left preaching for teaching, and now I was leaving teaching for university administration! I wondered how much of faith and how much of foolhardiness there was in my new adventure.

Not only had I come to a penniless institution but no one seemed concerned. The local people had been busy in using their capital grants to buy land and adapt the houses on it to their purpose. The Board of Trustees, as I soon discovered, was composed chiefly of members of the constituent Mission Boards selected to look after their respective denominational interests and with no sense of responsibility for securing funds. Dr. Harry Luce was the bright spot in the dark picture. The Board of Managers approved him as Vice-President, but the Trustees in New York opposed him. I replied with a letter of resignation, and they still refused to endorse him without giving an alternative suggestion. I then called the Managers together at Peitaiho and showed them copies of the correspondence. The Managers added their urgent recommendation and the Trustees came across!

Dr. Luce left promptly for the United States and began his tireless travels over the country, visiting friends he had previously won and through them making new contacts. He was working for an institution entirely unknown and without even a site on which to construct the buildings he was trying to secure. He wrote letters complaining of this as his biggest handicap. We were building foundations as of a wharf, under water.

3

It had meanwhile been agreed to seek a location outside the city walls, not more than a mile from the city. But this proved to be a baffling undertaking. For many centuries officials from other provinces residing in the capital had needed a burial site for members of their families and had purchased plots adjacent to the city. The environs of Peking are full of these unrelated private cemeteries, many of them in disrepair and belonging to owners who cannot be traced. Every effort of ours to buy up a sufficiently extensive tract of land invariably ran into one or more of these graveyards. Chinese prejudice against their removal is very deep. It became, therefore, a grave issue indeed.

We walked and donkeyed and bicycled all around Peking but were not able to secure a suitable piece of property. One day I was invited to Tsinghua College by some friends, and one of them said, "Why don't you buy that property across from ours?" I looked at it, on the main highway to the Summer Palace —five miles out, but really nearer to Peking because of a good road than many other nearer places already considered, and quite attractive. The location was toward the celebrated Western Hills upon the slopes of which cluster some of the loveliest temples and palaces of China's great past. It had been the ruined garden of a Manchu prince but was now used by Governor Ch'en Shu-fan of Chensi as a summer villa and ancestral hall. An official we knew said he would try to secure it for us. The Managers and Trustees approved the proposed site and the next summer I went to the capital of Shensi to see Governor Chen. The Governor showed great interest, sold us the property for $60,000 in Chinese currency, and contributed one-third of the purchase price for scholarships. The original purchase was forty acres in a solid piece. In course of time, wo bought adjoining gardens also in ruins or open land amounting in all to more than four times the original tract.

We had determined from the outset to use an adaptation of Chinese architecture for the academic buildings. Graceful curves and gorgeous coloring were designed for the exteriors while the main structures were to be constructed throughout of reinforced concrete and equipped with modern lighting, heating and plumbing. Thus the buildings were in themselves symbolic of our educational purpose in preserving all that was most valuable in China's cultural heritage. Our water tower was encased in the form of a thirteen-storied pagoda, perhaps the most distinctive feature of the campus. We restored the landscaping of the old garden and added to it by our own planting, by transporting carved monoliths from nearby ruins and by a few pavilions in scenic spots. One of these later was the island in the lake that perpetuated the memory of Dr. Harry W. Luce, given by his son Henry R. Luce. Another was for a clear-toned temple bell which still strikes the hours for the campus. So many visitors in years afterward spoke of Yenching as the most beautiful campus in the world that we almost came to believe it ourselves. It certainly helped to deepen the attachment of the students to the institution and its international ideals. In one respect at least the reality became fairer than my dreams.

4

But I was also learning that dreams cost money. Dr. Luce was being left to stray around the United States with no guidance or backing, as was true of a second man who was not even collecting enough to cover his expenses.

In 1921 an Educational Commission came to China headed by Professor Ernest D. Burton of Chicago University. Their purpose was to study Christian education in China on behalf of the mission boards and to make recommendations. Three Chinese and three missionaries were asked to serve as collaborators. Dr. Chang Po-ling, President of Nankai University, was one of the Chinese, and I was asked to serve as one of the missionary members. We traveled all over China, and as a result of our survey published a very elaborate report on the principles of Christian college, middle school and theological education, and developed a program for all China.

In 1922 I was asked to make a trip to America to help present this report to the mission boards. On this occasion I met for the first time with the Yenching Board of Trustees. It was one of the most disillusioning experiences I have ever had. I heard one Trustee twitting another as they were assembling because he did not seem to be aware which one of the numerous similar boards on which they both served this one was. Suffice it to testify that before long, through the resignation of some, the awakened zeal of others, and new personnel whom the Trustees themselves were extremely generous in urging me to nominate, they became as actively concerned and co-operative as could have been expected.

But on that first trip of mine, it was a bleak outlook. Dr. Luce was indefatigable in getting Yenching into the consciousness of possible supporters, and was winning friends widely, sowing the seed from which later on rich harvests were often reaped by others. Yet, very little actual money was coming in. Then one evening at the home of Dr. William Adams Brown I heard a teacher from the Women's College of Constantinople and Dr. Brown's son John talk about money-raising through professional firms. I left my friend's home feeling that here was the answer. The Trustees were very dubious. Where would the initial funds come from? One Trustee complained about commercializing foreign missions. The firm itself had never tackled an enterprise outside of the United States. But no one had any better solution and at last a contract was signed with Tamblyn and Brown.

The firm specified that I must be available. They had learned from experience that there is something about the psychology of the American "prospect" that makes him want to deal with the president of the institution concerned. So for the next few years I commuted between Peking and New York, spending most of the working seasons in the States, doing something for which I had no special fitness and neglecting what would have seemed to be my primary function. Altogether I made ten trips to the United States before the Sino-Japanese War. One of my colleagues remembers a remark that I made on returning from one of these money-raising trips. "I never see a beggar," I had said, "without a feeling that I belong to the guild." It was slow, hard work, all the money coming in voluntary gifts from the American people, not a dollar from the American Government.

Tamblyn and Brown used an ingenious technique. They had alert young college graduates who organized everything but never appeared. Dr. Luce and I, with Chinese and others connected with Yenching, would appear in a given city and speak on all sorts of occasions. Receptions would be given in our honor. Then we called on those assigned to each of us. And it worked. This was evident after the first season, but the goal had not been reached so the arrangement was discontinued. After trying to learn from others how this sort of thing was done I decided that I had better do it in my own amateurish way. Years later under a different firm which employed a more direct method I was sent to Boston with a go-getter from out West. He argued quite properly that the only way to get money was to ask for it. He took me to call on a list of Boston Brahmins, some of whom I had met before, to all of whom he applied his high-pressure salesmanship. I felt utterly chagrined and left that city determined that much as my University needed money I would never again be involved in that method.

This constant necessity for cultivating prospective donors and begging them for contributions was distasteful to me and involved a sense of strain such as I have never experienced in anything else. I even suffered from a sort of nervous indigestion which always ceased with the end of one of these trips. But it also led to many delightful friendships and other interesting experiences. I tried to follow two guiding principles. One was to keep the person solicited as a friend of the institution and of China whether a gift was secured or not. The other—which I can claim never to have failed to observe—was not to pass judgment as to how the person concerned had secured his money but to accept what he offered only when this was without any restrictions upon the University's authority in its use and with a full knowledge of its policies and purpose. This two-fold treatment of the question of moral right seemed to me to cover any concrete problem that might at any time arise. It stood me in good stead in later years when beginning similar efforts to raise money in China.

Another aspect of this money-raising problem, which should perhaps have caused me more anxiety than it did, was in striking a balance between recklessly plunging ahead and wise caution.

The physical plant involved not only academic buildings and faculty residences, gifts for which were relatively easy to secure, but unromantic things like a very expensive power plant. The more Yenching could show in the way of actual accomplishment, the easier it would be to secure additional funds. On the other hand, it was imperative that confidence in our financial integrity be preserved. The problem was one of taking calculated risks.

5

There was a Chinese named K. A. Wee belonging to a wealthy family in Singapore, brought to America as a small boy, who had been graduated from Ohio Wesleyan University and who had an M.A. from Columbia. His family had taken him for an extravagantly conducted tour across America and Europe before going back to Singapore. He, however, had caught American ideals of simplicity and service and wanted to return to his native country to do something useful. The family threatened that unless he returned with them they would disinherit him completely. His reply was that he would disinherit them instead, as he did. He had therefore to do something for a living. At this juncture Tamblyn and Brown heard of him and since they were about to launch a campaign for a Chinese college attached him to their staff, with only a vague idea how he could be used.

Meanwhile the Methodist Board of Foreign Missions had determined to commemorate the name of Bishop J. W. Bashford by a building on the Yenching campus. He had been active in persuading his North China Mission to go into the union project. He had also been President of Ohio Wesleyan University when Wee was a student there. According to a certain procedure, excess funds raised by Methodist churches in specified areas might be designated for this memorial building. With Wee rather aimlessly in our hands, it occurred to me to assign him exclusively to the job of getting pastors to sign the requisite slip by which their excess funds if any, would automatically go to this account. He revelled in it. Train travel resulted in much loss of time so he begged for a car to be used for this mission. He soon wore it out, to the disgust of the firm. But money was pouring in, and I interceded for him on condition that he be more careful with the new one. The Methodist authorities became alarmed, for this was piling up results beyond their calculations. But they were good sports. There was a maximum amount and a time limit. Wee promised them that he would scrupulously observe both.

As the deadline approached Wee trained another Chinese boy and then an irresistible girl—for whom one of the top executives of the Curtis Publishing Company supplied his private limousine—to help reach his goal. This is how we secured the handsome Bashford Administration Building in the center of our campus. Wee was held up some five times by traffic cops for speeding, but on seeing a Chinese at the wheel saying something about an errand for a bishop, the cop always passed him on. After this strenuous drive had been concluded, Wee told me he had been talking so much about Yenching that he had talked himself into wanting to stay with it. I replied that the only opening we had was in athletics. He was not too keen about this but agreed to take it to begin with. He is the only Chinese I know of who has been the coach of an American university baseball team. When he started in he was amazed to discover that Chinese teams would leave the field rather than lose face by being defeated, that a boy whose rival had been elected captain would have to ruin that rival's record in retaliation, etc. After struggling against this lack of sportsmanship, he told me one day that he had come to believe that about the most useful thing he could do for his country would be training students to develop the moral qualities of athletic contests which he had learned in his American experience. He added, however, that he had never had any technical training and asked to be allowed to return to Columbia to take a doctor's degree in physical education.

I did not then know there was such a degree. Dr. Wee built up at Yenching not only a new spirit of sportmanship which became contagious in all north China intercollegiate games, but a department of Physical Education and what became known as the "Yenching spirit" which did far more for campus life than the mere improvement of student health.

6

An industrial romance only possible in America proved to be of great advantage to Yenching. A professor of chemistry conducting a laboratory experiment at what was then Oberlin College told the class that this might lead to the discovery of a light metallic product of large commercial possibilities. Charles M. Hall acting on this hint continued the experiment and produced aluminum. The crude apparatus he employed is now in the Oberlin Museum. In his will, after various personal bequests, he provided that one-third of the remainder should go to Oberlin, one third to schools in the southern states, and one third to institutions of higher learning maintained by Americans in Asia or the Balkans. Two close friends, the President of the Aluminum Company of America and one of its legal advisers, were the executors. They were sought by all who had any claim and many who had none, and were extremely hard to reach.

Dr. Harry Luce with his untiring persistence and beaming friendliness had won over the lawyer in Cleveland and introduced me to him. He arranged that I should have lunch with Mr. Arthur V. Davis and himself in New York. Mr. Davis quizzed me mercilessly and I was fully aware that he was doing this to size me up. It was one of those horrible occasions when the nervous victim scarcely sees the food knowing only that the fate of his cause is hanging in the balance. I was perspiring when it was all over. Then Mr. Davis said, "I am going to Paris this afternoon, but I'll stand with my colleague (Mr. Johnson, who had agreed to give half a million if Mr. Davis could be convinced).

But don't let your agents come around bothering us. You go back and build up a college worth supporting and when the time comes we'll do our part. Good-bye." After a year or so when I saw Mr. Johnson again he said, "We've decided to give you that million—yes, we've been watching you, and we are going to double the amount." I went through another spasm later on when I asked them to make it a million and a half for reasons which they agreed were valid.

Having made all their allocations over Asia they still had stock with a book value of some four-and-a-half million, although one-half of this was not then paying dividends. They cabled me for consultation as to how to dispose of their undistributed balance. It seemed to me of fascinating interest that a man who was American big business incarnate and a typical corporation lawyer had between them conceived of an institute for helping Chinese to study their own culture with the apparatus and technical methods worked out in the West for research in a foreign civilization, and for helping Americans to learn enough about Chinese culture to spread the knowledge of this among their fellow countrymen. They confessed it was all very vague in their minds. None the less the germinal idea was theirs. Dean Donham of the Harvard School of Business Administration had been vainly exploring the chance of a grant from the Hall estate for his school. He happened to be a college classmate of Mr. Johnson, the lawyer, so they sent me to Harvard to work out with the people there something along the lines of their idea. The Harvard authorities were very gracious about allowing the fair name of their university to be associated with the little missionary college in China. This was the origin of the Harvard-Yenching Institute of Chinese Studies. Davis and Johnson drew heavily on Donham for assistance. He had been a banker and talked their language. He was unwittingly drawn into the new enterprise and became for many years the extremely active and competent chairman of its Board of Trustees. Among many other advantages to Yenching, the "Harvard-Yenching Institute" enabled us—and through us several other Christian colleges in China—to develop Chinese studies fully up to the best standards of any purely Chinese institution.

The treasurer of the Board of Trustees was Mr. E. M. McBrier. Early in the financial campaign I called on him at his apartment in the Woolworth Building. He opened the conversation, "I suppose you have come to arrange for a loan."

"No," I replied, "I leave all that to the Trustees. I have come on a more personal matter, to ask you to resign from the Board of Trustees." Mr. McBrier was startled. I went on. "Let me explain. You're obviously not interested in this project, as you are in other things. Why not relieve yourself of this responsibility?"

"What evidence have you?" Mr. McBrier asked.

"You are in a position to give to things you care about, yet you haven't given anything to Yenching except $260 to buy railway tickets for Harry Luce. You are treasurer of the Board. You know our needs, so I can't believe you care. There's no blame but I think you should be relieved of the burden so that we can get someone who doesn't have so many other interests."

Mr. McBrier was very angry at first, threshed around in his chair and spoke of other pledges. Finally he declared, "I'll promise you this: either I'll do something to convince you I'm interested or resign."

In a letter to me just before I returned to China, he promised $100,000 and later said he wanted a building started at once. I thought it might mean a change of plan. "Oh, no," he answered, "this is extra." Several times later he would mention other Trustees to me and say, "Why don't you go and talk to them as you did to me?"

After describing these bits of good fortune I could follow with a long and dismal chapter on failure in promotional efforts. Money-raising is at best a tedious and often disappointing task.

I wasted much time over "prospects" who lost either their interest or their money or became estranged over some trivial mishap. The most tantalizing aspect of this professional begging was perhaps success in getting on friendly terms with alluring "prospects" but none in "cashing in" on this relationship. For instance, I was able through Philip Fugh on one of his government missions to become fairly well acquainted with Henry and Edsel Ford who had me to lunch whenever I happened to be in Detroit and asked pointed questions about my University. Any American college president would have envied me this access and might have turned it to good account. But I followed an instinct which told me that if he made no offer he would probably not respond to my appeal.

After becoming trained in observing the idiosyncrasies of wealthy individuals, it was a greater joy to deal with officers of the Rockefeller Foundation with whom it was purely a question of having a sufficiently worthy cause that also fitted into their program. In any case, one could be assured of a friendly courtesy and understanding sympathy. The more I saw of the inner workings of the Rockefeller Foundation—and I was a frequent visitor —the more admiration I felt for the original concept and the way in which it was being realized.

So, over the years, funds were raised, first in America and later also in China, for buildings and equipment, for the growing cost of maintenance and teaching, and for endowment. By 1937 Yenching's endowment had reached the sum of $2,500,000 (in American currency).

7

In attempting to create the university of my dreams my task seemed to assume a four-fold aspect: its Christian purpose; its academic standards and vocational courses; its relation to the Chinese environment and contribution to international understanding and good will; its financial resources and physical equipment. The last of these I have already described.

Yenching had come into existence as an integral part of the missionary enterprise, in order to provide educational facilities for the children of church members and perhaps even more for training church workers. This ancillary function had supplied the only right it could claim for having been established on Chinese soil as well as its only hope for financial support. I wanted it to continue to be thoroughly Christian in atmosphere and influence while free from even seeming to be part of a propagandist movement. There should be no required chapel attendance nor compulsory religious services, no academic benefits from profession of Christian faith nor corresponding handicaps from refusal. It must by every test be a real university, where truth was taught untrammeled and faith or its outward expression was treated as a personal matter. In the choice of faculty members, by providing facilities and favoring influences, the administration would be creating conditions helpful to student initiative in religious affairs. For there can be no Christian university without a nucleus of actively Christian students. Yenching was regarded both within the institution and by the public generally as Christian, regardless of their personal attitude to Christianity. We tried to demonstrate the proper university standards and an avowed Christian purpose are not incompatible, that an integrated community a majority of whom were committed to the Christian view of life generated a quality of corporate life which is beneficent, and that the University as such was able to bear witness to the advantages of Christian faith for all forms of organized human life.

I came to feel that, after the earliest period of heralding a hitherto unheard Gospel had somewhat passed, missionary work might well take the form in many instances of adventurous demonstrations of the Christian way of life. The Yenching campus seemed to me pre-eminently to afford such opportunity.

The organization for religious life was the Yenching University Christian Fellowship, directed by an executive committee composed of faculty, student and worker representatives. Membership was conditioned on a pledge to follow and learn more of the way which Jesus himself had taught and lived rather than on any creedal basis. This had the advantage of detaching these functions from the University administration as such, as well as of avoiding denominational problems in a union institution. Those who wished to had their own special services, but this did not conflict with the Fellowship. This purely voluntary arrangement simplified matters also with Chinese public opinion which might have been aroused to oppose the use of an elaborate educational program for religious propaganda. The greatest benefit was the sense of spontaneity and realism. Only those who were genuinely interested took part but to them it was a matter of vital concern.

I can speak with immodest pride of the quality of work done in teaching and in research at Yenching because I had so little part in these activities. My job was to leave the teachers as nearly free as possible for their own duties. None the less there was a zest for me in all the details of our program. I have already spoken of the high standard reached in our department of Chinese studies, stimulated by gifts from the Hall estate and the Harvard-Yenching Institute. I also wanted to improve the teaching of English. The best way to make the mastery of foreign languages less necessary in China is to equip students for the task of mediating all aspects of western knowledge into Chinese life. Our students lived virtually in a bilingual environment. On entering they were supposed to be able to take any college subject in either language and the teachers were free to use either or both. Visiting lecturers were never interpreted, although there were nearly always some in the audience who suffered in consequence. In speaking to the student body, I sometimes changed my mind on the platform as to whether to talk in

Chinese or English. All this meant that the students gained flexibility in passing from one language to the other. Those who continued their studies abroad seemed to be able to do so with only slight linguistic handicaps.

The Medical College had been a more successful aspect of the local missionary union, as enshrined in its name, Peking Union Medical College, even before being supported by the Rockefeller Foundation. Another was the North China Union Women's College, the achievement chiefly of Miss Luella Miner, and the first attempt in China at higher education for girls. Their numbers were small and the standards not very high, but it was a significant beginning by a woman of rare vision and ability. Within a few months after I had taken office, it was decided to incorporate it as the Women's College of Yenching University. That was consummated in what was facetiously described as a wedding ceremony conducted by Chancellor Tsai of Peking National University who made the principal address. It proved to be an exceedingly happy partnership in our coeducational institution.

It was very gratifying to observe the progress made in our College of Natural Sciences. Chinese intellectuals had been belatedly influenced by nineteenth-century rationalism in which science had discredited religion. There was a special advantage, therefore, in the emphasis put on these subjects in a Christian university by teachers who felt no conflict between the two. A close relation had been formed with the Peking Union Medical College by which we almost served as its pre-medical school and our students received their B.Sc. after their first year in the Medical College. The same was true of our pre-nursing courses. The Peking Union Medical College had early felt the need for trained nurses fluent in English. But for a college girl to enter the career of a high-class *amah* was abhorrent to conventional Chinese thinking. Once the idea broke we had a steady stream of excellent material, and another career had been opened for Chinese girls. We had already faced a somewhat similar issue by introducing a course in leather tanning under industrial chemistry. Manual labor had been beneath the dignity of a scholar. Add to this the dirty toil involved in curing hides and would any of our boys be willing? And would they lose face among their fellows? We were surprised how quickly this course won its way.

Our College of Public Affairs took its name from the Princeton School of Public and International Affairs and was chiefly supported by an association of graduates of that university known as the Princeton-Yenching Foundation. This meant much more to us than merely the financial benefit. Princeton professors or graduates just out of college taught in the college for one or more years at a time. Our more promising students went to Princeton for a doctorate and not infrequently to return to our faculty. The departments included political science, economics and sociology, all extremely useful in the modernization of China. Perhaps the courses in social work were those for which graduates were most in demand by both private and government agencies.

My own opinion was that China had been mistaken in taking over the American four-year college curriculum and that mission colleges were partly at fault. Chinese economic conditions and other factors indicated as a preferable system grouping the last two years of Senior Middle School and the first two years of college into a single unit after which all courses would be more or less specialized. Most students could not afford a liberal arts collegiate education, and many of those in mission colleges used it therefore as what might be described as vocational training in English. In any case, I was keenly interested in stressing vocational courses, with an especial view to the outlet for expressing the Christian spirit or meeting social needs. Several of these have been mentioned. One that seemed promising until the Japanese destroyed our equipment was the attempt to recover the ancient Chinese ceramic industry by new scientific methods. My own special pet was probably journalism. The Trustees had authorized me to add this department on the explicit understanding that they had no financial obligation for it, and its hazardous existence may have endeared it to me. But newspapers were coming to be increasingly influential in Chinese life, and the inculcation of high standards of editing and ethics seemed especially worth-while at what was almost the inception of a new profession. From the outset, it was one of our most popular majors, usually vying with economics in having the heaviest enrollment. At one time the representatives of the Chinese News Agency in all the important capitals of the world were almost all the graduates of our department, and graduates were scarcely less conspicuous on the staffs of Chinese dailies.

One of the most gratifying developments in our technical courses came after the recovery of Yenching from the Japanese. A group of Chinese leaders in Tientsin and vicinity proposed that we start engineering courses with all the expenses to be met by themselves. They explained that they needed men less elaborately trained than those who had studied abroad or even in Chinese colleges with their too theoretical approach and their demand for high salaries. They had been watching the students we turned out and wanted men of this type who also had the requisite technical knowledge and the willingness to work in the shops and learn. It was arranged that students would start with two years of pre-engineering and then spend three years with half of each year on our campus and the other half in factories under expert guidance. The course at once attracted good students, but it became one of the many casualties of the Nationalist defeats.

Since I had for years been a teacher in a theological seminary, I naturally took an especial interest in the development of a School of Religion. It was to be primarily for college graduates, an integral part of the University, maintaining in this environment the same academic requirements. The dominant element in the faculty became increasingly Chinese. Fortunately, a splendid group of these was secured, the peers in their academic qualifications of any Chinese teachers in our own or any other university. They were absolutely free to work out forms of worship, doctrinal statements, etc., in harmony with their Chinese heritage, and to create a Chinese Christian literature. They revelled in this freedom and put it to excellent use. But they employed it more in their selections of western models than in anything startingly novel. There was, however, a wholesome lack of constraint among them and a sense of mission or responsibility as Chinese which was a notable advantage to the Christian cause and especially to religious life on our own campus.

8

Among the theories which I took with me to Peking, the most clearly defined was that the new University should establish itself in Chinese life independent of treaties with western countries or any other extraneous factors, with only such protection as the Chinese people themselves possessed and wanted to share with us. I believed that imperialism and missions could be and should be divorced. Foreigners and Chinese were to take part on equal terms in every aspect of University affairs, and live side by side in the same style of houses. At that time these were radical ideas. When the National Government was established at Nanking, Yenching was promptly registered as subject to all the regulations of its Ministry of Education. But these were largely internal matters. I set out to become acquainted with those who were in places of authority, including many whose previous careers or prospective ones made them important. In addition to their political influence, many of them were able to make substantial contributions, and these tended to increase their interest in the University and to identify it more fully with Chinese life.

After the University had become fairly well established through intensive financial efforts in the United States, I began to give more serious thought to building up interest in China, partly to win intelligently sympathetic and friendly good will in a suspicious and potentially antagonistic environment, partly to effect a beginning in Chinese financial support. With Philip Fugh I visited practically all of the more important sections of the country, including Manchuria, and became acquainted with almost all of the leading figures in government as well as with many others prominent in education, finance and industry. From these journeys many permanent friendships were formed, both personal friendships and friendships for our University. One immediate by-product was to enable Chinese to think of Yenching as at least potentially their own, and worthy of their generous support, rather than as an enterprise maintained for them by foreigners, however worthy their motives.

My original aim had been for Chinese to take an increasing share in educational, administrative, religious and other forms of leadership, as well as in financial maintenance, so that it would ultimately become essentially a Chinese university retaining its western origin largely as a historical memory. In so far as demonstrating their capacity for this and their loyalty to the ideals and principles of the University, my dreams were abundantly realized. The first chancellor of Yenching was Mr. Wu Lei-ch'uan, a *Hanlin* scholar who had become a Christian, for some years an honored member of our faculty and before then Vice-minister of Education. His title in Chinese was *Hsiao-chang*; my title was *Hsiao-wu-chang* but the English title was unchanged. He died after north China had been engulfed in the Japanese invasion. After V-J Day the Board of Managers elected Dr. C. W. Luh, head of the psychology department, as Mr. Wu's successor, and I retained my original title, being given leave of absence during my ambassadorship at Nanking.

However, I also awoke to the crucial importance of better

international understanding in securing peace and in leading ultimately to some form of world community. Universities, I felt, ought to be generating centers for this cosmopolitan outlook. The circumstances of Yenching's foundation might be turned into a permanent asset and broadened so as to include relationships with other countries. One dream of mine was in a small way beginning to be realized, but its fullest attainment is still in the future. This is that Yenching—while becoming Chinese in a more thoroughgoing sense than hitherto—should be at the same time more widely and avowedly international.

In the case of Yenching, we already had a start in this direction. Predominantly American in origin and support, but with a small British element, and established in China with the intention of becoming more completely and permanently Chinese, it had the framework. Furthermore, we began to have other relationships. The experiment of adapting the Oxford tutorial method in the honors courses known popularly as the "Oxford Modern Greats," with special British sources of support, and with the leadership of one who had himself taken these courses —Michael Lindsay, son of former Vice-Chancellor Lindsay of Oxford University—tended to strengthen the British connection we already had. Almost from the beginning a committee in Switzerland maintained two of their fellow countrymen on our faculty, Dr. and Mrs. Philippe de Vargas. The French Government had granted a fellowship for graduate study in Paris, and the first recipient of this had completed four years of study there, preparatory to joining our faculty, when the war broke out in Europe. The German Government had been making a small annual grant to our Department of Western Languages, which they renewed and we cheerfully accepted, even as late as the autumn of 1941. The Italian Government had in the spring of that year granted us eight fellowships with almost all expenses of travel and residence in Italy and the privilege of studying any subjects in any recognized university in that country. Eight students had been selected and were diligently working on the Italian language, but the acute international tension compelled the abandonment of the project before they were to sail in the summer.

I especially wanted similar ties with Japan and Russia. But wars and Communists shattered all such fantasies. None the less I am convinced that the idea is a sound one. What I hope can be achieved—assuming that Yenching can some day be reopened on its original basis—is a system of exchange professorships and student fellowships with as many other countries as possible, most of all with Japan and Russia, these to include especially the languages and literatures of these countries, present political or economic issues, etc. Such arrangements would enable students to specialize in one or another foreign culture, or to study a subject as treated in several different countries. They would come into personal contacts with these teachers.

But perhaps the main advantage would be in a certain atmosphere pervading the institution, making the students internationally minded, almost unconsciously, and bringing together like-minded persons from several countries into a community fellowship that would enrich and broaden the whole life of the campus. It would seem especially appropriate that such an experiment should be made in China. The moral philosophy of no other country has had a broader, more inclusive outlook. It is not in conflict with recently intensified nationalistic trends, unless indeed the Chinese people become convinced by unhappy experiences that a narrow patriotic loyalty is their only hope of national survival. That Yenching University may have its proper part in generating dynamic energies and in demonstrating the feasibility of friendly intercourse among those of all countries, seems not too chimerical an aspiration. Its foreign origin would then become not a historical necessity to be forgotten, but a permanent advantage to be utilized in bringing to Chinese youth on their own soil what many of them sought by studying abroad.

9

A few months after I had begun my work at Yenching, Charles Corbett, Lucius Porter and I met to find a motto. All of us had been born in China and shared in the conviction that a Christian university should represent a blend of religious faith, the scientific spirit and method, and fearless unhampered inquiry. One of the others urged the saying of Jesus about ministering rather than being ministered unto. I recalled the quotation Thomas Jefferson had carved in Greek over the main gate of the University of Virginia, which was similarly inscribed over the entrance to the Chicago World's Fair in 1893, "Ye shall know the Truth, and the Truth shall make you free." Somehow, as we talked, the inspiration came to combine these two great sayings of Jesus and thus sum up the essence of His teaching, "Freedom through Truth for Service."

This motto was soon woven into the whole fabric of the institution, embedded in its spiritual structure, in student publications and symbolic designs, in the popular college song and best of all in the consciousness of individual students. It is not too much to say that at least for the great majority it crystallized their philosophy of life, that they aspired to put it into practice, and that they made it the standard by which they passed judgment on their fellows. I had students who went over to the Communists come back and tell me with starry-eyed enthusiasm what they were doing for the common people in trying faithfully to live up to this motto. In no other college of my acquaintance has the college motto had so vital and dynamic an influence upon the student body.

10

In the building up of Yenching University, my faculty colleagues were an unfailing source of inspiration and guidance. From the beginning we were a team. I cannot overstate the

value and joy to me of that comradeship. I once heard Mr.
John D. Rockefeller, Jr. at a banquet tell an anecdote about
his father to the effect that when asked the secret of his phenom-
enal success he replied, "My associates." As I listened it sounded
to be like an overdone affectation of modesty, but before many
years had passed I came to understand perfectly what he meant.
On a much smaller scale I could say the same thing with the
utmost sincerity. I wish that there were space to mention each
one by name and describe his or her special contribution to our
common task.

A word must be said about Dr. H. S. Galt. In addition to a
theological training, he had specialized in education and had
been President of the College at Tungchow. He also had experience before and after coming to China in a wide range of
practical affairs. His attainments in both spoken and literary
Chinese were quite unusual among missionaries. There was
scarcely any aspect of university life in which he was not active.
Again and again on my frequent absences he acted in my place.
Almost continuously he was chairman of the Grounds and
Buildings Committee, which especially during the period of
construction was an extremely important function. His "History
of Yenching University" is evidence not only of his accuracy
in literary production but also of the first-hand knowledge he
has had of University affairs. However, it fails to give him the
credit he should have for all that has resulted from our combined efforts. By temperament and habit he tended to be careful
and conservative, to observe constitutional or other established
procedure. He was thus a constant safeguard against my more
carelessly adventurous tendencies. On any new proposal we
would be apt to take opposite sides with the result as a rule
that an agreement would be reached in the end which avoided
either extreme. Invariably we respected each other's point of
view and maintained a friendship unmarred by a single touch

of personal animosity. Happy is the administrator who can have so wise, unselfish and loyal a colleague.

A tribute should also be given to Timothy Lew, a friend from his boyhood, who accompanied me from Nanking to Peking when I assumed the administrative responsibility for the new University. He took all the scholastic and oratorical honors at St. John's University preparatory school and did the same in the United States as nearly as a foreign student could. He studied at the University of Georgia, Columbia, Yale, Union Theological Seminary (N.Y.), married a fellow student in the States on—as he expressed it—the American plan, and returned to join me in Nanking Seminary despite vigorous efforts of Southeastern University to secure him. I assured him that I would be delighted to have him with me as I began the untried adventure in the North but that he must decide for himself. Both the Seminary and Southeastern University wanted him badly and made their appeal the more formidable by offering him each a half-time position. But he decided to go with me which was in itself a striking instance of Chinese loyalty to a friend. It was not long before he was made Dean of our School of Religion and had begun to persuade others whom he had known in the States to join that faculty. He did the same with those desired for the College of Arts and Sciences (the other unit then of the University). With all of these highly qualified Chinese he argued that despite their skeptical misgivings this really was a missionary school in which Chinese were to share everything with foreigners as colleagues and that they ought to help in making this novel experiment a successful demonstration. His assistance at this initial stage both in selecting and then in securing desirable Chinese for the faculty had a very large part in the direction given to Yenching policy. Dr. Lew's subsequent career as a Christian leader is too much a part of the history of the Christian movement in China to be repeated here. He was one of its outstanding figures in religious assemblies and all kinds of organized activities both because of his impassioned eloquence and his rare capacity for literary expression in Chinese. He was a notable figure in most of the international Christian conferences of two decades until his death in 1948. I mention him here not only because of his beautiful friendship but because he symbolizes my relationship from Yenching beginnings with my Chinese colleagues, peers alike in their own scholarship and capacities, and in their rights in all administrative affairs. What has been suggested regarding Timothy Lew holds true of practically all of my Chinese colleagues in proportion to the time they were with Yenching or the extent of my personal opportunity of association with them.

II

In the preceding paragraphs I have tried to describe different aspects of the growth of the University as the realization of my fair dreams. But the last section of this chapter must be devoted to the students of Yenching. They are after all what makes a university. Some of them have been disappointing, most of them perhaps in some respects. But in view of what I had known of Chinese students in general, remembering also their historical background and the disordered conditions of contemporary national life, they have on the whole made their way against many obstacles and manifested a character and spirit which is far beyond what I would have prophesied. They gave ample evidence of what fine material is Chinese youth, of the vitality and mental capacity of the race, as well as of the effectiveness of education conceived as the self-expression of the whole personality. Through them the American people demonstrated their good will for China and contributed toward its advancement as well as toward more intelligent mutually friendly relations. The distinctively religious purpose of the institution was a powerful influence in these achievements and enabled it to have a not unworthy share in the progress of the Christian movement in China.

I had during my life in China ample opportunity to observe an unpleasant phenomenon of Chinese student life picturesquely described as *feng-ch'ao*, "wind and tide." These organized outbreaks gained force and their most effective technique in patriotic demonstrations. But, having discovered their power when thus organized, aggressive students in schools all over the country began to use such strikes as a means of remedying real or fancied internal complaints, anything from the personality of the President to the flavor of the food. When once swept by impassioned oratory or led into making commitments through skillful manipulation, even the most orderly and friendly students would join recklessly in these herd movements, and if not handled satisfactorily a hopeless crisis would be easily precipitated. We were very fortunate at Yenching in never having a *feng-ch'ao* that got out of hand, but we came sufficiently close to such a break for me to have a wholesome dread of mass psychology especially when this affected Chinese students with their peculiar weaknesses and social inhibitions.

In a more personal vein my own associations with thousands of Yenching *hsiao-yu* (alumni) has been an inexpressibly joyous one. One of the most beautiful traditions of Chinese life has long been the relation between teacher and pupil. Every foreigner who has taught Chinese of whatever age or social class can testify to the richness of this experience. It is something more warmly human than mere respect or even veneration on the pupil's part, instinctive and yet delightfully spontaneous. In my first years at Yenching, when the students were few in number and I was still wondering just what a college president really did, it was easy to know each one of them. But as their numbers increased along with my duties, and I was constantly away from the campus, this became impossible. I vainly tried in various ways to remedy this loss with only limited success. Yet in some strange way I felt toward an enrollment of a thousand or more mostly unfamiliar individuals as though I knew each one, and was subtly aware that they understood this. With the delicacy of perception which suffuses Chinese manners they would both while on the campus and in after life save me from embarrassment by telling me who they were.

Although my contact with them was necessarily slight, yet by some mysterious process they seemed to appreciate what I tried to stand for and how sentimental was my feeling for all of them. In the frequent anti-Japanese and other nationalistic outbreaks which swept the Chinese student world of the time and for other reasons I usually managed to get fairly well acquainted with their leaders. It was always inspiring to address the student body and to sense their eager responsiveness. Life on a coeducational college led to many a romance, and I was constantly called upon to perform a wedding ceremony, usually but not always according to the Christian form and in my own home. Incidentally, of these many campus engagements, whether I officiated at the wedding or not, I do not know of one which proved disastrous. It seems to be an argument in favor of this process for finding a suitable partner. This affectionate relationship between teacher and student, even when so nebulously generalized, would only be possible perhaps in China and had added significance in the case of an American. I was reminded of it in countless letters wherever I went.

My vanity over Yenching graduates was most unblushing in the case of those who had later joined the faculty, usually after taking advanced degrees abroad. We were aware of the bad ingrowing effects of having too many of them. But for an institution founded by foreigners for a special purpose and in process of becoming indigenous without losing its distinctive quality, there would be no better medium for effecting this transformation than our own old students. They appreciated and themselves shared the ideals and beliefs of the founders. They brought back memories of their earlier life as students and felt a loyalty not easy for other Chinese to acquire.

Whether the soul of Yenching can survive Communist intolerance, as it had recovered from the Japanese terror, only time will tell. During the first two years of Communist "liberation," the People's Government classified the University as a "progressive" institution and allowed it to continue with a minimum of interference. In 1951 it was forcibly merged with other universities in Peking and deprived of its name and identity as a private and Christian institution. But even though it has now lost the freedom which was one of its greatest strengths, I feel that it has been abundantly worth all that it cost in money and human effort. For thirty years it released spiritual energies both in its institutional witness and through the lives of its students. In the complex of conflicting ideas struggling now for the mastery of China these results cannot ever be completely liquidated.

5 Personal Experiences of Yenching Days

On moving to Peking I had the chance to learn Mandarin in its pristine purity, and at the time when it was beginning to be the *Kuoyu* or national language, which gave it additional prestige. But I was at once plunged into administrative details which were carried on largely in English and soon began to spend much of the time in or traveling to and from the States; thus I neglected to be properly drilled in the Peking pronunciation. Still less was I able to mingle in friendly, unhurried loquacity with the real "natives" of a city largely populated with those from all over China. The constant strengthening of the Chinese faculty meant that most of these had studied abroad and were more at ease in English than most westerners who had studied Chinese as adults could ever hope to be in their language. The improvement of our own English teaching fitted the students to understand it better, and led to its use by us in dealings with them as giving them further practice. Teachers and students alike were largely from other regions and dialects and their Chinese pronunciation might be a snare and hindrance to the eager learner of Pekingese. More and more I found myself either on the Yenching campus where English was current or traveling away from Peking. None the less I tried to make some progress in *Kuoyu,* in listening to and reproducing as best I could its beautifully clear and melodious sounds. It is certainly worthy of becoming the national language.

The study of Chinese ideographs and learning to read is of course an integral part of language study. Like the majority of western students, I found it a most fascinating feature and had to guard against overemphasizing this at the expense of learning to talk well. Even for this latter purpose a knowledge of the characters would seem all but indispensable. I tried to write every character as a test of recognizing it and to understand principles of structure and the order of strokes in writing. But I never undertook to compose in Chinese for the reason that to do so really well involves a vast amount of time spent in mastering what is difficult enough for the Chinese themselves and almost impossible for foreigners without betraying foreign defects.

Chinese literature is of course only a continuation of language study. The language course required by my mission included the *Four Books* (Confucian Classics) and one novel, *The Fortunate Union*. The necessity for reading these gave me my first acquaintance with a vast volume of great literature. The mission was wise in these requirements, and they were doubtless intended to stimulate a habit of such reading. But the actual pressure was all against this. American concern with practical results and a distorted sense of religious duty combined to drive most missionaries into keeping busy with petty details of mission activity. This was unfortunately aggravated by our superiority complex and our inability to appreciate how valuable even for our immediate purpose would have been a less superficial acquaintance with so rich a literature. It would help to an understanding of the people, their mental habits, their reaction to the Christian message, their social attitude to us. All honor to the few notable exceptions to the general rule among missionaries, those who despite all hindrances and the honest criticism of their colleagues, persevered in their studies to the point where they were really at home in the reading of Chinese books and who thus gained insight into the cultural background of this people. I felt all this and made resolutions which were too often broken, partly from yielding to the exigency of what was regarded as my "work," partly from lack of vision as to the desirability of perusing systematically such reading.

Between the classical literary style (*Wen-li*) and the now completely established simplified conversational *Pai-hua* or spoken language, I must confess to a personal preference for the former. I am quite aware that this is reactionary and old-fashioned, and that I am usually found on the other side. From the time when Hu Shih and his associates began their heroic Literary Revolution, which led in an incredibly short time to a sweeping victory, I watched the movement with enthusiastic approval and hopes for their success. It was as logical and progressive a development as when the scholars of each European country ceased to write entirely in Latin or Greek and used their own vernacular, from which came the Italian, German, English and other national literatures. I am merely recording my appreciation of *Wen-li* as a marvelously terse, elegant, expressive literary style, capable of delicate nuances of thought, subtle in its power of imaginative suggestion, in itself providing the material for the highest literary art. No wonder that its mastery has absorbed the energies of the ablest men of China for many generations, even apart from the career this led to in official preferment. For us foreigners I contend that the difficulty lies not in *Wen-li* as such but in the classical allusions in which it abounds. Not to recognize the quotation involved prevents an understanding of the passage. But to recognize such references requires many years of unremitting study even with the aid of dictionaries and is therefore impossible for any foreigner who has not gone through essentially the same courses as would an educated Chinese.

Looking back over my life in China I regret that I have failed to carry through a more systematic and extensive reading of the best of this rich literary deposit. As it is I have read in addition to the more important "classics" some of the greater philosophers in whole or in part, the most famous novels and specimens of recent ones, and other samples. But even this has been enough to give me some appreciation of the mellowed culture thus preserved and of the moral and spiritual ideals which are at least understood and accepted in theory by the humblest illiterates as well as by the scholars.

Of the philosophers my favorites are Mencius because of his advanced sociological teachings and Wang Yang-ming who combined the life of an active administrator with that of a teacher and thinker of rare spiritual insight. Motse is not far from the Christian position in his well-known but somewhat pragmatic advocacy of universal love, and he sounds almost like a contemporary in urging less extravagance in weddings and funerals. Hsuntse is hard reading because of his use of peculiar characters but is more Confucian than orthodox Confucianists—as well as much more logical—in arguing that since human nature is not naturally good it needs all the aids of proper education and government.

That such reading—apart from deepening my respect for Chinese civilization—has molded my character, I am confident. Though to what extent and in what forms I hesitate to say. It has made me more tolerant, and more concerned with the ethical and social values of Christianity. I have at least learned to admire the gentle humanism of Chinese literature; its emphasis on personal relationships, loyalties and rights; its cardinal belief in the moral order of the universe with which man as an individual and in his social organization should strive to be in harmony.

2

I refer to Chinese art not because of any expert knowledge, for which I have never taken the time, but merely as a tribute to such features as I learned especially to admire. Any study of Chinese ideographs leads to appreciation of calligraphy. Painting is very closely allied to this. Without any technical study I have come to revel in Chinese paintings, especially landscapes and birds. The former seem at their best in the soft browns of the Ming period. So fond am I of bronze objects that I thought at times of attempting to collect these, but constant preoccupations and economic limitations prevented. Porcelains need no special capacity for enjoyment; most of those I possess are precious alike because of their intrinsic beauty and as carefully chosen gifts from Chinese friends.

My experience with theatricals has been a curious one. Because popular performances were usually connected with temple-worship, Chinese Christians were supposed to eschew them, and the missionary could not too openly indulge. Such glimpses as I had aroused mild amusement or curiosity, the accompanying music being meaningless clatter. As the religious prejudice ceased to inhibit, I remained too busy and indifferent. But shortly after moving to Peking I saw Mei Lan-fang give a short operatic performance as an item in a charity entertainment, and was at once attracted by the exquisite grace of his motions. It was much later before I could enjoy with any intelligent appreciation the singing of this most famous of Chinese contemporary actors. Since women were not tolerated in Chinese theatres until very recently, Mei Lan-fang always impersonated feminine roles. In course of time we became acquainted, and as the plans for his American tour took shape, he consulted me not only about business arrangements, but also about the plays to be selected and their adaptation to American taste. I protested that I knew nothing about Chinese and very little of American dramatic affairs, but his insistence led to my going to see him perform and, with this added stimulus, to observe the plays critically. Absurd as was Mr. Mei's deference to my opinion in preparing for what proved to be an amazingly successful tour, it led me to read up in English about the Chinese drama, to watch the best performers under competent guidance, and incidentally to

a personal friendship with this idol of the contemporary stage.
Architecture became a practical issue when we determined to construct the Yenching academic buildings in a modified Chinese style. Except for the unusually graceful pagodas around West Lake at Hangchow, and the location of temples in beautiful natural surroundings, I had not paid much attention to Chinese architecture until moving to Peking where I became at once fascinated—as is true of all visitors—by the superb specimens there. The palaces and temples of Peking and the nearby Western Hills, with their sweeping curves and splendid colors, exhibit this art at its very best. To me its distinctive excellence is, however, the balanced proportion of its lines. There is no better instance of this than the T'ien An Men leading to the old Forbidden City. Another feature not so generally noticed is the delightful way in which the rigid symmetry of the main buildings is relieved of monotony or severity by so-called nature architecture in which pavilions, bridges and even buildings are scattered in deliberately irregular patterns, built into natural or artificial hills or valleys or bordering on pools, all off the points of the compass and in line with nothing. In Yenching I liked to think of the Chinese exteriors and modern interiors as symbolic of our synthesis of the best in Chinese culture and modern knowledge.

In closing these comments in Chinese art, I cannot resist referring to the skillful use of form and color in ordinary life, whether it be the knack of selecting the most picturesque spot for locating temples or pagodas, the artistry in a "hundred crafts," the graceful elegance especially of masculine attire, traces of orderliness and beauty even in humble shops and homes, stylized penmanship in any serious writing or its twisting into individualistic fancies when in lighter mood. One gains the impression that artistic appreciation is a racial heritage and that it permeates Chinese life quite generally.

3

After my father's death in 1913, my mother had moved to live with us in Nanking, and naturally had accompanied us to Peking. At first she thought of herself as a useless old woman away from all of her old haunts and activities, but actually she became one of the busiest persons in the community. She kept up with the news, never missed a meeting to which she might go and really enjoyed talking to all sorts of callers coming to our home. She had arrived in Shanghai on a Christmas Day in 1874 and soon after had helped to start the second girls' school in all China. Then only the poorest of the poor would have thought of sending their daughters to the strange foreigners where everything was provided free—food and clothes as well as books and pens. The teaching was as elementary as possible. The school made only two conditions for entrance: the feet must be left unbound, and the school had the right to veto the marriage engagement (made of course by the parents). Fifty years later it occurred to my wife and me to celebrate Christmas by keeping open house all day for our students to pay their respect to my mother on this golden anniversary of her arrival in China. As these sophisticated college girls tripped gaily in with their boy friends, many of them from leading families of the country and from all parts of it, this dramatized for my mother the progress in education for girls since those simple beginnings in Hangchow.

She was taken ill on her eighty-third birthday two weeks later, and she died in a few days. Chinese as well as western feelings led me to bury her beside my father and a brother in Hangchow. But there was a civil war at the time and I had to travel by sea from Tientsin. The government kindly supplied an ornate private car, designed for the Empress Dowager and therefore embossed with huge gilded dragons, for the railway trip to

Tientsin. I thought with quizzical humor of the way my mother would have smiled at this ending to her life in China.

Miss Grace M. Boynton, a teacher in Yenching, wrote about my mother, "Her sweetness and gaiety exerted a peculiar charm over us who knew her. Even at the age of eighty, her energy seemed inexhaustible but it was never of the bustling kind. Rather, it was benign. It carried her into the hearts of us all. I do not know when it began, or who started it, but I remember that for the whole Yenching community, faculty and students alike, she was known as 'Mother Stuart.' "

A year and a half later my wife died. She had never recovered from an injury when our son was born, and she was a semi-invalid, chiefly concerned that my work was not interfered with by her weakness and fairly frequent ailments. She and my mother supplemented each other admirably. My mother's interests were intellectual or in public affairs, my wife's in housekeeping, notably in desserts up to New Orleans standards, in the beautiful products of Chinese craftsmanship, in simple, kindly deeds for people in trouble. We had planned to advance our closing exercises that year in order to move out to the new campus before the summer rains began. She knew that her end was near, but it must have been sheer will power that enabled her to survive until after commencement. She died on June 6, one week after the spring term closed and just as the University was being moved to its new site. The funeral was held on Sunday afternoon in the chapel of the Medical College, conducted by Dr. T. T. Lew, a service beautiful in arrangement and expression. The casket was taken to the new University cemetery near the new campus, in which hers was the first grave.

Our married life was so richly satisfying a memory that she unfitted me for caring to repeat the experience. Apart from personal disinclination, this was probably no disadvantage. Yenching had become my rapidly growing family. The students constantly spoke of themselves as my children, and I had very much of a fatherly feeling for them. I was able to put all of my time and energies into the single engrossing job. Several faculty wives took turns in overseeing my domestic needs. I was free to travel constantly both abroad and in China.

One of the most pleasant events at Yenching for me personally was the construction of a President's house, the gift of Mr. and Mrs. George W. Currie of Philadelphia. They stipulated that this was to be in Chinese style as well as near to the lake and the center of campus life. Since my wife had died I pled with them that I could stay in a student dormitory apartment or an academic building, but they continued to want to donate the President's home or nothing. Then I had an idea of my own, that the living room, dining room and two or three bedrooms should be for University use while my own little suite of rooms could be private. Everyone was happy with this arrangement. Whenever after this I went to Philadelphia it was understood that the Currie house should be my home. We at Yenching gained a very handsome and comfortable official residence, and I made two of the best friends I have ever had.

My only son, named after me, went to the United States for his college education and has continued to live there. He was spared my childish misfortune in the transition from Chinese to American life, not only because I had determined to see to it that he be prepared, but also because conditions in Nanking and Peking where he grew up were wholly different from the time of my boyhood in Hangchow as well as because Americans had become more cosmopolitan in outlook. Among his school-mates and other acquaintances during that sensitive period of first adjustment to American life he derived perhaps a slight thrill of prestige and novelty from his China connections. His religious growth seemed quietly normal. Shortly before his entering college he asked for my ideas on his lifework, especially with reference to the ministry. I advised him to let the matter wait at least until he was well on his college course, and when he said he was already inclining toward this career I warned him to resist it, that it was in his blood and he ought to be on his guard against drifting along the line of least resistance. As I became convinced, however, that he knew what he was doing I assured him that there was nothing I would rather have him do than maintain this succession.

Through Washington and Lee University and Union Seminary (Richmond, Va.), "Jack" seemed to combine normal religious behavior with a healthy enjoyment of youthful fun and human qualities generally. But it was in his attitude to the theological tensions of our time and to the missionary call that I have found an especial satisfaction. Everything about his personality, to say nothing about my own prejudices, seemed to point toward his remaining in the South. He had imbibed from association with me and his Peking environment a somewhat broader outlook than if he had grown up under typical southern conditions, and had learned to do his own thinking. I had also tried to share with him something of my own ideas and experience. The result is that he appreciates truth on each side of the argument and puts the emphasis, where it belongs, on preaching to meet popular needs and on pastoral service. As to the missionary call, it was inevitable of course that he face it. He had none of my antipathy to it; on the other hand his memories were rather alluring, although these could not include much that was typical. The exaltation of foreign missionary work as the supreme test of consecration had, however, ceased to seem as axiomatic as had been the case in my time. Wisely, I think, in view of his own special qualifications and of changed conditions in China, my boy decided to work in the home country. But this was with no struggle such as I had gone through. Especially since his mother's death we have been very close to each other in understanding, though usually separated geographically. We have written to each other regularly and I have felt that I knew what went on in my boy's inner as well as in his outer life, as fully as could be desired. In him much that I once thought of for myself has been continued, first in Virginia and now in a church of the "deep South" at Summit, Mississippi.

4

My frequent trips from China to the United States brought me some unusual and interesting experiences not immediately re-- lated to my work for the University. I had occasion to visit two Presidents of the United States. The first such visit was to President Woodrow Wilson, while I was still teaching in Nanking. He had heard me speak in the Central Presbyterian Church in Washington and asked me to call upon him, and tell him something about conditions in China. I took my nine-year-old son with me and he was both thrilled and scared. The President asked him, "Are you named after Dr. John Leighton Wilson?" "No, sir," the little boy replied, "after my father!" President Wilson was very simple, human and kindly in his manner. He gave John a card inscribed "To J.L.S. Jr. from his friend Woodrow Wilson" which he still keeps, framed in his study.

It happened that I arrived in the United States in 1933 just in time to listen to the new President deliver his first fireside talk immediately after taking office and as bank failures were giving alarming evidence of the seriousness of the depression. Less than two months later I was summoned to the White House. President Roosevelt must have heard that someone who had lived long in China happened to be in the country. This was not long after Japan's ill-timed attack on Shanghai which aroused public opinion both in China and abroad.

What interested me most was that in the midst of that frightful depression he was thinking about affairs in faraway China. His technique was also of interest. I was kept waiting some time which they told me was the usual experience. He put me at ease at once by asking about my University, then by speaking of the connection of the Delano family with the Canton clipper trade. I countered by telling him of the tragic death a year or so earlier of Mrs. Delano, the wife of a captain of Marines, when I had been asked to conduct the burial service at a dismal Japanese crematory near Peking under peculiarly distressing circumstances. By that time I was no longer nervous. He wanted to know what America could do short of war to prevent the Japanese from overrunning the whole of China, stressing the point that a war would last five years and must be avoided if at all possible. As the conversation became more earnest, I realized that I in my turn was staying overtime and was wondering when or how to leave. But he solved the problem by remarking that a certain South American delegation was probably getting impatient outside.

On June 17, 1930, Princeton University conferred upon me the honorary degree of Litt.D. The citation read by Dean Augustus Trowbridge, read as follows, "John Leighton Stuart—Founder and President of Yenching University in China. Born in the ancient empire of the Orient and influenced early by its culture rich in the knowledge of human nature, he came for his later training to Virginia, cradle of western democracy. After returning to China he won widely recognized leadership in the Christian educational movement in the Far East. Through long association with the leaders of China he is giving effectual help in the momentous and perplexing affairs of the young republic."

5

My birthdays were usually spent with family and friends. During the Yenching years a group of faculty intimates generally carried me off for two or three days to our favorite temple in the Western Hills, or, if other engagements prevented, for a picnic supper afloat on the Summer Palace Lake.

My sixtieth anniversary was made much of by my friends in

accord with a gracious Chinese tradition. One need not to have achieved anything more than to have existed for this number of years to enjoy such a celebration.

Rather than attempt to describe that occasion myself I shall rather immodestly quote from an account written by my dear colleague Lucius C. Porter entitled "Yenching Celebrates Leighton Stuart's Cycle of Cathay." Dr. Porter wrote:

Sixty years have a special significance in China, marking the completion of a series of cyclical names by which Chinese chronology has been measured since the far away days of the Shang dynasty. These sixty cyclical names used, for year, month, day and hour, appear repeatedly on the Oracle Bones from the Waste of Yin, which are the oldest objects that have come down from Chinese history; on one of these bones in the museum of the Harvard-Yenching Institute at Yenching the whole list of sixty names is inscribed. Mindful of the traditional significance of this cycle in Chinese thought and life, the Chinese faculty and students of Yenching University have been, throughout the year, anticipating the completion of such a cycle in the lifetime of their beloved President, John Leighton Stuart. These preparations, carefully worked out, culminated in the grand celebrations at Yenching on the President's birthday, June 24, 1936, and on the evening before; while Yenching alumni in a number of important centres throughout China also held gatherings in celebration of the day, the most notable of these being the gathering of the Shanghai Alumni Association, which, for the greater convenience of its members, was held on the preceding Saturday, June 21, when two hundred and fifty gathered under the chairmanship of T. T. Chang, editor for the foreign department of the Commercial Press.

The celebration at Yenching began with a grand dinner on the evening of June 23. The fine hall of Boyd Gymnasium made an ideal place for this gathering. The long U-shaped tables seated 186 diners, the company being made up of the entire administrative and teaching staff of the University, members of the University Board of Managers, and a few distinguished guests headed by his Excellency the American Ambassador and Mrs. Nelson T. Johnson, and including the Presidents of the various universities of Peiping and their wives, the directors of various cultural organizations of Peiping, the Director of the China Medical Board, and the chairman of the Peiping Union Medical College (Rockefeller Foundation), Dr. Hu Shih, Dr. J. C. Ferguson, doyen of American Sinologists, and a few others. The numerous complimentary couplets and banners presented to President Stuart, with all their beauty of Chinese calligraphy and the brilliance of their shades of red, the traditional color of joy, were used effectively in decorating the walls. There were forty-nine of these congratulatory sentiments headed by those from Lin Sen, president of the Chinese Republic, and including tributes from many Alumni Associations throughout the country, from the entire student body, and an especially imaginative sentiment from the women students in particular. Tall stalks of varicolored hollyhocks, which grow abundantly on our campus, alternated with the complimentary banners along the walls, while behind the presidential seat was a huge branch of the beautiful lantern tree now in its glory of golden blossoms.

As the guests entered they were greeted by a reception committee which presented each guest with a souvenir program for the evening, which, with a cut of our beautiful pagoda, also indicated the number of his or her seat at table, and with a chronicle of Dr. Stuart's life prepared according to Chinese tradition by Professor T. T. Lew giving the record of events year by year. Chinese lanterns overhead, with red candles and bouquets of flowers alternately placed along the tables, made the whole scene beautiful and festive.

The spontaneous spirit of joyful congratulation which filled the
hearts of all present was shown in the animated conversation
around the tables until it could be expressed in the form of
the speeches of the evening. These were given by His Excellency, the American Ambassador for the Westerners, and by
Chancellor Chiang Monlin, of the Peking National University
(the oldest university in China), on behalf of the Chinese
present. Chancellor Chiang's speech was given in Chinese,
since, as he said, the company was bilingual. In felicitous
and well-matched phrases he itemized some of President
Stuart's outstanding qualities, noting particularly the union
of Greek intellectual elements, Hebrew religious spirit, and
the genial humanism of Chinese culture in a warm, out-
going personality that won interest and friendship, just as the
springtime sun calls for the the burgeoning of leaf and flower.
Chancellor Chiang referred particularly to the central place
of the religious spirit in Dr. Stuart's character, noting that it
was without the narrowness that some critics have attributed
to missionary character. He expressed his admiration for
Leighton Stuart as a true representative of the spirit of Jesus,
and praised him for the contributions to Chinese education
which he has made. He regarded as most noteworthy the
fact that President Stuart's ideal for Yenching had been to
create an institution in China with the hope that it would
increasingly become supported and controlled by the Chinese
themselves. Those of us who remember the early days of
Yenching, when anti-Christian movements were current in
many parts of China, will realize something of what it means
for the non-religious chancellor of China's foremost intellectual
centre to refer so graciously and sincerely to the religious
inspiration that lies back of the President and his colleagues
in their achievement at Yenching.

The toast-master of the evening was Yenching's chancellor, Wu
Lei Chun, and although he endeavored, evidently under

previous instructions, to dismiss the company following Chancellor Chiang's speech, the guests refused to leave until they had heard from President Stuart himself. He finally was forced to his feet and made a very characteristic reply, testifying to a strong feeling of unreality with regard to all the proceedings since he found it difficult to conceive of himself as the centre of any such interest. The whole affair, he said, was but another expression, in the beautiful forms of Chinese courtesy, of that kindly friendliness and concern for human relationships which is perhaps the chief characteristic of Chinese culture; a concern which makes sixty years of mere existence an occasion for elaborate ceremonial and congratulation. The hearty, spontaneous joyfulness of the entire dinner company—the larger Yenching family circle—was perhaps a finer recognition of President Stuart's quality of life than any of the more formal expressions of congratulation.

. . . On June 24 most of the visitors began by calling at the President's House to wish him many happy returns. His beautiful Chinese-style courtyard was gaily decorated, the large character "Shou," meaning longevity, was placed over the door, with streamers of bright colors radiating from it. In the evening colored electric lights intensified the beauty of the decorations. These decorations, and particularly the lights, were a birthday present from the Power House staff, one more sign of the close fellowship which exists between the workmen, students and faculty that is a distinctive mark of Yenching life. But the really great event of the afternoon was the presentation to President Stuart by the servants and workmen on the campus of a "Pien"—the typical Chinese expression of appreciation consisting of a lacquered board on which is carved a complimentary phrase in all the delicacy and beauty of Chinese calligraphy; the "Pien" after presentation, is hung over the recipient's doorway that all the world may know how he has been honored. And before presentation the honor is more generally proclaimed by carrying the "Pien" in procession, with a band, through the streets to the recipent's residence. In this case the "Pien" was paraded over the entire campus with a band engaged to give color and rhythm to the occasion. Headed by the foremen of the campus workmen and the gatekeeper of one of the residential compounds, almost all of the workmen and servants of the University, with the children of the campus and adjacent villages following, the merry procession made the round of the campus and residence compounds ending up at the President's house, where amid a din of firecrackers, the presentation was fully made. The workmen were invited in and served punch in the dining room on complete equality with the dignified alumni and distinguished visitors who took tea there half an hour later. The ladies on the refreshment committee said that never in history had such an amount of supplies for tea been consumed so rapidly. The "Pien" bore the inscription "His instruction knows no class distinction."

Immediately after the workmen's presentation the children of the campus headed by William Leighton Wee and John Leighton Li, dressed like two miniature Chinese gentlemen, presented their congratulations in the form of two congratulatory scrolls.

The great day ended with a grand entertainment in Bashford Hall for which the usual elaborate and lengthy program, which delights all Chinese audiences had been prepared. When the President had been duly escorted, bouquet of flowers in hand, to the front of the hall, the curtain rose. The first item was, of course, a congratulatory address beginning with a tribute to the President which said that his personality expressed the spirit of Yenching just as his successful securing of money made possible its realization. The speaker went on to greet the alumni and closed with a farewell to the seniors, noting the significance of their leadership through this year of confusion and national difficulty, and wishing them well in their future work as they seek to carry into wider circles the spirit of Yenching; they were urged to become like its President, pathbreakers and centres of united effort. Following this speech the President himself appeared upon the platform and the student body presented to him an elaborate embroidered picture, symbolizing "the spirit of old age," which was carried down the aisle by two of the women students amid applause. Following this the entire audience, which packed the house, rose and bowed solemnly three times in his honor. The President made an appropriate, well-phrased and modest response in Chinese. The representative of the senior class responded for that class and then the entertainment began.

. . . The entertainment which began at half past seven did not close until well after midnight. The courtesy and tact which have made Leighton Stuart so beloved by Chinese, were perhaps never better exemplified, than on this evening, when after a long and tiring day, he sat with unabated interest to the end of the performance. At about eleven-thirty your reporter, who had been an intermittent attendant throughout the evening, met one of the girls of the student committee responsible for the entertainment, who was out for a breath on the Bashford terrace; in reply to a query regarding the proceedings, the latter said in tones of respectful wonder, "And President Stuart is still sitting in the front seat."

Reference should be made to the fact that President Stuart had requested that no presents be given him but that any wishing to remember him should contribute to a Stuart Scholarship Fund. This request could not head off the complimentary couplets and banners. However, many contributions were made to the scholarship fund by faculty, students and workmen.

6 Personalities
on the Chinese Scene

During the years spent in Hangchow my friendships had been primarily with mission employees, such as preachers and teachers. They represented the better type of faithful, reliable, but subservient dependents who, having made the break with their social *milieu*, had identified their interests with those of the missionaries. Their outlook tended to be narrow and not very different from their employers', except in their realistic understanding of their own people both inside the Church and without. Of these church members, not many were naturally congenial though there was a constant give-and-take of friendly intercourse. There were midday meals with farmers who, ravenous from a morning in rice fields or mulberry cultivation for silkworms, would finish five bowls of steaming rice while I managed to consume one and a half. All such experiences helped me to know the daily life of the people and led occasionally to something more obviously beneficial.

In Nanking, however, my closest friendships naturally began with Chinese colleagues on the Seminary faculty. These were a superior type of mission-trained product and there was more of a mutual feeling of equality. My personal teacher or writer was a typical scholar of the Confucianist tradition and through years of close association we developed a pleasant intimacy. There were also Chinese members of the University of Nanking faculty and a few people in the city whom I came to know fairly well, as well as students both in the Seminary and the University. One of the Seminary teachers, a Christian of the second generation, had been a playmate of my boyhood who after a

mastery of English in Hangchow College had worked in the
Post Office Service until he decided to go into Christian work.
It was early in this period that I met Dr. P. W. Kuo, the son
of a matron in a Shanghai mission school, who had been enabled to study in the United States where he made a brilliant
record, returning to China with a Ph.D. Later on he was appointed President of Southeastern University, the prototype of
the modern government higher educational institutions and at
that time easily the best. He collected some fifty "returned students," each one outstanding in his own subject, and gave the
impetus to education based on American models. But when I
first met him he represented almost an unknown species. I
scarcely realized that there were Chinese of this kind. About the
same time I met C. T. Wang (later to become General Secretary for the Y.M.C.A. in China, Minister of Foreign Affairs and
Ambassador to the United States), and heard him speak. His
father had been a preacher in the Anglican Mission in Ningpo,
and the treatment he received as seen in entering missionary
homes via the "service" or "traders" entrance made C. T. at first
bitterly anti-Christian, although afterward he became a strong
Christian lay leader.

During all those years before moving to Peking, I became
acquainted with not a few western "returned students," and
found them quite congenial while not unconscious of their
faults and of the exaggerated prestige they enjoyed in Chinese
society because of their coveted new knowledge, or the degrees
which were supposed to prove their fitness for remunerative
jobs. These students sometimes suffered from fictitious importance in demanding high positions and salaries, in arrogant pride,
and in possessing a theoretical knowledge of subjects which they
could not apply to Chinese needs. None the less they have been
an immense service to the nation. Indeed it is difficult to see
how China could have developed as she has—and imperatively

had to—without the service these men and women have rendered.

2

One of my earliest impressions of China as a missionary was of the awakening nationalism. This had probably always been dormant, but successive humiliations from foreign countries were arousing it. The naval defeat by Japan and the consequences of the Boxer uprising had come within the decade before my arrival. Partitioning between the Great Powers was widely feared, and we of today have almost forgotten how near that was to being realized. American policy as formulated by John Hay did more to prevent it even than is popularly supposed.

The Russian-Japanese war ended during my first year of missionary residence (1905), and the desire to learn the secret of successful resistance against western aggression was spreading among Chinese youth. Hence they went in large numbers to Japan to study. The Manchu Dynasty was tottering.

As I moved to Nanking (1908) the Empress Dowager and the imprisoned Emperor Kuang-hsu simultaneously died, and the succession fell to an infant born the same year as my three-year-old son. Despite the secrecy and the attempts at suppression, revolutionary sentiment was in the air, and when the outbreak came prematurely three years later (October 10, 1911) it spread easily everywhere even without carefully planned organization. The only resistance that held out for any time was in Nanking where we were living. We had some exciting times. Most of the students had cut their queues off, but to be seen without one meant instant death. We western teachers in all the mission schools worked together to get our students safely out of the city during an hour each day when the gate nearest the Yangtze River was opened and such queues as had not been discarded were pinned to the hats of many boys in succession as we steered them by the guards at the gate, and often carried their baggage because of the lack of coolies and the care they must take not to dislocate their none too securely attached pigtails.

When Sun Yat-sen finally came to Nanking I was asked to serve temporarily as Associated Press correspondent and thus had the privilege of seeing him frequently.

I was the only foreigner present in the Provisional Assembly that met at Nanking in 1912, when Dr. Sun made his famous speech refusing the presidency—on the ground that he had been so much out of the country that he was unfitted for the constructive administrative work then required—and urging, for the same reason, that Yuan Shih-k'ai (who had persuaded the Emperor to abdicate) be urged to accept it on his guarantee to support a Republic. After much protest from his youthful followers and a more cynical fear of Yuan among Dr. Sun's seasoned comrades, this was reluctantly approved. The others proved to be right for Yuan later did let them down when he tried (unsuccessfully) to become Emperor, led on by his family and friends. I came to know a niece of Yuan Shih-k'ai, Pauline Yuan, who once read to me faked editorials from Shanghai newspapers urging her uncle to take the throne, thus making him think it was desired "by the people."

In all this development I was in touch with the inner core of revolutionary idealism. I am convinced that Sun Yat-sen was absolutely honest and sincere, unquestionably and unselfishly patriotic, but he had been out of China so long that he was out of touch with things Chinese. His influence served to preserve a republican form of government through the period of civil wars, and his famous lectures in 1924, "The Three Principles of the People," became a charter for the revolution of 1926-27 led by his aide Chiang Kai-shek. He himself died in Peking Union Medical College Hospital from cancer in 1925. His Christian funeral was conducted by Dr. Timothy Lew of Yenching University.

Madame Sun Yat-sen, a sister of Madame Chiang Kai-shek, was devoted to her husband and to the "Three Principles" which he enunciated. She came to feel that her relatives were not living up to these ideals and finally threw in her lot with the Communist People's Government in which she now holds a high though nominal position.

3

When I visited Peking in the spring of 1919, a new national consciousness was boiling up among the students, and on May 4 a delegation of these attacked the homes of three officials whose assistance to the Japanese had been especially scandalous. They with their families and hastily collected possessions fled to the safety of the Legation Quarter. The student leaders were arrested and confined in a law college hurriedly improvised as a student jail. Their fellows clamored to be allowed to share their captivity. Similar movements flared up all over China. The local prisons were soon crowded to capacity with yet more students seeking admission. The shaky government was in a ludicrous dilemma. If it treated the students as offenders because of a genuinely patriotic outbreak, it virtually condoned the pro-Japanese traitors, and the publicity was becoming most embarrassing. If, on the other hand, it justified the students it impugned the integrity of some of its officials, and the Japanese might exercise their dreaded power in some form of reprisals. The wily old President therefore ordered that they be released, but like Paul at Philippi they refused to leave unless formally set free and cleared of the charges against them. This would be an impossible loss of face for the government.

Meanwhile I had promised to visit Peking for commencement and preach the baccalaureate sermon in a large Methodist church nearby. But President Hsu had compromised to the extent of promising to send two high officials to "comfort" the students after which they were to be released, and that particular Sunday morning had been selected for the ceremony. All of their fellow students were to go to meet them as they emerged and escort them back in triumph to their respective schools. Having prepared a sermon for college graduates, I had to deliver it with such hasty adaptations as I could to a congregation in which students were conspicuously lacking. This was to have been the first contact with my future students. The next morning when I did meet them I made clear my hearty sympathy with them in their patriotic efforts. In all the troubled years that followed, whenever the students felt the urge to join in similar demonstrations, they knew my attitude. It was a very real bond of understanding and had a profound influence upon the status of Yenching University during that turbulent period of Chinese history.

4

Soon after moving to Peking I began to cultivate Chinese officials in order to help them understand the purposes of our Christian university and to secure gifts from them if possible as evidence of their good will toward Christian education. Many of these officials were retired after having made a lot of money through "honest" or "dishonest" graft. Under the Manchu Dynasty there was not sufficient distinction between public and private funds; an official was entitled to make some profits but was limited by his superiors and by custom. In the early Republic the same habits and traditions continued, but there were no checks other than danger from rival warlords. The Japanese aided all this corruption to cause disunion in China. The National Government of Chiang Kai-shek brought better government organization and improvements in methods of tax collection and public finance. In all this period of conflicting interests I felt that it was the best insurance to know the prominent officials in various camps, the different rivals and their entourage.

Dr. W. W. Yen was a son of an Episcopal clergyman, graduate of St. John's University, returned student from the States and prominent in Chinese political life. He had served as Minister to various countries and as Premier in the Peking Government. He was a man far above the average in statesmanship and character. He served for many years on the Yenching Board of Managers and occasionally as chairman. When I first came to know him I persuaded him to help us solicit funds for a men's dormitory. Just then, as the University was moving out to its present campus, came the revolution of 1926-1927. With Dr. Yen's permission, quickly and easily given, and with Philip Fugh's planning, the money raised was used instead for a wall to enclose the campus and protect it during the months of civil disorder.

Another quite different type of official with whom I early became acquainted was General Ch'en Shu-fan, the Military Governor of the inland province of Shensi. He had sold us our new University site and had remitted one-third of the purchase price on condition that we reserve a spot where he could build a villa for his aged father, to be finally transformed into a memorial hall. He proposed that I visit Sian with a view to advising the provisional authorities on educational matters. I was eager for the adventure and set out in the early spring of 1921 with all sorts of fond imaginings as to what might be the outcome. I took a personal servant. We traveled by the Peking-Hankow Railway to its junction with a new line being constructed from the sea to Sian and then on this one as far as it went. From there we spent a week in overland travel. The Governor had sent a squad of soldiers to escort me as we were to pass through a bandit-infested region. There was a mule litter for me (two mules carrying poles for a covered frame on which bedding is spread and one or more passengers get what comfort they can). Fortunately for me and for my servant the Governor had provided an extra horse which I preferred riding as much as my servant did lounging in the litter. This method of travel gave me a fine chance to see rural life in this part of China unspoilt by modern or foreign inroads.

I spent about a week in Sian as the Governor's guest, visiting scenic or historic remains of the ancient capital and contemporary activities. At one of the official feasts in my honor the civil and military governors were sitting next to each other as joint hosts, each eating specially prepared food to avoid being poisoned, each with guards standing unobtrusively behind his chair. One of these accidentally dropped his gun which for an instant caused a panic. The two governors then affably resumed their easy conversation with each other as though they were the best of friends.

I was fascinated by Sian, the old capital of the T'ang Dynasty, and its environs. I had visions of educational development in this virgin territory and of special ties between the Governor's middle school and Yenching University. When I left the Governor gave me a horse which I brought home with me. But scarcely had I reached Peking on my return journey before news arrived that the civil governor had staged a successful revolt against his colleague who soon retired to private life in Tientsin. There I often called on him. The whole incident was typical of the disorders of the time and of schemes which came to nothing. But I had been given an idea of the value of this sort of cultivation.

5

Another provincial Governor of the Civil War years was General Yen Hsi-shan of Shansi Province. I first met him in connection with my travels with the Burton Educational Commission. Later I made several visits to see him and was impressed in general with his ability and character. He tried at first to be a "model governor," and then became disillusioned. The people were not ready for reform, and he was tricked by foreigners and Chinese alike. He set out to keep Shansi a part of the Republic, but it became practically separate. Because of opposition at one time to Chiang Kai-shek he had to flee to Japan; after that the Japanese tried to woo him to their side but unsuccessfully. Later he identified himself loyally with the Nationalist cause. In 1936 he invited me to Shansi to help him make contacts for industrial development of the province. Some plans were being made; then came the war against Japan.

Sun Ch'uan-fang was a governor of Kiangsu Province who once fought the governor of the neighboring province of Chekiang. He was defeated in 1927 by Chiang Kai-shek in the latter's northward advance. Once in an interview with him he asked me, "Why do foreigners come to China to educate the Chinese?"

I said, "Civilization is not national, but international. If it is mingled then a deeper understanding can be achieved. Our purpose is to co-operate with the old Chinese culture and help to produce a new."

"Thank you for your intention; but why do you come to see me?"

"I came to see you for a contribution."

General Sun then stood up with obvious lack of interest, "I'd like to see you some other time." However, later he gave Yenching $100 and still later $20,000 in Chinese currency. One of General Sun's sons attended Yenching afterward and worked hard; then left at the time of the Japanese invasion to "do something patriotic." The General himself went later into retirement and was shot while worshipping in a Buddhist temple, by the wife of a man he had once executed.

Han Fu-ch'u was another independent type of provincial governor who was able to continue in power under the National Government. He cleared Shantung of bandits and in many ways was a progressive ruler, though quite dictatorial. The Japanese worked on him constantly. He wanted to take a strong stand

President Chiang Kai-shek and Ambassador Stuart
in conference at Kuling, summer resort, 1946.

General Marshall and Ambassador Stuart at Nanking, 1946.

against them but wondered whether Chiang Kai-shek would back him.

Governor Han in 1935 asked Philip Fugh and me to see the Generalissimo if possible and ascertain his attitude. Chiang was at first very angry. "Local governors," he declared, "have no right to ask about national policy; they should do their job and let national policy be handled by the proper authorities."

I countered, "All that's a very good abstract principle, but China for centuries has been governed by men, not laws. Therefore, personal loyalty is a matter of prime importance. Here is a man who will be your true friend if you'll establish a personal connection."

Chiang again blazed out, but finally said, "All right, you go tell him that if he'll stand firm I'll not let him down."

On our return to Tsinan we advised Han to go to see Chiang. Han went, had a friendly interview and achieved an understanding. Later, Chiang sent his own representative to Shantung to establish closer relations. But when the Japanese attacked in 1937 Han vacillated instead of standing firm, and he and his armies fled to the West. Generalissimo Chiang sent for him, had him court-martialed and executed.

Governor Sung Chê-yuan had a similar story except that he finally backed up against a wall and died fighting the Japanese. When in charge of Hopei Province (where Peking is) he temporized constantly both with the National Government and with the Japanese. I tried to convince Generalissimo Chiang that with proper backing Sung would be loyal and would resist the Japanese armies. After the Marco Polo Bridge incident, Chiang urged him to go to Paotingfu, the capital of the province, and make a stand there. But after a kind of Japanese blitzkrieg he slipped away at night. If Sung had obeyed Chiang's orders the situation in north China might have taken a very different turn. Sung later repented and made a struggle against the invaders of north China, but it was too late.

6

I visited Manchuria several times during the years of Marshal Chang Tso-lin and later of his son Chang Hsueh-liang, finding both of them friendly and responsive to our appeals for Yenching. The first time I saw Chang Tso-lin he was seated on a thronelike chair with two lifelike stuffed tigers beside him. He was a small man with clear and black piercing eyes. He had acquired a reputation as a village vigilante leader, gradually built up his position and finally came out on top in the struggle for power in Manchuria. All his life he had to work with the Japanese, but he was never entirely subservient to them. In April, 1928, he came to Peking and occupied the city temporarily, but he was driven out.

In June, 1928, I was hurrying back to Yenching for commencement by way of Europe and the Siberian Railway. On reaching Mukden I learned from Scotch missionary friends of the fate of the uncrowned King of Manchuria. He was returning from Peking and had been seriously wounded in an explosion as his train was crossing a bridge a few miles out of Mukden. The missionaries confided to me the knowledge that he was already dead. This information came to them through medical sources, although the report was being spread in the city of his improvement and all the people were ordered to make no change in their daily life. His son, Chang Hsueh-liang, the "Young Marshal," a youth of twenty-two, was flying back to take over, and told me later that the Japanese had three times attempted on that train ride to persuade his father to sign a document greatly enlarging their rights in south Manchuria. On the last occasion they warned him that otherwise he would not reach Mukden alive. A British engineer who had visited the scene of the explosion explained to me the technical reasons why it must have been perpetrated by Japanese. They had 40,000 troops

awaiting the signal to "restore order" when the death of the Old
Marshal became known.

Whatever his shortcomings he had therefore died as a patriot
and his people had foiled the Japanese plot to seize control by
maintaining the fiction of his recovery. I was already back in
Peking when some weeks later his death was announced. The
Young Marshal told me also how the Japanese had sent Baron
Hayashi on a mission of condolence after which he secretly
presented the same document and asked for Chang's signature.
Chang Hsueh-liang described how he shut his eyes on refusing,
expecting to be shot. These details throw light on the "Mukden
Incident" three years later—a similarly faked railway accident,
and the barefaced rape of Manchuria.

That Incident was another of the turning points of history.
It was perhaps provoked in part by the Young Marshal's contemptuous rejection of insistent Japanese demands. Four colo-
nels, impatient over the delay, determined to force the issue and
on a flimsy pretext took control of all Manchuria in the name
of the Emperor.

Henry L. Stimson, then United States Secretary of State, used
the transatlantic telephone to consult with the British Foreign
Minister as to a protest, but Sir John Simon replied that he was
not interested. Living close to the situation as I was, I am confident that if these two countries had led in an emphatic
démarche, the Japanese Government would have disowned the
action of unauthorized subordinates as it could easily have done
at that stage with no loss of face. When the League of Nations
finally took up the matter and sent the Lytton Commission to
investigate, it was too late. The Japanese had tested out the reluctance of the Powers to get involved and their lack of cohesion.
Mussolini saw the point and followed with Abyssinia. The Span-
ish Civil War was the next consequence. Hitler soon followed
the lead. All this could probably have been averted by prompt,
stern and united action in Manchuria. In China the date of the

Mukden Incident, September 18, 1931, became an anniversary observed annually, especially by students, with bitter shame and high resolve. It made a profound impression and colored the thinking of patriotic Chinese from then on. I had the feeling of a murky miasma coming in from the sea and settling down especially upon north China with the inevitability of fate.

When the news of the Sian revolt in 1936 and the kidnapping of Generalissimo Chiang Kai-shek reached those who knew the Young Marshal it did not seem possible that he had acted from other than patriotic motives. Both in the most public way possible and in private conversation he testified without qualifying phrases that what he had done was wrong. This need not therefore be further argued. That he meant to end a domestic conflict disastrous to all concerned and fraught with danger to the whole nation can be safely assumed, despite the folly and impropriety of the means employed.

7

A colorful figure on the Chinese scene for over twenty years was General Feng Yu-hsiang, sometimes called "The Christian General." He was a man with a tremendous physique and a big genial face, a forceful character and a quite sincere though mercurial temperament. He became a Christian for emotional reasons, and he was always a rather superficial and immature believer. His army in the early years was like Oliver Cromwell's with strict regimentation and discipline. For a time Christian chaplains served in his army, but they all disappeared at the time of his defeat by Chang Tso-lin. General Feng veered from Christian faith to communism, then back to Nanking republicanism. During the war he was an ardent patriot though never given any really responsible position. After V-J Day he again showed his Communist sympathies and died rather mysteriously on a trip to Russia.

I became acquainted with him first in Peking when he was

looking askance at Chiang Kai-shek's government. Later he went to Nanking and was given a post, and then disgruntled retired to the famous sacred mountain of T'ai Shan in Shantung Province. Philip Fugh and I called on him once there. He was reading an old classic and practicing his well-known calligraphy. "I'll go back to Nanking if they'll sink their differences," he said emphatically. "I'll do anything, I'll take the highest position or the humblest if they will only fight Japan."

On another occasion I visited him with my left arm in a sling due to arthritis in the shoulder. When he learned what my ailment was he at once offered a remedy in the form of a plaster which he had bought from a famous Peking medicine shop and always carried with him. It consisted of bear's grease and ground tiger's bones. He insisted on doctoring me himself so I bared my shoulder and he administered the plasters one in front and one behind, having an aide take a photograph of the operation. Whether this plaster was as efficacious as he claimed or whether the treatment of an American missionary doctor helped, or whether it was the change from the damp Nanking climate, I was entirely free from pain on reaching Peking. Once at a reception in Chungking General Feng described this incident in a very humorous way and drew uproarious laughter from the guests.

The last time I saw him in Chungking he had been reading a Chinese life of George Washington. He spoke of the details of our eight revolutionary years—traitors, debts, hunger, cold, dwindling army, etc., and added, "We Chinese haven't suffered anything like that yet. There is no reason why we can't go on a lot longer."

8

In 1933 Generals Li Tsung-jen and Pai Ch'ung-hsi were allied with General Ch'en Chi-t'ang of Kwangtung against the National Government. Ch'en and his ring were thoroughly corrupt and only wanted independence from the Nanking regime because this would give them greater possibility of graft. Li and Pai, on the other hand, were high-minded and patriotic but feared Chiang Kai-shek would appease Japan. At that time I had two long talks with General Li.

I said, "If you could be convinced that Chiang is not going to attack you, and will fight Japan, would you support him?"

"Yes."

I continued, "I am convinced he will; what about Pai?"

"He's a harder nut to crack but he could be won over."

"Very well," I concluded, "I'll try to get evidence to convince you both beyond any doubt."

Returning to Shanghai I talked with several National Government officials. One said, "We've been sending emissaries for some time, with no success."

"Yes," I replied, "but this must be done—how about T. V. Soong? I am convinced that you can get the League broken up and enlist the loyal support of Li and Pai if a major figure will go."

T. V. Soong was terribly busy, so I asked him about General-issimo Chiang's going. "It's too dangerous," was Soong's immediate reaction.

However, Chiang eventually did go, putting himself at their disposal. After that Chiang and Pai and Li were very good friends and worked together well during the resistance against Japan. When the Constitutional Assembly elected Chiang Kai-shek President of the Republic in 1948 Li Tsung-jen was chosen Vice-President.

Wang Ching-wei was a very different type. He was a good speaker and writer, affable, but lacking in fundamental moral principles. He never got over his revolutionary-adventurer attitude. He was the only prominent Kuomintang official who broke with the National Government at Chungking and sought to make a separate peace with Japan. He made a tragic mistake in

going to Japan after leaving Chungking, without any real support from patriotic Chinese, and in consenting to head the
Japanese puppet government at Nanking. He probably thought
of himself as the hero of a great peace movement. As I knew him
he seemed to be motivated too by three other reasons: an honest
difference of opinion with the National leaders over various
matters, deep jealousy of Chiang Kai-shek and a psychopathic
fear of war. He died in Tokyo, before the world war ended, un-
honored and unmourned by the people of China.

9

Shortly after the National Government was established under
Chiang Kai-shek (1927), I visited Nanking in order to get
acquainted with the new leaders. In my first meeting through
Dr. H. H. Kung with Chiang I was impressed by his masterful
personality and magnetic charm. I also met most of the prominent
members of the new government. They all had an eager desire to
live up to the ideals of Sun Yat-sen which was very cheering. I
was reminded of the same spirit in the revolution of 1911.

Early in that same year Generalissimo Chiang Kai-shek made
one of the fateful decisions which influence the course of human
history. As Sun Yat-sen watched the breakdown of his Republic
in the dissensions of the warlord period, he determined to carry
a punitive expedition from Canton to Peking and restore peace
and unity. He solicited help from various countries, including
ours, but found no response except from the Soviet Union which
sent advisers and other aid under two extremely able men, Boro-
din and Galen. Beginning in 1920, they organized the Kuomintang on Soviet lines. This reorganization continued after the
death of Dr. Sun on March 12, 1925. The "Northern Advance"
was planned by them. They were in the section which followed
the Canton-Hankow Railway and set up a provisional government in the latter city. That march was accompanied by much
unrestrained burning and slaughter of "bourgeois reactionaries."

The Generalissimo led another section on a route nearer the coast and somewhere on that march determined to break with the Russian advisers and start an independent policy. In this he was supported by the substantial business classes in Shanghai, which has of course given the Communists ever since a ready-made accusation that he sold out to the capitalists. The first consequence was the liquidation of the already active and vocal government in the Wu-han cities and the homeward trek of the Russians and some of their Chinese followers. These included Madame Sun Yat-sen and her devoted secretary, a Yenching boy. After a brief sojourn in Moscow she decided—despite many stories to the contrary—that Russian communism was not the panacea for China, and withdrew with her staff to Berlin where I saw them a year or so later.

On March 24, 1927, right before the defection of the Generalissimo, the strongly communistic Wu-han leaders attempted to embroil him in difficulties with western nations by sending a contingent of soldiers to massacre all the foreigners in Nanking. Most of these were missionaries, and the soldiers found them so friendly and unsuspecting that their inherited Chinese instincts of decency prevented them from shooting these harmless people down in cold blood. My brother Warren had taken my place on the Seminary faculty. His wife had been sent with other women to an American gunboat lying at anchor in the river, but the men had all stayed at their posts. Warren was talking with a group of soldiers outside the gate of his home, persuading them against violent action when another one further away took a shot at him splintering the woodwork behind him. At this juncture a poorly dressed man in the crowd which had collected came up and advised him to get away. Warren followed this man who was a rickshaw puller whom he had happened to have befriended when sick. The man took Warren to his squalid hut amid a cluster of these, charged his neighbors to keep quiet, took Warren's valuables, hid him in his own tattered bedding and fed him with what he himself had. Twenty-four hours later he reported to Warren that Nanking University students were hunting for foreigners to convey them to the University for greater safety, restored his valuables and escorted him to the students.

The Vice-President of Nanking University, John E. Williams, a dear friend of mine, was killed—as were five others, representing in all four countries—and several others were seriously wounded. The most spectacular feature was the flight of a group led by the American Consul, John K. Davis, son of my father's mission colleague, who scaled the city wall from "Socony Hill." Among these was the husband of the well-known authoress, Alice Teasdale Hobart, who injured his ankle in letting go the rope after his descent from the wall.

The whole plot was a barbarously inhuman attempt to frustrate the Generalissimo whose change of heart was destined to delay the process of sovietization of China for more than twenty years. By a curious coincidence, the then American Minister in Peking, Mr. John V. McMurray, had asked me a few days earlier to drop in to see him when next in the city and I had done so on the afternoon of that day, March 24, 1927. He had wanted to ask me whether, if some local incident occurred in the Yangtze Valley tinderbox, I thought that would mean the flaring up of anti-foreign feeling all over China. I thought not. That evening a Chinese member of my faculty was exhibiting his collection of paintings at his home and wanted me to be present. Shortly before the hour an American colleague brought me the word of wireless news from the city that all foreigners had perished in a Nanking massacre, he not knowing that I had a brother there. I decided to go to the exhibit despite my grief and learned the next morning from Mr. McMurray that Warren was still apparently unharmed.

To return to the Generalissimo. From 1927 until the present time he has not wavered in his opposition to Russian communism as a political philosophy or program for China. The progressive unification of the country in the decade between 1927 and 1937 in spite of Communist wars and Japanese aggression, and the remarkable economic and other achievements of that period, are well known. I came to have a sincere respect for the Generalissimo and his capable wife and rejoiced with the Chinese people when he was released from his strange captivity at Sian in December, on Christmas Day, 1936.

My estimate of the Generalissimo at the time when Japan launched aggression in China may best be given by some quotations from an article which I wrote for the Peking magazine *Democracy* on May 15, 1937. I said in part:

For all I know the descriptions appearing in print of General Chiang's manner of life and his summary treatment of political enemies up to ten years ago may all be true. If so, there is the greater credit to him because of the changes since then for the better. But from the time of his emergence into national importance in 1926-7 I have followed his career with the interest of one who had become intensely concerned over the fate of China and was not unfamiliar with the prevailing characteristics of the warlords who for the past two decades have been struggling among themselves for power and self regardless of democratic principles or the people's rights. These men inherited the mandarin theory of public office for personal gain with neither the imperial sanctions nor the old scholarly tradition to restrain their rapacity and irresponsible rule. Would the new Kuomintang leaders under the ideology of Dr. Sun's Three Principles merely reproduce the age long vices of Chinese officialdom? That many of them have is common knowledge; that many more have exploited the situation more or less to their own advantage is unpleasantly apparent. It is against this background that the character of General Chiang should be studied. Much of the criticism against him is doubtless because of what is [in China] taken for granted of one in his position: They alleged that he intends to make himself a dictator; that he has amassed a fortune which has been largely transformed into American securities for safe keeping; that he has made a secret agreement with Japan or is at least too intent upon holding power to risk this in resisting aggression from that source; and that he has a hopelessly medieval mind.

These and other assertions have been in constant circulation often with more specific charges. There has also been much genuine misgiving or suspicion or simply lack of confidence. Nor is any of this surprising. What is surprising is his steadily growing popularity. That he has stayed continuously in one or both of the highest active offices in the National Government could be accounted for by political astuteness.

But the esteem in which he is held is primarily on moral grounds. This phenomenon is the more suggestive because no other people have been trained as have the Chinese to look for ethical qualities in their rulers, nor perhaps have any developed a more sophisticated disillusionment in this respect. Chiang's fiftieth birthday, the end of last October, was the occasion for a nation-wide and spontaneous celebration unprecedented in China's long history. Even more convincing was the almost universal anxiety during his detention in Sian and the wild exuberance of the relief and joy on the news of his release.

The explanation does not lie in the magnetic charm or social graces of a winning personality. Even with his associates he is taciturn, preoccupied with affairs, lacking in capacity for "small-talk." He has the innate affability and courtesy of a Chinese gentleman but is business-like enough to satisfy American requirements and can be very curt or severely frank on occasion. On the whole the steadily increasing popular respect for him must be accounted for on other grounds. Consummate skill in dealing with people of widely diverse types, highly trained intelligence, capacity for quick and shrewd decision, forcefulness and courage, indefatigable energy, are among the qualities that have made him a great soldier and sagacious executive, and have given him a natural pre-eminence in the counsels of his party. But there is something more in the attitude of his people than respect for the one holding his high office or performing efficiently his functions. It would seem that cynical distrust and easily understandable skepticism have been slowly dissipated by the recognition of his genuinely patriotic purpose and unswerving devotion to the national welfare. Conversely, the suspicion of his motives or opposition to his authority or dislike amounting often to hatred which still abound are due to lack of conviction as to his patriotism and nobility of character.

Assuming then that General Chiang is worthy of the esteem in which he is now held by so great a majority of his countrymen and by many competent foreign observers, what are the influences which have molded his character? The earliest perhaps was the political idealism of Dr. Sun Yat-sen and the intimacy which developed between him and this highly gifted young disciple. His acceptance of his leader's revolutionary philosophy and the demands it imposed seems to have been genuine. To a marked degree he was helped by the saintly mother of his present wife who has herself been a potent factor in his broadening outlook and deepening moral emphasis ever since this marriage. The staggering size and perplexity of his task, with its almost insuperable difficulties and their kaleidoscopic variety, have perhaps served to no slight extent to awaken a sober consciousness of responsibility. This may have been accentuated by the note of urgency in a time of national crisis. Every one who works for China's betterment has a heartening sense of the improvableness in existing conditions, and the response to his efforts must have given him a zest which grows with enlarging experience.

General Chiang has been a Christian for some ten years, very unobtrusively but living up to the principles and practice of this faith as he learned of it more clearly. He knew not much about Christianity at the outset and yet in the midst of strenuous activities and harassing anxieties he has found the time for and developed the habit of personal religious culture to the point where it has become a conscious source of guidance, inspiration and moral strength. The writer, as himself a Christian, cannot but believe that the observance of the teachings and dependence upon the spiritual resources of this faith does have a transforming effect on character, and since General Chiang himself in public statements regarding his Sian experience attributes much of his present attitude and behavior to what he has learned from the teaching and example of Jesus, it would seem quite rational to recognize the working in him of cause and effect.

It may be permissible to add a word in conclusion to the effect that the writer's personal contacts with General Chiang have led him through the same stages of opinion as the people of the country have been described as reaching, resulting in an unquestioning confidence in the transparent sincerity of his patriotic purpose and in the stern purity of his personal life, an admiration tinged increasingly with affection, and a clear conviction that China is extremely fortunate to have one with his character and capacity actively leading the nation in this supremely critical period of its rebirth and rebuilding.

10

The reader will already have noticed several references to Philip C. Fugh and there will be more. Any description of my life in China, especially in my association with Chinese officialdom, would be incomplete without a section about him.

About the time of our removal to Peking in 1919, a departing Y.M.C.A. secretary left with me as a sort of legacy a seventeen-year-old boy whom he regarded as the most promising member of a Bible class of his. It happened, however, that this was not our first contact. A year or so earlier there had been a National Y.M.C.A. Conference in Tientsin which this boy had attended. In that faraway period foreigners rather than Chinese were in the majority as speakers on such occasions and I had been asked to make an address. Although he claims that my southern dialect was unintelligible to him yet something about my personality seemed to envelop me in his imagination with an aura which for some inexplicable reason all our subsequent intimacy has not wholly obliterated. After he became a sophomore at Yenching, my mother, my wife and I tried to take an interest in him and were more solicitous when he had to drop out of college for a year and a half in order to help his father in his unfortunate business adventures. On resuming his studies he was not only physically weak but harassed and dejected about family affairs. He was the descendant of a long line of Manchu Dukes, and after the overthrow of that Dynasty the family had lost much of its wealth. His father, inexperienced in such matters, had undertaken various commercial ventures which were not going well. The boy had an exaggerated idea of the share we had in his spiritual recovery and was correspondingly grateful.

When Philip was six years old his grandfather, who then held the title, had taken him to Court to be presented to the Empress Dowager. She gave him the name *Yung Ching* which means "Eternally Pure," but could also imply "Forever Loyal to the Dynasty." This became his name in the family and with his intimates. He is more generally known as *Ching Po*, a reference to the principal river in Kansu Province where his grandfather had been Governor. He seems to have inherited a political acumen from ancestors who had been high officials for generations. An instinct for dealing with the Mandarin psychology was in his blood, and I have profited greatly from it. He had been urged to enter the Christian ministry, but I advised against this, arguing that with his special aptitudes he could do more by carrying Christian principles into government service.

This talent was soon discovered by officials who enlisted his help for various tasks. Chiang Kai-shek soon after taking office in Nanking employed him on several confidential missions. One of the most delicate of these was to win the Young Marshal, Chang Hsueh-liang, away from Japanese blandishments and lead him to include Manchuria in Kuomintang China. On his trips to Mukden, Philip was shadowed by Japanese spies, taken to a lavatory, stripped in their search for documents and constantly questioned. Toward the end of December, 1929, the Young Marshal announced his decision by unfurling the Kuomintang flag about his headquarters. Philip was also sent on missions to the United States and seemed to ingratiate himself at once with prominent Americans whom he had occasion to meet. The then Chinese Ambassador in Washington arranged for him to pay a purely courtesy call on President Hoover, who kept him in conversation long after the appointed time. When he told me about this in a casual way and when I asked him if he realized what an exceptional treatment this was he appeared quite surprised. On the first of these trips I happened also to be in the States and he asked me what he could do about his name which was then spelled in the usual way as Fu. He said hotel clerks and telephone girls always asked him, "*Fu* what?" I suggested that he tell them *Fugh*. After that he had no more trouble, and the addition of the two redundant consonants has long since become fixed.

In his twenty-fourth year Philip was married by me to the bride chosen by his parents, in a colorful ceremony which blended the elaborate decorations and lengthened festivities of old China, in a big restaurant taken over and transformed for the purpose, with the simple dignity of the Christian wedding ritual.

Soon after Yenching had become somewhat established, I

began to endeavor to have it win for itself a welcomed and recognized place in Chinese life, independent of western treaties or American protection. The best security in China lies in personal relationships. I had in mind not only this benefit but also the cultivation of a Chinese supporting constituency. Philip soon discovered what I wanted and offered to help. He managed to be released from time to time from whatever he was doing. Thus began a campaign of cultivation which took us all over China from Manchuria to Hongkong and during the Japanese war (before Pearl Harbor) to Chungking and other places in free China. An endowment fund made a good start, with endorsements which were even more cheering than the money. But the apprehensions of Japanese invasion and then its actuality put an end to all such efforts. What had been accomplished, however, was of incalculable value in various ways to the University. In every place we visited there was a group of former Yenching students and invariably a reception of some sort by them. They would have been the nucleus for the campaigns we had in mind for the future.

My academic colleagues were naturally suspicious of Philip's devotion to my interests. There must be some ulterior motive. They tried to discover this in his ambition for government office, utilizing me to become acquainted with high officials and thus secure some luscious post for himself. They often warned me to be cautious. These anxieties were quite natural. I knew, however, that the reverse was true and that Philip could easily get a good job without any help from me. Apart from his attachment to me, he had become very fond of Americans generally and of our country. To him the promotion of good relations between the two countries seemed to be about as patriotic a cause as he could work for. It is still his primary enthusiasm. Meanwhile his political sagacity and his transparent integrity were leading him to one opening after another. But he has always kept his political independence.

The part that Philip Fugh played in my release from Japanese detention and in my work of the postwar years will be described in later chapters.

11

One more personality comes to my mind who serves to dramatize the changes in relationships between my early and later years in China. I recall once walking on a street in Hangchow (this in itself being undignified then for anyone with social position) when the Governor of the province came by. He was in his richly caparisoned sedan-chair with eight bearers and numerous liveried attendants before and after. I gazed with awed curiosity at a mandarin to whom I could never expect to come any closer, and the carelessly contemptuous glance with which he took note of the lone barbarian standing aside to let him be carried by can easily be imagined.

But this official's wife, as it happened, was the daughter of the famous soldier-scholar, Viceroy Tseng Kuo-fan, and for many years a devout Christian. In her eighty-third year she visited Peking and came to Yenching as my guest, meeting faculty and students with charming graciousness and regarded by them with the greatest respect because of her parentage, her own attainments and her vigorous old age. After returning to the city she sent me a scroll written in the exquisite calligraphy she had learned in her father's home, describing her visit to the famous institution she had long wanted to see because seventeen of her grandchildren had already studied there and more were to follow.

7 The Japanese Occupation and an Island of Freedom

The months of the Chinese calendar are numbered, and several important events happened on "doubles." Thus Independence Day, October 10, is known as the Double Tenth. So when the Japanese created another of their faked incidents near Peiping on July 7, 1937, this became the hateful Double Seventh. They had probably realized that in view of the Generalissimo's success in unifying the nation, they must strike without further delay. They took the city on July 28. I was awakened soon after dawn that morning by the dropping of Japanese bombs on a military barracks located near our campus; it was my first experience of aerial bombing and a terrifying one. There was panic on the campus, and the wildest rumors gained easy credence.

The immediate problem for me was whether to follow other universities in a hasty withdrawal to some spot in Free China or to take the consequences of staying where we were. No one could predict what the Japanese would do. I consulted friends of all types who saw the problem clearly enough but had no definite opinions. I finally decided to stay. The disrupted entrance examinations were resumed. We flew the American flag for the first time on our rather high pole. Previously we had flown only the Chinese national flag or our University pennant.

We had incidents almost daily, usually minor ones but always with the possibility of becoming serious. This was especially true because of linguistic limitations on both sides and the natural suspicions of an occupying army in unfriendly territory. It was not long before I called to my assistance one of our graduates whose family circumstances in childhood and later on his graduate study in Japan enabled him to speak the language as fluently as a native. He was invaluable in all our constant dealings with Japanese military officers and others. We had the Oriental problem of face in fixing his status. It had to be high enough to give him proper access and dignity with Japanese while not hurting the sensibilities of Chinese on our faculty older or with higher academic rank. Resentment against the invaders was so intense that he was almost included in this sentiment as teachers and students saw him fraternizing on easy terms with the detested invaders.

Whenever he proposed it, I would entertain Japanese civil or military officials as part of the price paid for better relations in so delicate a situation. The Japanese High Command arranged from time to time for delegations of their fellow countrymen to visit north China in order to promote their cultural control and perhaps to impress the people "back home" with their own success. They invariably included Yenching in such an itinerary, and I had to impress my western colleagues into helping me entertain the visitors. A few Chinese were occasionally also asked and consented as a supreme evidence of a good will that rose above nationalistic pride. The delegations were commercial, educational and once even a group of Christian pastors. This last drew out a few more of our more actively religious Chinese, and it was pleasant to watch the triumph of Christian ideals struggling against racial feeling and mutual embarrassment.

Japanese were never permitted to enter the gate except by special arrangement and were always escorted over the grounds by my secretary or someone else. I soon discovered that the secret of dealing with them was a blend of firmness and friendliness. Their military power and the brutal use they made of it caused the Chinese to cringe before them. On the other hand, they met with little more than a forced compliance. Despite their blustering they were not too sure of themselves and stood in a certain awe of the unrevealed American attitude. Courteous treatment was all the more appreciated by them under these conditions. To show no fear of their armed might while heartily cordial in manner enabled me to meet their truculence or break their nervous reticence in many a delicate encounter.

With the protection the students enjoyed on an American-owned campus, it was understood that they should not take advantage of this to carry on anti-Japanese activities. More than once I had to remind certain patriotic individuals among them that they should either leave our campus and do whatever they had in mind or desist entirely and thus avoid endangering their comrades as well as themselves. The Japanese were constantly on the watch for underground hostility and had a horde of secret police and spies whose reports led to numerous cases of arrest and torture. Our own students were under especial suspicion. The usual procedure was to pull them out of the University buses when they were making week-end trips to the city. My resourceful secretary was remarkably fortunate in getting them released without too much delay or hardship.

One boy was, however, so horribly treated that when he was finally set free he lived for months in abject terror even of his mother, and when I was permitted to call at the home he was still in this state of pathological dread. When I last saw him several years after this experience he was still unable to resume any normal activity. His case made graphic my fears over continuing university work in occupied territory. Another boy confessed to me with an obvious sense of shame that when under interrogation by the dreaded secret police he was given the alternative of prison and torture or acting as a spy on the Yenching campus he had agreed to the latter. He was to report to them weekly what went on. I told him that I had no condemnation of him nor any objection to his reporting whatever he observed on the campus, but asked him to inform me occasionlly of their reaction. Before long he told me that they had dismissed him because there was no interest for them in his reports.

2

Students were constantly trying to slip away through the lines to Free China for patriotic or other reasons, and I arranged with certain junior members of the staff, themselves former students, to work out suitable routes for them. One was down the Peking-Hankow Railway and overland, another was via Shanghai, and another safer but much longer one especially used for girls, via Hongkong, Rangoon and the Burma Road. I had friends along the way who were authorized to advance funds and otherwise assist them. After Pearl Harbor, early in my captivity, I was taken to Gendarmerie Headquarters for four lengthy and grilling inquisitions. One of the points about which they were most solicitous was this clandestine traffic about which their highly efficient secret agents had learned just enough to make them anxious to know more. I tried to tell them with disarming frankness that I felt myself to be toward these students *in loco parentis* and therefore duty bound to assist them in trying to travel elsewhere, but that their reasons for doing so were not my concern. It was hard for them to object to this but they tried their best to extract information as to who were my Chinese helpers. Knowing too well what their fate would be, I refused on the ground that these men had trusted me, and that my inquisitors themselves would have no respect for me if I in my turn were not faithful to them. I added that I was an old man and a few years more or less of life could not mean much. I would answer any questions about myself, and they could do anything to me they wished, but I would not endanger the lives of my loyal associates.

Another question on which they quizzed me was as to the nature and purpose of Yenching University. I knew that this had long puzzled the Japanese military mind which simply could not conceive of an institution of its dimensions being on a purely private basis from religious and philanthropic motives. While we were still functioning, one of their higher officers had asked to call on me on an important matter which put me into a tremor as to what offense I or someone else among us had committed. But when he arrived he merely wanted to know whether in view of our possible financial needs we would care to accept a substantial annual subsidy, nominally from the puppet Chinese local government. When I explained that we were dependent entirely on voluntary private gifts, that the American Government had never contributed one dollar, nor would we accept any contribution from that or any other political source, he was so astounded that he forgot his instinctive Japanese manners and left the room without the customary formalities. My inquisitors revealed the same incredulity and actually became so interested in this strange phenomenon that they ceased to probe for evidence of American governmental infiltration and put further questions out of sheer curiosity.

3

A third topic of more serious questioning was my relations with Chiang Kai-shek. After the Double Seventh, Philip Fugh and I had made an annual spring trip to Hongkong to attend meetings of the China Foundation for Education and Culture (American Boxer Indemnity) of which I had long been one of the Trustees. That meeting had previously been held in Shanghai or Peiping. I took advantage each year of this occasion to fly from Hongkong to the war capital, the first year in Hankow, afterward in Chungking. This was the shortest—in fact the only —route to reach either of these two cities from Peking, even though it meant traveling the whole length of China, from Peking to Shanghai by rail, from there to Hongkong by steamer, then by air westward despite the hazards of watchful Japanese pursuit planes.

I made this annual trip chiefly for two reasons. It was a way of demonstrating to all concerned that Yenching, although carrying on under Japanese occupation, was none the less loyal to the Chinese cause. I wanted also to learn first-hand how that cause was faring. We had only Japanese-controlled news. The morale of our campus would be sustained by authentic information, especially if—as proved in the main to be the case—the news was reassuring. I carried with me the usual reports for the Ministry of Education, not only from Yenching but from other similarly situated institutions. These trips had fascinating interest. I always had interviews with the Generalissimo and with various other government officials. There were gatherings with missionaries, Yenching *Hsiao-yu* and as many other groups as time permitted. On my first trip to Chungking I experienced my first air raid there late one afternoon as I was waiting for their car to take me to supper with the Generalissimo and Madame Chiang. I saw twenty-seven bombers coming over the hills in a perfect "V" formation. The night that followed was ghastly, as was the walk the next morning through a mile and a half of utter devastation littered with portions of charred corpses.

On my return from the first of these journeys, I reported my impressions to my old friend, Wang K'e-min, head of the north China titular government. He had long debated whether or not to take this seemingly unpatriotic position under Japanese overlords. After listening to my rather cheering description of the determined will of all classes of the population, under the Generalissimo's inspiring leadership, to carry on the resistance, he asked me if I would be willing to have him arrange for me to tell this to the ranking Japanese military officer. They had, of course, known of my travels but could not prevent a citizen of a neutral country. It was a challenging proposal, but I finally undertook it with Philip Fugh, who had accompanied me as usual, and my courageous interpreter. On my subsequent trips, I made bold to inform the Japanese authorities in advance and ask if I could do anything for them!

It was about what had transpired on these journeys that my

inquisitors wished especially to learn. I described the Generalissimo as an ardent patriot defending his country against invasion and reminded them that Japanese ought, with their
own intense patriotic devotion, to appreciate him better than
those of any other race. I went on to explain that for myself I
was anxious to see these two countries on friendly terms of
mutual good will and economic and cultural interchange. I knew
this also to be true of at least the great majority of my fellow
countrymen. Unfortunately, the Japanese policy-makers had
adopted a course which prevented this. None the less my relations with the Generalissimo and all other Chinese were pred-
icated on the hope that there might yet be a happier development. I knew full well that he and the rest of them were not
anti-Japanese as such but only opposed to aggressive violence
and conquest. There was not much they could take exception
to in this attitude, although they argued that their intentions
were badly misunderstood.

4

The fourth issue was my supposed connection with Japanese
peace efforts. There had always been an element in Japan opposed to the "China Affair"—as they preferred to call it—and as
their armies became more bogged down in the vast morass of
China and the war dragged interminably on, many influential
civil and even military leaders were eager to end it as best they
could. Some of these had been in touch with me, and my secretary had actually made two trips to Tokyo, largely on his own
initiative but of course with my approval. In my answers I dealt
in harmless generalities, refusing to give any names or details,
but referring them to my erstwhile secretary knowing that he
would be quite able to take care of himself. Actually, however,
I had been asked on my later trips by members of that peace
group to take messages to the Generalissimo asking what his
terms would be for ending hostilities and, brought back—un-

officially, of course—his answer. His terms were then exceedingly reasonable.

In all of the four sessions those in charge were scrupulously courteous. There was none of the menacing intimidation of which I had heard so much. Each time I was kept sitting alone for an hour or two before being taken to the inquiry room, but after the first experience I realized that this was a technique for unnerving me and, forced myself to take it casually. The desk was piled high with my dossier in Japanese script, and reference was constantly made to one or another of those documents. On the last day we parted on good terms, and the presiding officer told me that he had come to respect my point of view.

Not long after the occupation began, I was urged by one Japanese after another to add a Japanese teacher to our faculty, the assignment to be made and all expenses paid by their government. Sometimes this was proposed on grounds of better cultural understanding, at other times with veiled threats. They were in a position to be very troublesome, but I had made up my mind that it would be better to close the institution than to sacrifice our independence. When finally I was convinced that this decision was accepted by them, I consulted with my colleagues as to the desirability of inviting on our own initiative a Japanese scholar whose reputation would preclude the suspicion of political inducements. They agreed, notably the Chinese, that this would be a splendidly Christian and broadminded action, thus refuting also Japanese criticism.

We selected one of the three or four internationally known scholars, Dr. R. Torii, whose sociological and later on archaeological research had been chiefly carried on in China where his publications were highly esteemed. He was then seventy years old but still vigorous, living quietly in Japan, entirely out of sympathy with his government's military adventures. I informed a secretary of the Japanese Embassy of our decision and, when he exclaimed that we could not possibly get a man like that, told him that the invitation had already been accepted. Dr. Torii made only one stipulation, that we protect him from pressure on him by his own military. We assured him that this would be easy as long as he stayed on the campus. He had a wife and two charming daughters, one of whom was his assistant in English and the other in French, all three working with him in his studies. An only son was conscripted in the armed forces. It was gratifying to watch how they steadily won their way in our little community despite all anti-Japanese prejudices. They were in themselves the best type of cultured Japanese and were genuinely international in outlook. They had an instinct for joining freely in our social life while avoiding embarrassing issues. Advanced students were allowed as a special privilege to accompany Dr. Torii and his family on field excursions and learned the better to appreciate their spirit. One of these married one of the daughters. After Pearl Harbor they lived in the city, almost in penury, the daughters supporting the family. He refused all Japanese offers, being as he expressed it "once Yenching always Yenching." When peace had been restored and we were back on our campus, I took a special pleasure in carrying him out to his former residence in my own car after the others—including his son—had preceded him. He was showing the effects of age and the strains of the war upon so sensitive a spirit, but we determined to treat him to the end on the terms he had himself formulated.

5

In course of time I had a visit from Dr. Walter Judd. As a medical missionary in Shansi he had been watching the brutalized conquest of that region by the Japanese military until he could endure it no more. It was not enough to agonize in spirit with the Chinese Christians and the whole community he was serving. They were not only defenseless but pitifully inarticulate, whereas he was well aware of the Japanese dependence on

America for the sale of basic war materials, and he could talk. The logic was unanswerable. He must tell the American people of the iniquitous traffic which made us participants in these depredations. It meant leaving China for as long as the Japanese remained in power, resigning with no resources of his own from his Mission Board, starting on a crusade with no slightest assurance that the American public would care to listen to him or that even his minimum travel expenses could be provided. He had had some success in public speaking as a student, and that along with his burning conviction of having a burden on his soul of which he must deliver himself were his only assets. It called to mind the Hebrew prophets and was a magnificent adventure of faith. As he related to me instances of Japanese cruelty and described the consequences to China if this were allowed to go on unchecked, he became passionately excited. When he asked for my advice I could only urge him not to waste his energies on persons like me but to expend his fiery eloquence on the people at home. This he accomplished with marvelous success, and it opened the way for his continuing usefulness to China as a distinguished member of Congress. Fortunately for all concerned, a committee had already been formed for the very purpose he had in mind, and they were on the lookout for speakers when he arrived.

6

For over four years we were able to maintain our little oasis of freedom against Japanese oppression and to strengthen thereby the principles we had tried to demonstrate against every other form of domination over the human spirit. This witness was widely appreciated both in the passionately felt immediate issue and in its larger implications. In normal years we had students literally from every province in China and from overseas, but during this period these were almost confined to the

Peiping-Tientsin area. But so many were anxious to escape the Japanese attempts at cultural control that we violated sanitary and other considerations in overcrowding our dormitories to accommodate them. All in all, these four years were an exacting but exhilarating experience.

8

Incarceration and Release

For weeks before the Pearl Harbor attack, we had been anxiously waiting for something to shatter our illusory calm. We could only speculate as to what it would be. North China weather is at its best in the slowly cooling, windless autumn season, but there seemed to be something sinister about our tranquil campus. The Tientsin Alumni Association had been asking me to visit them, and after postponing it repeatedly for fear that something would "break," I finally decided to make a brief trip for the week-end of December 7, during which I blandly assumed that nothing would happen. But early Monday morning as I was quietly planning to return, it was evident that the Japanese had for some reason taken swift control. I was soon discovered and taken back to Peking by two military police, who were polite enough but evidently under strict orders not to let me out of their sight.

On that railway journey I spent the time in uneasy guessing as to what had happened. I might soon be facing a firing squad or something worse. The Peking station is just outside of the imposing South Gate—the famous *Ch'ien Men*—and the American Consulate is immediately within it. I was made to walk this short distance, which was somewhat reassuring, and escorted into the entrance of its marine barracks. There were some two hundred marines interned in its main building. I was taken to the third floor where I was welcomed by old friends, which was a further relief. There were some fifty British and Americans, separated by a partition with an open door. It was a motley crew. I soon spotted Dr. Henry S. Houghton, Dr. I. Snapper and Mr. Trevor Bowen, all of the Peking Union Medical College, who were to be my companions in a long captivity, and by a prophetic instinct I chose a bed near them.

Among the Americans there were also a journalist or two, one lone missionary, some ex-marines who were engaged in the nefarious drug traffic and usually themselves addicts, and a nondescript residue, the common feature being apparently that we were all somehow objectionable to the Japanese. There were, of course, initial discomforts such as lack of bedding and other essentials. We ate with the marines and thought at first that in this respect at least we would be fortunate. But the Japanese soon took charge, and as food became more short alike in quantity and quality, I had my first experience of the bad manners of grown-up Americans when in real privation.

2

There had been all sorts of wild rumors among us as to the outbreak of war, but at first we refused to believe the devastating news about Pearl Harbor, the sinking of two British battleships off the Malayan coast, and all the other appalling calamities that followed in swift succession. After my first discomfiture I began, however, to feel an unholy satisfaction over the dastardly Japanese attack on our navy. For years I had been sending highly confidential reports to our Yenching Trustees about the Japanese menace and the advisability of our doing something to stop this before too late. These were circulated among a carefully selected list of leaders. It was discouraging to observe how unheeded were all such warnings. It came over me that some such disaster as this was needed to arouse our people to action, and once that happened I was not seriously worried as to the ultimate result. The Japanese were woefully deficient in their understanding of the American temper. This was probably the most costly victory in all history when—as a Chinese adage has it—the clever failed because of their cleverness.

One month passed in relatively mild confinement. We had to do our own work. Some of our companions created problems. The news was continuously bad. But we had a few callers and many pleasant reminders on Christmas Day. Those first four weeks passed rather rapidly. Then all of a sudden the others were allowed to depart, and the three mentioned above and I watched them listening to a farewell speech by a spick-and-span officer while we moodily wondered why we had to stay behind and what our fate would be.

Later on that same day we were conveyed to the home of Dr. Houghton, Director of the Peking Union Medical College. This was a charming old Manchu princely residence, equipped with modern conveniences and a staff of well-trained servants. In this lacquered, if not gilded, cage we spent four months, each of us with room and bath, enjoying central heat, the usual cuisine, a large yard and a very occasional glimpse of friends through an aperture in the gate. We even were permitted a few visitors on Dr. Houghton's birthday. It was imprisonment de luxe. Moreover, the unvarying bad news did not entirely crush our hopes that things would take a better turn and that we would soon be repatriated.

3

Suddenly our guards informed us that we were to be moved elsewhere. After much argument, they allowed us to inspect the new premises not far away—the absolutely bare rear quarters of the residence of a British businessman—and to take with us such furniture as belonged personally to Dr. Houghton. We had seven guards who occupied the residence in front, including the only bathroom, and we lived in the little offices behind this around a twenty-by-twenty foot court of crumbling cement. This was our world for the remainder of the three years and eight months.

Dr. Snapper was a very distinguished Dutch physician, a

visiting professor at the Peking Union Medical College. His wife had been allowed to visit him at will in the Houghton residence, but upon removal to the new prison, he had to choose between her joining him inside or not seeing her at all. He naturally took the former alternative which further restricted our living space but made our social life more pleasant. We had been assured by underground routes that we were destined to be repatriated by SS *Gripsholm,* the connecting ship for which, the SS *Conte Verde,* after various delays sailed from Shanghai in June. We, therefore, endured our sequestration quite jauntily in this confident expectation. When the time came, however, the ship sailed without us. Then in September the Snappers were included as passengers on the British exchange vessel. Again the three of us left behind were comforted by secretly delivered messages to the effect that we would certainly be passengers on the second sailing of the *Gripsholm,* which took place a year later. By that time we were much more weary of our rigid confinement. Long afterward we learned that our friends, including the Rockefeller Foundation and the Yenching Trustees, had been exerting themselves to the utmost on our behalf and that the State Department had put us at the top of the list and had announced that there would be no further exchange of nationals without us. This was said to have been finally agreed upon in Tokyo.

But for some inscrutable reason the local Japanese military authorities refused, and we knew that we were there "for the duration." Poor Bowen had fewer resources within himself than the other two of us and had literally been existing until this liberation. He believed until the last that we might even be flown down as the ship was leaving port. We told him that all the logic was on his side, but all the signs pointed the other way. We feared that he would have a nervous collapse when he realized our fate. But the morning after he calmly announced that he was going to study Chinese, to which he had hitherto

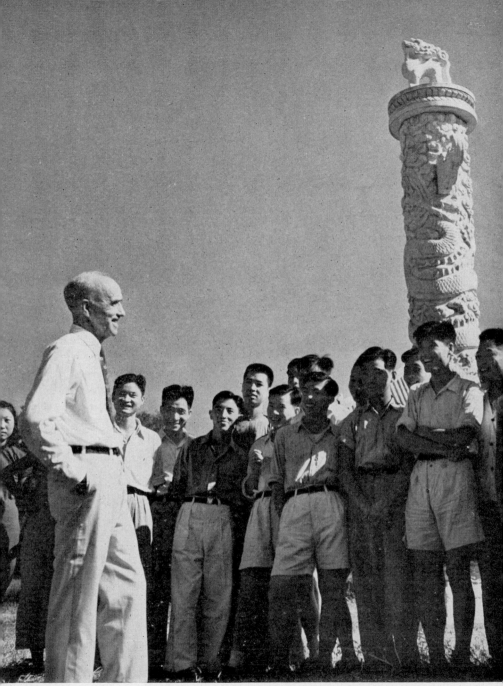

President Stuart chatting with a group of newly enrolled
students by one of the imperial pillars on campus of
Yenching University, 1946.

Ambassador Stuart conferring with Admiral Louis E. Denfield, Commander of U. S. Pacific Fleet and Admiral S. S. Cook, in Nanking, 1946.

been entirely indifferent. Sure enough, this typical New York financial district accountant worked unremittingly on the Chinese language from then on and was doing so the day we were released. It gave me one more diversion to be his teacher. But this episode was a grim reminder of what misery it would have been for all if any one of us had become neurotic. For that matter, it would have been almost intolerable if one of us, in this enforced intimacy and segregation from all others of our kind, had developed any idiosyncrasies or disagreeable traits. Fortunately the trio had started out good friends, and much more fortunately we remained so to the end.

Our seizure on the very morning of Pearl Harbor must have been premeditated. The other enemy nationals in north China were relatively free until put in an internment camp well over a year later. But why this special treatment of three elderly men? The answer has never been found. The military police, who were in charge of us, were solicitous about our health and reasonably so about our comfort. But they seemed to be under the strictest orders to keep us *incommunicado*. This was all that mattered, but on this they took every precaution. The only tenable theory seemed to be that the Japanese military mind simply could not conceive of institutions like Peking Union Medical College and Yenching having been created by private philanthropy or religious zeal. They must be instruments of the American Government for winning the hearts of Chinese youth and thus thwarting their own imperialistic designs. By putting their executive officers out of all contact they may have imagined that they were destroying the influence of these colleges. What actually happened was just the opposite. If they had let us be quietly repatriated, we and our schools would have been forgotten. Had we been sent to the internment camp we would have been lost in the crowd. But the mystery of our seclusion stimulated curiosity and sympathy. We became almost legendary.

Our food was to have been the same as our guards. For those

accustomed to western diet it would have been bleakly unappetizing, and Dr. Houghton could not have survived. But the Swiss Consulate in Shanghai had set up a branch in Peiping for cases like ours, and the two men in charge happened to be professors respectively in our two institutions as well as very good friends. Among many other kindly deeds, they persuaded the Japanese Gendarmerie to allow them to supply our food. A Chinese banker advanced the money. A young Norwegian missionary had been caught in the city and—being regarded as on the Axis side—was permitted to do the marketing and bring her purchases to our outer gate. This she did two or three times a week and was a veritable angel of mercy. She also wrote us occasionally, sent mementoes, and every Saturday evening cooked a delicious Norwegian dinner which we learned to look forward to as eagerly as children. One of our earliest and pleasantest meetings after our release was with this unseen ministrant. When we moved from Dr. Houghton's home, his cook and another servant went with us, promising that whatever happened they would stay with us to the end. The cook had to leave, but the other one kept his word. He was allowed to spend a night at home once every two weeks and very occasionally went by devious routes to Philip Fugh's home. Philip was almost a prisoner himself but had a concealed radio, and it was immensely interesting to get first-hand news. But it was also highly dangerous for all concerned and—especially after we knew that the trend had turned in favor of the Allies—we used enough self-control to abandon this device.

Bowen and I played badminton or something else in our cramped court every day that weather permitted. Houghton had to give up even this mild form of exercise, but cleaned his own room with scrupulous care for about an hour daily—a task which would have been far more irksome to me than the games. Houghton and I played anagrams in the evening in which the Snappers joined as long as they were with us. After our release

Time magazine wrote up our whole experience under the caption: Fifteen hundred nights of anagrams.

4

Soon after our arrest I was permitted to go to Yenching under guard to get needed supplies. I walked into my office which was then used as the headquarters of the force occupying our campus and which was filled with Japanese officers. As casually as I could, I found the file of communications to our Trustees referred to in a preceding paragraph and handed this to Dr. Galt of our faculty to take care of. He burned the whole lot at the first chance. But not a Japanese seemed to take notice. Had they known the contents they might well have shot me. Contrary to the regulations, the petty officer who had me in charge allowed me to stay for lunch and to talk freely with a small faculty group while he sat close enough to watch but not to overhear.

As long as American and other foreign friends were at large we were the happy recipients of letters, flowers and birthday and other remembrances. Many of these really came from Chinese who got into trouble with the Japanese if they sent us anything directly. We were most grateful for books, and even after the others were sent to the internment camp, our Swiss benefactors searched the city to keep us supplied. For some enigmatic reason the Gendarmerie required their interpreter to furnish them with an abstract of each book. His own knowledge of English was none too profound, and he frequently had to bring a volume for us to see in order to write his summary, and perhaps after weeks had elapsed this book would be received. Why the Gendarmerie concerned themselves over our reading matter is another of the mysteries of our peculiar treatment. If there was any danger of our minds being corrupted they had seen to it that we could not corrupt anyone else. Our hardships really amounted to little more than loneliness, monotony and of course haunting suspense. But compared with what we might have suffered and with all that I have since learned about what many others did, we were exceedingly fortunate. We were not always comfortably warm in winter. We had our meals in an unheated passage-way where the water in our glasses often froze while we were at the table. It was hot in summer in our cramped quarters. But we lived in Chinese wadded gowns, put on over much else in cold weather and were correspondingly denuded in the heat. For the one thing of which we were certain was that we would have no visitors, and that every day would be precisely like every other one.

Even so there were breaks. One such was caused by the "Peking Man." Her famous bones (I believe this is the correct gender) had been deposited in the Peking Union Medical College, after replicas had been so perfectly made that only experts could distinguish them from the original. But apparently some Japanese scientists felt that the new position of their country in the world—and in Peking—entitled them to have this prehistoric treasure. At any rate, Gendarmerie officers came one day to interrogate Houghton and Bowen on the matter. They replied truthfully that they did not know where the bones were. Actually the precious case had been sent for safety to Chingwangtao where an American transport was to call about the Pearl Harbor date to take away a contingent of marines. Whether the bones had been delivered to the transport, or scattered on the sands, or met some other fate, my two companions were of course utterly ignorant.

There was much argument and the officers went away obviously unconvinced. A few days later Bowen was carried off to Gendarmerie Headquarters and came back five days later bearing all the signs of having had a horrible experience. On arrival at headquarters he had been stripped of everything by which he might commit suicide and forced to crawl on hands and feet through an aperture into a cage too small to recline in at length. A leering guard would not allow him to attempt to do so during the day. A leather thong hung conspicuously in view. He was too miserable to touch the food supplied twice a day but eagerly drank the little cups of water. After five days of this they evidently felt that he had been sufficiently unnerved to confess to anything and questioned him once more about the relics before sending him back.

One aspect of the matter that added greatly to Bowen's jittery condition for many days, comical as it seems in retrospect, was his hurriedly snatching two hundred-dollar bills as he was being led away. This was on the general theory that money on his person would come in usefully, as residents in China have all discovered. These were immediately taken away from him on arrival and when returned it was with a query as to how he was in possession of notes so recently minted. As our time of detention lengthened and the limited funds we had collected dwindled, we had surreptitiously secured an additional supply from an American friend. Bowen's two bills were from this lot. We agreed on the most plausible explanation we could concoct, in case we were questioned further, and drilled our servant on it.

Their interest seemed, however, to have been merely casual, although they would have derived a sadistic pleasure from knowing how Bowen trembled for days afterward at any sound which might be their coming after him again. As to our financial affairs, we had all been sufficiently worried over our naughty adventure to agree never to try that again. Meanwhile the American Government had arranged a monthly stipend for each of us through the Red Cross which eased the problem. The Gendarmerie had given us the alternative of eating their food or receiving an allowance which, with the mounting inflation, would have enabled us toward the end to purchase one egg apiece monthly. Yet with humorless precision, we were given the original amount through the whole period duly receipted for. Nor did we dare to fling it back at them or refuse to accept it.

Bowen continued to be our controller, just as he had been of the huge Medical College establishment. He managed all of our simple domestic affairs, cared for our two canaries, our brief spell of trying to find diversion in rabbits, etc.

To be strictly accurate, I had one visitor on two separate occasions. This was an old Japanese friend named Tagawa, for over thirty years a member of the Japanese Diet and a Presbyterian elder for about the same period. On his first call he was allowed to stay ten minutes. Something over a year later he came again, accompanied by one of our guards and a Gendarmerie officer who made full notes of the conversation which lasted half an hour. Mr. Tagawa had for years been going back and forth between Japan and China trying to reconcile the conflicting aims or opinions of the two countries. This was his fourteenth trip and he was then seventy-five years old. His coming was a cheering reminder of the reality of Christian fellowship in a time of all-out war and of intense racial bitterness. A year and a half later, after my release, I learned that he was sick and destitute in a Nanking hospital and was able to help him get back to Japan. He had apparently been penalized by his own military for being too active in the cause of peace.

5

It may be of interest to transcribe here some reflections on the religious aspect of this experience as I recorded them early in its duration. They can best reveal my mood at the time if left unaltered:

It can easily be inferred by this description of my religious history that life has thus far treated me very kindly. Not only direct religious influences have on the whole been favorable, but the external circumstances have been pleasant . . . Then came suddenly the event long foreshadowed and feared which has brought to me the greatest sense of disaster which I can imagine, the wreckage of all that has been suggested in the preceding sentences. This will not be merely in the nature of an interruption, annoying or disturbing, but may well be permanent . . . We are caught on the surface of a catastrophic storm and are flung—as are innumerable others, most of them less fortunate—into an eddy from which we cannot foresee when or how we shall be released. But looking forward to that time, and unless my old life can be restored—which at this writing has only slight objective cause for optimism—I shall be an old man, bereft of the only home in which he could be usefully contented, unfitted for ordinary employment in America, my slight resources practically wiped out by what has taken place, a lonely survivor from an enterprise in which those once comrades cannot but be scattered and with its organized existence hopelessly defunct. There has thus come upon me that aspect of religion which gives consolation in sorrow and frustration and a better understanding of those who suffer. I have often noticed how largely religious, especially devotional, books deal with problems of human grief, discouragement, despair, whereas in my own case religion has been chiefly the source of an *élan* inspiring congenial activities and tending to neutralize their more selfish or sordid motives. I now have the opportunity to test out and to profit by Christian faith as a solace in a time of bitter disappointment and when facing a future full of harrowing uncertainties. If—as I have often preached or urged upon others in private—it does not so much matter what happens to any of us as how he takes what happens, then I now have a chance to apply my own medicine. In this sense I can almost welcome the present experience and prepare myself not to lose its possible benefits.

6

Our chief interest in captivity was, of course, the war news. We were allowed to subscribe to the local English daily, a scrawny specimen of the effects of Japanese military control, and also to the English edition of the *Osaka Mainichi* from which we learned a great deal. It was well edited and, being intended for readers within the country, contained much information that would not appear elsewhere. We assembled for what we called our cocktail hour before the evening meal to discuss the day's news, sometimes with real cocktails or a substitute. One of us, usually Dr. Houghton, would have been studying the *Mainichi* and would read relevant passages as a basis for comment. In the nondescript assortment of books brought with us from Houghton's home was an excellent atlas, and it was fully put to use. We developed quite a respect for the daily German *communiqué*, which seemed to be essentially factual. The opposite was true of Japanese publicity, but they unwittingly allowed much that was damaging to leak out. The news of the first year is an awful memory. The indisputable facts were invariably bad enough even without the jubilant Axis version of them. I remember vividly the news that the Germans had been turned back at El Alamein as marking the first sign of the long hoped for reversal in this dismal record, but it was weary months after this before the trend toward victory was reflected clearly enough to enable us to look forward to rather than dread the reading of the news.

We became quite proficient in interpreting the Japanese dispatches. When, for instance, we read that American marines had attempted a landing on a certain island in the Pacific but had been driven back with sanguinary losses and that this had happened a second time, after which this island dropped out of the news until Japanese airplanes took to bombing it, we came to assume that these attempted landings were successful. We deduced so much from unmistakable references to shortages of aviation gasoline, cargo steamers, food etc., that we decided that —regardless of American performance—Japan could not last long after the defeat of Germany. We fixed this as from four to six months. We could only guess as to American production until one day we read under big headlines and quoting an American source that airplane production had fallen off two percent from the previous month to only some 7500. This was our first glimmering of the enormous scale American war production had reached. Whatever consolation the Japanese derived from the differential of two percent they were welcome to. In the spring of 1945 the delivery of the *Mainichi* became irregular and then increasingly intermittent, with occasionally much abbreviated editions, until it ceased altogether. We could not decide whether we were more pleased over this convincing evidence of the effectiveness of our bombers or grieved over the loss of our primary source of news.

7

Soon after the German defeat there was a sudden change in the Japanese cabinet, with an eighty-year-old man as Premier and one nearly as old as Foreign Minister. It took no special acumen to divine that this meant a shift toward peace, although it was announced in the grandiose English the Japanese affect that this had been done to accelerate their war prosecuting potentialities. As it came out later, it was decided in May to seek mediation with America through the Soviet Union and if that failed, through Chiang Kai-shek. The Soviets refused flatly so the Cabinet passed an action setting me free, and a commission of two diplomats escorted by military officers was ordered to take this word to me in the form of an Imperial Rescript and with the plea that I proceed at once to Chungking to persuade the Generalissimo to assume this function. We had then one more proof of the stranglehold of our blockade for this delegation encountered constant dangers along the route. A flight normally of a few hours had taken them two weeks, dodging our fighters in the air, sighting two submarines and three destroyers when crossing the straits to Korea by ferry, and otherwise taking risks in sneaking through our blockade. On finally reaching Peiping they met new obstacles in the unwillingness of their own military and were compelled to go to Nanking to get permission from the Commander in Chief of the Japanese Expeditionary Forces. The real issue seemed to be that the military chiefs wanted to be in on the negotiations whereas the men from Tokyo sought to get me safely out of their clutches and away from Gendarmerie espionage. It seems strange that when they must have known they were facing national destruction, they were still struggling to maintain their own prestige.

The first I knew of all this was on July 24 when one of the guards asked if I wished to see Mr. Fugh, in a tone of voice as though this were a daily routine. Philip followed him almost immediately, escorted by the military officer from Tokyo who left after briefly explaining his mission. Philip gave me further details and brought me up to date on the military situation. My two companions were not included in the order so I slipped across promptly to satisfy what I knew would be their bursting curiosity over so unprecedented an event. Philip's function was to "sweeten me up," as they expressed it, in anticipation for their proposal, on the assumption apparently that I had gone sour in the long isolation. The two diplomats were still arguing in Nanking. A guard sat in the room throughout the first interview, but Philip was allowed two more visits with this feature eliminated. Finally he came with the chief delegate who had won the consent of the military, and they stayed on to lunch with our trio. Mr. Kawai was an experienced diplomat who talked very freely of the desperate plight of his country and the necessity for ending the war without delay on any terms whatever. I reminded him that the Potsdam Conference of July 26 had announced that these were "unconditional surrender" and that Chiang Kai-shek had given his concurrence. Therefore, there was nothing that I or anyone else could do to help except to advise the Emperor and the new Cabinet to agree to this promptly, despite whatever opposition might still be offered by the recalcitrant military leaders whose folly had brought this overwhelming disaster upon their nation. He concurred in all of this and started back to Japan with this reply.

What Mr. Kawai told me of the exhaustion of war effort in Japan amply confirmed our impressions from reading the *Mainichi* and from other sources. If this had been realized by our Joint Chiefs of Staff, they need not have urged President Roosevelt at the Yalta Conference to make sure that Stalin would enter the war against Japan, which he did by promising enormous concessions in Manchuria at the expense of China. Their Intelligence Service was apparently less accurate than the sources upon which Admiral Zacharias based conclusions essentially the same as ours. The Yalta Agreement, from the blunders of which China and the non-Soviet world are destined increasingly to suffer, were due, therefore, not so much to President Roosevelt's failing health as to our faulty military intelligence system.

The day after the departure of Mr. Kawai, his substitute—a Colonel Ojeki—came with Philip and an interpreter who spoke excellent Chinese which is not generally the case with Japanese. The conversation which lasted several hours was extremely friendly. It was a dramatic experience to listen to a Japanese military man, after beginning with the characteristic Oriental unwillingness to put unpalatable truths in plain language, finally break down and admit that the situation in his country could scarcely be worse. When we shook hands as he departed, his eyes filled with tears and he rushed out of the room.

I had refused to be released unless my two companions were included, but this had to be referred to Tokyo. This voluntary detention proved to be somewhat advantageous, as illustrated by a caller who forced his way past the guards. This Chinese pretended to be overjoyed at my prospective liberty, and then tried to learn all that he could about the results of my conversations with Mr. Kawai and the report he was taking back to Tokyo.

He was doubtless an agent of the Japanese military who had
been instructed that he be admitted. I found myself therefore
in the absurd position of hoping that the guards would maintain
their rigid refusal to admit all callers.

8

Meanwhile we heard in quick succession of the weirdly
terrific explosion which seemed to have devastated Hiroshima,
of the Russian entry into Manchuria and of the Emperor's
broadcast proclaiming surrender (August 9, 10, 11). On August
16, Colonel Ojeki and Philip Fugh came again to inform us
that we were about to be released, and we begged that one or
more of our Swiss and Norwegian benefactors be allowed to
call. Our ministering angel, Signe Skrövseth, counted so on
getting permission that she brought four little cakes for each of
us to have one with her at four-o'clock tea. But the utmost concession was that I could go to the gate and speak to her. I could
at any rate report to the others that she not only existed but
was as nice as we had imagined. One of the Swiss was also
allowed to see us for a few minutes that day and the other one
the next morning.

On the afternoon of August 17 we were suddenly summoned
to Gendarmerie Headquarters. At any time earlier we would
have had the jitters, but after all the recent happenings we were
adjusting ourselves to accepting every new event as good for us.
We went the short distance in automobiles with guards and
were shown into the Commandant's reception room. He came
out followed by his staff in full regalia. There were two in-
terpreters from the Japanese Embassy. He made a short speech
regretting that we had been "inconvenienced" and informing
us that we were now at liberty. We tried to make a suitable
reply. He then shook hands with each of us, as did the others,
and the ceremonious meeting was ended. News spread rapidly
that the Americans so long and mysteriously hidden from view

had been taken away and when we returned a large crowd had assembled. Among them were some of our Chinese friends. The gate was left open and the hitherto implacable guards allowed people to stream in and out at will.

Our strange incarceration of three years, eight and a third months, to us seemingly interminable, was over. I think we now understand one reason at least for it. In the impossible event of the Japanese Army having had to surrender I would have been used as a mediator for peace with Chiang Kai-shek. Dr. Houghton would have had the responsibility of keeping me physically fit for this, and we two being administrative officers for our respective institutions Bowen was held as a third hostage. But what was of infinitely more importance—even perhaps to us— was that the thirty years' nightmare of Japanese subjugation of China was also finally dispelled, with only the agonizing memory of the sufferings and slaughter of many millions of Chinese, and the vast sacrifice in life and treasure by Americans as well as those of other nations, in order that this hideously militaristic ambition might be forever quelled.

9

The release from confinement, the reunion with former friends and colleagues, was a thrilling experience. This was true of every trivial detail. I had told my two companions, when we discussed what we would each do first when free again, that I was going to revel in a warm bath. This I did daily in soapy luxury. Peiping colors are at their best in August and to drive —at will—past flowering lotus ponds and other familiar scenes had for me a childish delight. I had vowed in my loneliness that never would I complain again if callers were numerous or their visits lengthy, and in those first crowded days I whimsically reminded myself of this pledge.

It was on the second day that I met with the committee of Chinese faculty members who were the last relic of Yenching administrative planning. I at once asked them to reconstitute themselves "The President's Advisory Committee." Every one of them had suffered the cruel horrors of Japanese imprisonment in the attempt to make them transfer their allegiance, but they had remained staunchly loyal. One could not have desired a more intelligently alert and faithful group of colleagues. When I proposed that we start something at once on our university campus, stripped as it was of all equipment and still occupied as a Japanese military hospital, I discovered that they had already begun to plan for this. We would take in a freshman class of about four hundred, and have a formal opening on the Double Tenth (the Chinese Independence Day, October 10). Our friends told us that it would be impossible, and we ourselves rather feared that it would be, but there was an enthusiastic determination to achieve it and we did.

We arranged to have an opening ceremony with as much of the usual colorful academic procedure as possible. It happened, however, that the newly established government had fixed on the same day and hour for the formal Japanese surrender and the dignitaries, including the principal speaker, had to attend. We were disappointed but felt that this added to the historical interest of the occasion, the hour of ten in the morning making it a "Triple Tenth," and the speeches were no doubt at least as good. Professor William Hung had resolved never to make a public speech until the Japanese Army had withdrawn from Chinese soil and this gave him an opportunity of which he made brilliant use. The weather was perfect, the auditorium packed, and the assemblage was vibrant with joy over our "comeback" after four years of what the Japanese took delight in describing as "the now defunct Yenching University."

10

Less than two weeks after our final release on August 17, I started for Chungking on an American Army airplane. The first military mission had arrived in Peiping, and the chief was most considerate in helping in my desire to make this trip. But it was not as simple as he expected. We were all taken to Kunming and required to be "processed" (the first time I had met with this use of the word) in the large American military hospital, along with hundreds of other Americans from all over the Pacific who were being prepared for repatriation. I protested that I was only trying to get to Chungking and could not therefore carry infectious diseases or vermin into the States, which not only failed to secure exemption but caused me to be regarded as something of a freak. After escape from the Japanese Army I was now in the clutches of the American, and my Chinese companion, Philip Fugh, had to be processed too. Despite my annoyance over the delay I was impressed with the efficiency and the unfailing courtesy of all of those who dealt with us.

We reached Chungking on the first of September, the first three days of the victory celebration. President Chiang gave a diplomatic reception on the second, where I met many old friends. Ambassador Hurley stood by the side of the host. He had recently brought Mao Tse-tung, the head of the Communist party, from Yenan, going there for that purpose in his own airplane. When Mr. Mao saw me in the crowd, he greeted me with the remark that there were present many of my former students at Yenan. I laughingly replied that I was well aware of that and hoped that they were proving a credit to their training. A few days later he and Mr. Chou En-lai had Philip and me for lunch where the household service was supplied by eager young students. Little did I suspect then that less than a year later I would be in constant conference with Mr. Chou as head of the Communist delegation in the peace negotiations organized by General Marshall.

Soon after our arrival sudden changes in temperature gave me a severe cold and a lingering cough which was apparently a common malady known as the "Chungking cough." It kept

me awake at night and bothered me all of the three weeks before
I could finally leave for Peiping. It was an ironically distressing
experience. The war capital was full of old friends and all sorts
of interesting people whom I enjoyed seeing after my long
sequestration. I was also constantly being entertained and asked
to speak or had opportunities to learn from others what had been
happening in the world to which I had now returned. All of
this was fascinating and would normally have been eagerly
welcomed. But that wretched cough made me as exhausted
physically as I was aglow spiritually with pleasure and excitement.

Both of these conditions were intensified by two days spent in
Chengtu where a group of splendidly loyal Chinese teachers
had organized Yenching University in exile. They had about
400 students in borrowed buildings. What they lacked in library,
science equipment, textbooks and everything else can only be
imagined by those who had seen other refugee institutions from
the coastal provinces or other aspects of the devastation wrought
by war. The boys were housed in an ancient and charmingly
picturesque Confucian temple, infested by rats and crowded to
the limit. The chief complaint of the girls was the bedbugs
which no way could be found to exterminate. But the spirit was
wonderful, and despite my harassing cough, the numerous
speeches I had to make and my gnawing fatigue, I felt it worth
the nearly four years of imprisonment to experience the rebound,
to see how my beloved colleagues and their students had been
bravely carrying on in the face of so many difficulties and to
revel in their hearty welcome. In Chungking, on my return
there, the hundreds of Yenching graduates had a rousing reception in a restaurant attractively located on a bluff over the river
where, despite tables hastily put in order for the stream of new
arrivals, the management was unable to meet the demand, and
a number had to go without their dinner.

After repeated delays, I was at last able to travel on an airplane scheduled to stop at Weihsien in Shantung where all British and American nationals in north China had been interned by the Japanese. So without any warning I literally dropped from the clouds upon this camp where the unfortunate internees were still being kept, although it was then almost six weeks after V-J Day. Among them making possible another delightful reunion were Yenching faculty colleagues and many friends or acquaintances. During the twenty-four hours of the stop there, I was able to compare their circumstances with those of our trio. Physically we had undoubtedly been better off. In housing, food, service, etc., we were more comfortable. They were very crowded and had to do all their own work, while forced to an intimacy with all sorts of people. We had privacy and leisure in abundance, but it was deadly lonesome and monotonous. They were able to organize not only for cooking, laundry, scavenges, etc., but also for social, religious, athletic and educational activities which gave occupation and a sense of being usefully busy.

When finally back in Peiping the doctor put me in bed with orders to see no one and neither say nor do anything for at least three days, and for once I was entirely ready to obey.

11

After my release, the New York headquarters of the University had been urging me to return there for consultation, and the Navy had agreed to repatriate me by air. But when I appeared before the proper officer in Shanghai, I must have looked quite pathetic, for he suggested that I ought to be sent back on a "hospital ship." So under his solicitous care I was put on an airplane equipped with stretchers and a nurse, my fellow passengers all being sick or wounded naval men. We were in Guam for two nights and a day during which a traveling companion and I borrowed a jeep and went all over the island. I was amazed at the extensive naval program, impressed by the two beautifully kept cemeteries and much interested in the evidence of care for the welfare of the natives. Having read Japanese descriptions of our B-29 bombers, it was fascinating to be taken through one. We ended our tour with a swim which had all the glamour associated with a tropical island. We spent two and a half days in Pearl Harbor where, as always, I was cared for in the sick officers' ward, carried—despite my protests —on and off the airplane in a stretcher and to and from the hospital in an ambulance, and permitted "shore leave" whenever I asked for it. The second day happened to be Thanksgiving and the Yenching graduates in Honolulu caused me to feel heartily in that mood. There was a Chinese lunch and in the evening an American Thanksgiving dinner with all the trimmings, a reception the day following for all my friends and theirs in the city, and the happy consciousness that if there were gastronomic penalties from overeating I was staying in a superbly equipped naval hospital.

When we landed on the Oakland airfield I was conveyed by the usual process to the Oak Knoll Hospital and entrusted to a doctor whom I asked what would happen to me next. He was baffled at the appearance of a civilian with nothing more than a slip giving my name as a "patient without disease," entitled to travel by Naval Air Transport Service from Shanghai to the United States. But after learning that I wanted to get to New York City as soon as possible and consulting with his colleagues, they said that since NATS had taken care of me thus far they might as well see me through. So I was sent across the continent and landed in Brooklyn at nine o'clock at night in a wild storm of wind and driving rain but with perfect precision. As we had been bouncing about in the air like a ship at sea I speculated with sardonic humor as to whether my long and placid flight would end in disaster. It is pleasant to recall the unfailing courtesy and thoughful kindness of everyone in NATS who dealt with me as I experienced my first transoceanic flight. This was so true, in fact, of all my contacts with our armed forces that I asked a nurse in the Kunming Hospital whether they had any special instructions or training in this, and she was evidently puzzled at my question.

It was thrilling to meet my old associates at the University's New York office, members of the Board of Trustees and other staunch friends, as well as to read letters from many others. I had further evidence of how solicitous they had all been over the fate of my two companions and myself in our mysterious captivity and what tireless efforts had been made through the State Department for our release.

The University needed money very badly of course for reconditioning after the damage done by the Japanese, as well as for current expenses. All agreed with me, however, that it would be extremely bad taste for me to solicit funds while exploiting the sympathy our friends would naturally feel for me. Chiefly on medical grounds it was also decided that I should not make public addresses. I was scheduled therefore for a "promotional campaign" across the country under arrangements much more easy and delightful than previous ones had been. This usually took the form of luncheons, dinners or receptions at which I was the guest of honor, the others and I myself being alike free from the haunting embarrassments of a financial appeal.

It was tantalizing not to have time for my own part of the country where I have widely scattered relatives and friends and for which I still feel a very sentimental attachment. But the closest I came to the South was Washington where I spent Christmas with my brother Warren and my son. The latter came up from his pastorate near Winchester on each of my trips and acted as a chauffeur for me.

9 Call
to Diplomacy

Soon after I reached New York City, it was announced from Washington that President Truman had requested General George C. Marshall to go as his personal representative to China in an effort to help find a solution for ending the civil strife between the National Government and the Communist party. A few days later, December 15, 1945, he issued his message on the subject [see Appendix]. General and Mrs. Marshall had just bought a picturesque old farmhouse in Leesburg, Virginia, and were in the act of settling there for well-deserved retirement. But, true soldier that he is, the General responded at once to a call that could have no personal attraction.

Thus began a mission unique in international relations. The Chinese could have resented it as a meddlesome intrusion into their internal affairs or even as a bit of arrogant imperialism. The fact that they did not was due to the unsolicited generosity implicit in such a gesture and the prestige of the special envoy against the perspective of a long record of what Woodrow Wilson had finely described as "friendly helpfulness to another nation." It was typically American in being a blend of ingenuous idealism and enlightened self-interest, carried through with highly organized efficiency. I shall attempt in the light of subsequent events to reconstruct what happened in Chungking during and following the Political Consultative Conference called by the Chinese Government after General Marshall's arrival early in January. His personality and prestige and the lofty yet reasonable ideals which had brought the delegates together created an atmosphere of good feeling and high endeavor which made possible the five resolutions [see Appendix] which, if approved, would have ended the controversy, formed a coalition government on a democratic basis and led to a reorganization and training of the troops on both sides under American advice. All those who took part were probably sincere in subscribing to this agreement whatever reservations they may have had as to details or ultimate objectives. The Communists were quite frank then, and in subsequent discussions, in stating that they aimed at a communized China but that the people were not yet prepared for this, and it would be better for them to go through the stage of bourgeois democracy. The government representatives were skeptical of Communist good faith and their colleagues outside —untouched by the mood of exaltation pervading the conference—were even more dubious or frankly opposed to any attempt at co-operation with so treacherous a foe. None the less, if General Marshall could have remained a few months longer in continuous contact with all concerned the probabilities are that at least a beginning might have been effected in co-operation. But in early March he was recalled to Washington and was away from China until the latter part of April.

Immediately upon his departure, the smoldering animosities broke out afresh. Each side began to accuse the other of violating the agreements, and each began to protect its own interests by still further violations. The most serious of these was the Communist entry into Manchuria where the Soviet Union turned over to them very large stocks of Japanese military equipment. After this flagrant disregard of the terms, the Nationalists felt naturally justified in any form of retaliation. Mutual suspicions and hatreds became rapidly intensified and were aggravated by acrimonious charges and countercharges. As in all Chinese history since 1927, the personality of Chiang Kai-shek was the storm center. His finer qualities had been quickened by the idealism of the Political Consultative Conference and by the character of General Marshall. But he had never been thoroughly convinced, and he was susceptible to the plausible arguments of his trusted associates once he had left the high plane of conference discussions.

He had during the previous November summoned the National Assembly to convene on May 5 at which time the constitution was to be approved and the new coalition government inaugurated. But realizing the futility of meeting at a time of violently conflicting emotions, he announced that the meeting would be postponed to a later date. He felt himself to be within his rights to do so on his own authority—the more so since no one had questioned his original action. But the Communists charged him with violating the Political Consultative Conference procedure, and, although there was no formal protest at the time and no record kept of what happened in the "Steering Committee" to which the decision was first reported, this was one of the points at issue in all subsequent discussions. The Communists later on branded the National Assembly, called for November 12, as illegal because of the procedure in fixing the date. The same applied to the Constitution then approved. This is an instance of the way in which points at issue between the two groups—often, as in this one, unimportant in themselves—were wrangled over bitterly, each side sincerely believing its case to be right. General Marshall was occupied daily in conferences with those primarily concerned, in listening to those who had opinions to offer or causes to plead and in trying to repair the damage during his absence.

2

I had reached Shanghai from America about the end of April, 1946, and was detained there for various reasons for about two weeks, anxious to return to the Yenching campus where many problems were awaiting me. But Philip Fugh who had flown to Shanghai to meet me urged that I ought to stop off in Nanking to pay my respects to the Generalissimo. For an ordinary civilian,

travel by air was not easy to arrange—the railways had all been
cut by the Communists—nor were living quarters easily available
in Nanking where the only modern hotel had been pre-empted
for the American Army Advisory Group. But as usual I followed
his uncannily astute political instincts, and it altered subsequent
history for me.

The visit with Chiang Kai-shek was well worth the incon-
veniences involved. My last one had been in Chungking the
previous September, and it was pleasant to see him settled again
in the capital. In the course of our talk, he asked me my impressions of the situation, and I replied that they were much
worse than what I had gathered from American press reports.
He then asked what suggestions I had and, after thinking a
moment, I told him I would like to sum these up in one that
went to the heart of the issue. This was that he should himself
lead in a new revolutionary movement for internal reforms with
something of the adventurous enthusiasm with which he had
originally joined the Kuomintang under Sun Yat-sen when
this was really dangerous and that I felt he could thus again
rally the students and younger intellectuals now so discontented
but eager for a leader whom they could wholeheartedly follow.
With them as volunteer propagandists he could win back the
waning public confidence and be again the symbol of the national
will, as he undoubtedly had been during the Japanese war. This
was the only way to overcome the Communist menace, but, in
doing so, he would also be carrying into effect the third of
"The Three Principles," the People's Livelihood. He nodded
assent, but as I was to learn later it was one thing to secure
this, and quite another to stir his will to resolute action.

With the encouragement of President and Madame Chiang,
I called on General Marshall. I did not suppose that he had
ever heard of me, and on my part, it was chiefly curiosity to
meet the man who had such a magnificent war record and such
a unique mission to China. An appointment was fixed, and he

talked to me for about an hour and a half, reviewing the whole history of the negotiations to date. I put in an occasional question or comment but otherwise listened with keen interest. At the end, he said that he was telling me all this because he wished me to help him, and I assured him that I would be glad to return to Nanking whenever he cared to send for me. This happened once or twice, and toward the end of June I happened to be in Shanghai again attending an educational conference. While there, Mr. Chen Li-fu paid me two visits and talked at length on the Communist and related problems from his point of view. General Marshall had frequently referred to him as the leader of the reactionary forces which were blocking his efforts.

Chen Li-fu is one of two brothers, nephews of a martyred revolutionary leader who had been Sun Yat-sen's and then Chiang Kai-shek's patron. This, especially in China, meant a very strong bond, and the brothers had been devoted workers for the leader who had also taken the place of their late uncle in personal relations. Both brothers were very intelligent, free from any suspicion of avarice or venality, but fervent believers in the Kuomintang and its leader as well as in the necessity of eradicating communism from China. The so-called C-C Clique, named after them, was not so much a clique as the members of the Kuomintang organization which they had built up and controlled in all of its ramifications. This and the patronage which went with it gave them enormous influence. Their minions exploited this for blackmail and other selfish ends, or were stupidly brutal and repressive, but they themselves worked with singlehearted loyalty to build up their leader against all rivals within the party and to suppress all outside opposition. It is ironical that the technique for this was learned from Russian advisers who, coming to Canton about 1923, reorganized the Kuomintang on Bolshevik lines. Chen Li-fu argued with trenchant sarcasm that, although denounced, especially by Americans, as a reactionary he was in reality more of a pioneer or prophet in that he saw clearly the menace of communism long before others had come to the same conclusion.

I sent General Marshall a message asking whether he wished to hear a report of these interviews. He replied immediately that he would have his own plane ready for me as soon as I could come. The results were highly dramatic. We arrived Saturday afternoon, June 29. A truce between Nationalists and Communists arranged early in that month was to expire at noon the next day. All concerned admitted failure to reach an agreement. The Generalissimo had prepared a press release which would have almost precluded any further attempts at negotiation and had ordered all his field commanders to be ready for action. General Marshall himself had told his staff to draft the priorities for their return home. In such a situation Chen Li-fu was forgotten. It was too late to do more than suggest to General Marshall that he ask the Generalissimo to withhold his announcements and that all concerned merely let the truce lapse. This is what happened and the next days I spent quietly learning what I could and making comments based on this.

3

I was anxious to get back to my University and its many postwar problems as soon as I could be released. Then came the Fourth of July with its American reception which, in my efforts to keep out of sight, I was debating whether to attend. But as I was dressing, a message came from General Marshall asking me to call at nine o'clock and stating that his private airplane would be ready to take me to Peiping at ten. The problem of the reception was safely settled, and I supposed that the final call on General Marshall was merely to enable him to express appreciation for what I had been trying to do. But he amazed me by asking if I would be willing to become the American Ambassador to China. I remonstrated that I had just passed my seventieth birthday and had sent the University authorities my resignation, that at this age one should be retiring from active duties rather than taking on new ones and that I would be a tyro in diplomacy, etc. I finally told him, however, that his task was so difficult and so significant that anyone he wanted to help him should be willing to do so and that I would leave it with him. We agreed to think of it as an assignment for a year or less. He worked quickly, for on July 10 the President had presented my name to the Senate where it was unanimously approved. At that time, General Marshall could have had from the American people whatever he wanted.

Back on the campus I was busy with an accumulation of detail until the news broke and excitement ran high. But my colleagues agreed that if I could help at all to bring peace to the country this would be the best use of my time even for the University. I then presented my resignation as President to the Board of Managers. They unanimously refused to accept it but granted me a leave of absence. I went to Nanking almost at once for what was intended to be only a brief preliminary trip, but it was about a month before I was able to return to Peiping to adjust University affairs.

The Generalissimo was spending the hot season at Kuling with his wife, and Mrs. Marshall was comfortably housed nearby. General Marshall took me and the retiring and incoming Embassy Counselors to Kuling so that I might present my credentials. The journey involved a flight of an hour or more, a ferry across the river to Kiukiang, a motor trip across the plain, and a sedan-chair up the mountain—in all about five hours. The ceremony was simplified for this mountain setting, and in the personal conversation which followed, I told the Generalissimo I wanted to treat him on the basis of our long friendship and not primarily in my new capacity as an American official.

4

General Marshall made eight or nine week-end trips to Kuling that summer to join Mrs. Marshall at that beautiful mountain resort and escape the intense heat and interminable conferences in Nanking.

My share in these conferences began promptly after my return to Nanking, sometimes sitting in with General Marshall, more often talking with the Communist delegates and all sorts of other Chinese in my residence. The Communist leader was Chou En-lai, a graduate of Nankai Middle School and afterward a student in Paris. He was a man with a brilliant mind and rare personal charm. In talking with him and others, I realized how deep was the mutual distrust, and how near to a solution in accord with the Political Consultative Conference resolutions they were if two or three moot points could be cleared up. It was actually a remark of Chou's which led me to suggest the formation of an unofficial committee of two from each side with me as a sort of moderator—the Committee of Five as it came to be known—which could discuss these issues without involving either group in any commitments.

Chou concurred heartily in the idea (later vetoed by Yenan), and it seemed sufficiently promising for me to offer to accompany General Marshall on the next week-end trip to Kuling to put it up to the Generalissimo. The news that I was going there again started all sorts of speculations among Chinese reporters, twenty or more of whom were on the mountain, eager for any item implying progress in the peace talks. I ate something that deranged my stomach and perhaps got chilled in ascending from the heated plain to the cool hilltop. At any rate, after a visit from the Generalissimo's private secretary, Mr. Shen Ch'ang Huan—a Yenching boy—I lay down a while before going to the Marshall's for lunch. But I became dizzy and word was sent to General Marshall who came over and literally put me to bed himself. The Generalissimo sent his personal physician whose vague comments gave free play to the imagination of the reporters hovering around. The Generalissimo was dictatorial in ordering me to stay on the mountain and in bed and not to try to see him until I was well. The reporters, balked in getting any political items, dispatched sensational stories of my illness, the delicacies sent by Madame Chiang or Mrs. Marshall, and so on. These all grew with the distance, and in course of time I heard from an anxious relative in America of her relief when the radio finally announced that I was at last out of danger!

After a few days I was allowed to see the Generalissimo, and I explained my plans for the informal committee. He agreed but stipulated certain prerequisites for the meeting. I returned to Nanking the next day and that evening had a five-hour session with Chou En-lai and his associates. When I announced the prerequisites Chou leaned forward and for some minutes remained silent with drooping head and downcast mien. This was one of several occasions when it seemed that a reconciliation was almost in sight. But in each instance the suspicions or fears of one side or the other as well as the conflicting aims or ideologies were the chief obstructions. Whatever their motives the evidence seemed to me convincing that the Communists wanted the coalition but only on their terms. The Kuomintang were more hesitant or skeptical. But never in my experience with human beings have I encountered anything like the suspicions on both sides, especially among the Communists.

I held further discussions with Chou En-lai and the other Communists who would have served on my informal committee, as well as with the Kuomintang appointees. Chou objected in principle to the Generalissimo's right to lay down any condition in advance and became increasingly embittered. Then he dramatized his discontent by withdrawing to Shanghai where he sulked for weeks, although his colleagues were left in Nanking.

Meanwhile, General Marshall and I had issued our first joint statement in which we attributed our lack of progress in the negotiations to the intransigence and suspicions on both sides. My little committee never actually met and this was perhaps the beginning of the final break, though the more obvious cause was a combination of events in October—the summons for the National Assembly on November 12 and the fall of Kalgan. These two occurrences may be more fully described as typical of the controversial issues and of the mental or emotional factors.

5

Late in the previous year the Generalissimo had on his own authority announced the convocation of the National Assembly to pass the proposed new constitution for May 5, 1946. During the subsequent Political Consultative Conference, this meeting was accepted without challenge. But as the date approached and war had broken out anew the Generalissimo informed the Political Consultative Conference Steering Committee, which was still functioning, that there must be a postponement and made a public announcement to that effect. Although the Communists claim that there was a protest at the time as to his right to do this alone, yet he remembers nothing more than that some questions had been asked. No minutes were kept. It seemed to him that he was consistently exercising his prerogative as implicitly recognized at the time of the Conference, and that this justified him later on in announcing the date as November 12, the birthday of Sun Yat-sen. But to the Communists this appeared to be a proof of his arbitrary disregard of agreements already made. To them the Steering Committee was supposed to exist for dealing with all such matters.

The fighting was at this time generally favorable to the Nationalists, and they were evidently converging on Kalgan, a strategic Communist stronghold northwest of Peiping, and a gateway to Peiping. Chou En-lai and the remaining delegates revealed their earnest desire to avert this disaster to their cause. General Marshall and I did our utmost to effect a ten-day truce before this would happen and had no easy time in securing the Generalissimo's consent to terms that the other side could accept. But we finally did and then we tried with less success to lure

Chou En-lai back from Shanghai. General Marshall went to the extreme of flying to Shanghai to urge him to return to Nanking. We pointed out that they were committing themselves to nothing more than a willingness to resume negotiations and that, if successful, the advance against Kalgan would be halted whereas every day's delay carried that closer to the city. But they demurred: "the time was too brief, the Generalissimo could not be trusted," etc.

Again we had failed, and Kalgan fell on October 10. By a coincidence this was almost exactly one month before the opening of the National Assembly, and it was required that a formal summons to all delegates should be issued one month in advance. The emotional reaction of the highly temperamental Chou En-lai and of his companions was the more intense because these two events were thus synchronized, and this precipitated the end. They declared the Assembly to be illegal primarily because of the procedure in fixing its date and the consequent illegality of any constitution passed under these circumstances. Chou himself returned to Yenan, and though the others stayed on in Nanking and there were fairly frequent meetings with us, these were all informal and fruitless.

The Assembly date had been changed from May 5 to November 12 in the hope that the Communists might participate. However, the Communists were simply not interested in this constitution-making meeting. They were more interested in getting a coalition government started in which, they insisted, they and their friendly allies (such as the Democratic League and such "no party" fellow travelers as Kuo Mo-jo) *must* control altogether fourteen seats in the State Council of forty. As the Political Consultative Conference resolution had stipulated that all actions of the State Council required a two-thirds vote of the forty members, fourteen votes would have constituted a veto—twenty-seven votes being necessary to pass any measure. So the government could only consent to giving thirteen seats to the

Communist bloc. That was one of the main reasons why the Communists refused to join the coalition government and why they also refused to take part in the National Assembly. At the last minute the Assembly date was postponed three days to wait for the Communists to come in. It opened only on November 15. When the Assembly began to elect its fifty-five man Presidium, it reserved nine seats for the Communist bloc. But they never took part.

The draft constitution submitted by the Generalissimo to the Assembly was the one agreed on by an all-party subcommittee of the Political Consultative Conference. This draft, however, was much more democratic than the one prepared ten years earlier, and this registered the progress in the Generalissimo's own thought. There was strong opposition to these more liberal features among the Kuomintang extremists, and they worked hard to secure a revision in the direction of its earlier conservative character. It would never have been approved by the Assembly except for the determination of the Generalissimo. He exercised great pressure on the die-hard group, and he told them he wanted the constitution passed, and that they were either to listen to him as head of the party or break with him completely. Finally, they agreed to go along with the majority. The Generalissimo at once called me up and told me not to worry because the constitution would be safely passed.

In other words, ultimately, and after lengthy debate, a democratic constitution was actually adopted by the Chinese Assembly. This was no small feat to accomplish with an Assembly which was composed of 2,045 members of divers political opinions from all over China.

It may be worth-while to quote General Marshall's own words in his personal statement issued on January 7, 1947: "In fact, the National Assembly has adopted a democratic Constitution which in all major respects is in accordance with the principles laid down by the all-party Political Consultative Conference of last January. It is unfortunate that the Communists did not see fit to participate in the Assembly, since the constitution that has been adopted seems to include every major point that they wanted." [see Appendix]

6

In view of all that we Americans have since learned about Communist aims and techniques, including the self-declared Chinese variety of Marxist-Leninist Communism, it may not be without value to record the impressions of these few months of almost constant dealings with their delegation. As has already been stated, they were entirely frank in admitting that their ultimate objective was a communized China but that the people needed to be prepared for this by passing through a period of "elementary indoctrination." They were ready, therefore, to co-operate in the coalition government with a democratic constitution as a stage toward that consummation. The hindrances were their fears of nonsurvival unless their areas were protected by their own armed forces and their suspicions in general of the government group. Unfortunately, most of the leaders on both sides had been the same persons for some twenty-five years, and in a nation where personal relationships are supremely important, this added much to the problem of reconciling the two parties.

For myself it had always seemed essential to end the military phase of the conflict. It was apparent to almost everyone that a solution could never be reached by this means, even though one side or the other were victorious. American assistance in reorganization of all troops and their demobilization seemed to offer the best available guarantee that neither side would attack the other and that the process of reducing the huge military costs might be begun. Whatever difficulties or dissensions might result from the attempted coalition, these would be of a political nature and would avoid further bloodshed and economic devastation.

These six months, ending with the passing of the constitution on Christmas Day, were spent in almost constant conferences, in suggesting proposals or in listening to their rebuttal, in helping the Generalissimo to draft public announcements, and in similar efforts to end the war. The emotional tensions shifted in violence from one to another of the triangular grouping. Chou En-lai became more and more incensed and revealed this toward the end in unreasonable demands and abusive publicity. The Generalissimo would then lose his temper and appear hopelessly recalcitrant. General Marshall became so indignant that he almost decided more than once to ask President Truman to recall him. Frustrated hopes would be revived by some new turn of events or promising proposal only to be again dispelled. Toward the end of October, various "Third Party" leaders undertook what we Americans were so egregiously failing to accomplish. We readily withdrew and would have rejoiced to witness successful Chinese intervention. But in less than a month they too gave up the attempt.

Through that summer and autumn the public waited expectantly for news of peace. All of us were watched by Chinese reporters, and all our movements were published in detail. My calls on General Marshall were usually fixed for a period before dinner. He found his relaxation after the incessant interviews by seeing a movie in the evening which was always shown in his home immediately after the meal. As a rule I stayed on for this. Once or twice the Chinese papers reported that something important must be under discussion because I had been seen going to General Marshall's at five-thirty in the afternoon and had not left until after eleven!

7

From the time of my appointment it was assumed that I would be chiefly occupied with the peace negotiations. Shortly before this, W. Walton Butterworth had been sent to the Nanking

Embassy with the rank of Minister-Counselor, and he most efficiently conducted the administrative routine until promoted to the Office of Far Eastern Affairs in the Department of State. But his successor, Lewis Clark, proved himself to be equally competent and congenial, with the result that I did not even try to master the routine of Embassy business and relied on the trained personnel to attend to this. It is a pleasure to testify to their efficiency in general, in so far as I am qualified to appraise this, and to their unvarying courtesy and consideration for me. What I timidly entered upon as an ignorant novice was made surprisingly easy by those who initiated me into all the mysteries of diplomacy from "top-secret" messages to the seating at official dinners. This kindly helpfulness applied also to Mrs. Butterworth and Mrs. Clark and all the other wives and members of the staff in their treatment of a solitary and inexperienced widower. In fact, I soon felt toward all of them as though they were my new faculty family.

As I was leaving Peiping to assume office a Chinese-American association gave me a farewell party, and as I was making the ineluctable speech, I espied my friend of many years, Dr. Hu Shih, among the guests and proceeded to draw a contrast between his good fortune in ceasing to be an ambassador abroad in order to return to Peiping as a university president whereas I was leaving that loveliest of cities and that satisfying career for the unknown vicissitudes of a function from which he had escaped.

8

In its broader aspects I was also rather pleasantly surprised. That the Chinese public would welcome my appointment was on the whole to be expected, but the unanimity of the editorial and other comments was far in excess of what I might have imagined. Nearly all of the higher officials had been friends or at least acquaintances for years past, and my new official status did not make much difference in our relations. I had also been widely known for my educational activities and my strong sympathy with the Chinese nationalistic aspirations. In fact, the Chinese constantly said that they regarded me as one of themselves.

But I felt much less confident as to the American reaction. There has always been a measure of estrangement between the American missionary and non-missionary groups in the Orient. In that exotic environment, the characteristics of each seem to become unhealthily pronounced, and this is aggravated by economic standards of living, social habits, etc. The business community could well have disapproved of me, therefore, as coming from a calling which would seem to them to have unfitted me for knowing or caring much about their affairs and one, moreover, which was associated in their minds with narrowly pietistic religiosity or visionary sentimentality in the treatment of Chinese.

Incidentally, the Standard Oil Company and the British-American Tobacco have long operated well into the interior, as is true also of course of the missionaries. This has led to the witticism that these are the three principal American activities in China and that the motto of all three is, "Let there be light." As to the American public at home, insofar as they felt any interest at all, it might be to wonder—as did one columnist—why the President had appointed "an ancient missionary" to this post. It may be that I was mercifully kept in ignorance of adverse criticism, but the cordial friendliness of my fellow countrymen of all types in China and most of the comment reaching me from the States was extremely reassuring. These attitudes of Chinese and Americans alike helped to make the adjustment quite natural. The style of living, the emoluments, the prestige, were all very different from the simplicity to which I had been accustomed. The distinction between sacred and secular had never seemed to me to lie primarily in matters of church attendance or in taboos against smoking and drinking but rather in a quality of life which was its own touchstone as to what was right or wrong in behavior, acceptable to God or offensive to man. In any case I determined simply to be myself, there being excellent authority for the confidence that "It follows as the day the night. He cannot then be false to any man."

10 The Dream
that Did Not Come True

General Marshall spent a year in untiring efforts to help the Chinese establish a coalition government and thus to bring peace, economic recovery and democracy to this sorely distracted nation, doing this with a courtesy, patience, wisdom and tenacity which was the finest possible expression of America's friendly concern over the welfare of China. Even during the last two months, when formal conferences had been discontinued, we held constant meetings with government leaders or the Communist delegates in an endeavor by all concerned to reach a solution. But General Marshall had been compelled to recognize that his mission had failed and began making his plans to return home soon after New Year.

On January 6, 1947, General Marshall was called back by President Truman to succeed Mr. Byrnes as Secretary of State. We visited the Generalissimo that afternoon, and he was told of General Marshall's departure after one more day but not of the new appointment. The Generalissimo was very outspoken about the Yalta agreement concerning which China had not been consulted, and he added that although he himself was able to forgive those who were responsible, yet the Chinese nation bitterly resented this treatment, and he hoped this would be reported to President Truman. He also asked if General Marshall would be willing to come back and act as his own Supreme Adviser. Madame Chiang did most of the interpreting. It was agreed that we four should meet again alone the next afternoon and follow this with a farewell dinner.

That final conversation was one of dramatic intensity. The

Generalissimo renewed his invitation to General Marshall to continue his great service to China by acting as his Supreme Adviser. He pled with great earnestness, offering to give him all the power which he himself possessed and promising to co-operate with him to the utmost. He asked General Marshall to consider whether he could do anything more valuable, not only for China, but even for the United States than by assisting him to make of China the kind of country which Chinese and Americans alike desired. As he conceived it, General Marshall would have under him not only the Army Advisory Group which he himself had created but also a similar group of American advisers in civil administration. General Marshall was deeply moved, but did not feel at liberty to say more than that he fully appreciated the honor done him as well as the magnitude of the opportunity and that he would give it careful consideration.

But as we drove away that evening, he asked me to take the earliest occasion to explain to the Generalissimo why he could not accept the offer. The next morning I was one of a large crowd, including the Generalissimo and Madame Chiang and Chinese Communist representatives who were at the airfield to see General and Mrs. Marshall depart. The lonesome feeling which lingered long was compensated by the thought of having him still in somewhat the same relationship in Washington.

2

The morning of that last eventful day General Marshall asked me what form, in view of the breakdown of peace negotiations, American policy should take toward China. I replied that, as it seemed to me, there were only three possible courses: to give active assistance, especially in the way of military advice, to the National Government, in the expectation that the needed reforms would be undertaken and to condition further aid at each stage upon evidence of this; to drift along with no strong program of our own but only an opportunistic one of "wait and see"; and to withdraw entirely from any participation in China's internal affairs. I added that I was all for the first of these but would much prefer the third to the second.

He thought a moment or so, and then he said that he agreed with me in principle and that he understood me to favor "an affirmative policy."

3

Because of the importance of the issue it may be advisable to elaborate these three courses.

National policy must perhaps be based primarily on self-interest, and we Americans have long felt it to be of great importance to us that China develop into a strong, united, progressive nation with a government acceptable to its own people, friendly to us and a stabilizing influence in the Pacific area. We were forced into war with Japan chiefly for this reason, and in that conflict we invested vast amounts of money and materiel in China. This and the losses in human life throughout the whole area can in a sense be made chargeable to our concern for China. To spend relatively very small additional investments in order to accomplish our original purpose would seem to be "good business." For world events since then have demonstrated the danger to us of a communized China and the consequences of this to Japan and all of southeast Asia.

As an ally during the war and operating extensively over Chinese territory and through the efforts of Ambassador Hurley and the mission of General Marshall, as well as in many other ways, we had already become so involved in Chinese affairs that we could scarcely avoid continuing the attempt to help toward a settlement of the civil strife.

There was the responsibility also for the Yalta Agreement by which, without China's knowledge or consent, we made promises to Russia which forced upon China a treaty ceding to that country joint operation of railways in Manchuria and very special rights in Dairen and Port Arthur for thirty years. This permitted Russian troops to enter, just as the war was ending, Manchuria where they brutally slaughtered Chinese, publicly raped their women, looted their possessions, and plundered this allied nation of two billion dollars worth of industrial machinery.

This was followed by making available to the Chinese Communists the enormous stock piles of Japanese military equipment which enabled them to fight the National Government the Russians had pledged themselves in the treaty to recognize and protect. Whatever dubious justification there may have seemed to be at Teheran and Yalta for us to encroach upon these sovereign rights of China, we had a moral obligation to rectify this as best we could. Almost immediately after General Marshall's recall to Washington in March, 1946, Chinese Communists had violated the Political Consultative Conference agreement he had secured, by invading Manchuria, where they controlled all but the city of Mukden and a shifting perimeter around it. This rich northeast region has immense agricultural and industrial value to China, to say nothing of its political importance. I thought then that if it should become one more Soviet satellite state, we could not escape a share of the responsibility.

My hope was that by giving outright military aid, especially in the form of technical advice, we could enable the National Government to recover and hold a certain area north of the Yangtse River, and to give to its population a sense of political and economic security while introducing the needed reforms primarily in local civilian administration. I had in mind the railway zone from Nanking to Tientsin, on to Mukden and Peiping or beyond to the northwest, the branch line across Shantung to Tsingtao and if possible the Lung-Hai line running east and west north of the Yangtse. This could be regarded not as fighting Communists so much as containing them and freeing the hapless population of both sections from the horrors of marauding soldiery. It would reduce the conflict, for a period at any rate, to guarding the lengthy frontier line. Meanwhile, the struggle could shift from harassing the population to a competition in working for their welfare and allowing the better system to win. My confident expectation was that the Communists, who are thoroughgoing realists, would not be long in proposing a renewal of the peace talks. I remarked to General Marshall that I thought his mission would succeed after all. In retrospect, with what we now know of the Communist intentions and methods, it seems clear that it had no chance; but at that moment it seemed to me that it could and would bring about a helpful agreement.

If we felt unable to adopt this strong "affirmative" policy, I much preferred that we promptly and completely cease our political activities in China, except of course the usual diplomatic relations. No humanitarian relief nor economic rehabilitation nor currency stabilization could be of much real help till the military phase of the Communist issue could be ended or at least reduced to frontier defense. The war was costing approximately eighty percent of a budget in which expenditures were three or four times the current revenue. Transportation and productive enterprises were being paralyzed. This would not be a militaristic intrusion on our part but an effort to complete the task we had already assumed by hastening the end of the armed conflict. Otherwise the struggle would drag on. The whole nation wanted peace. The party members on both sides were a mere fraction of the huge, disorganized, inarticulate, amorphous population. These were neither Kuomintang nor Communist but merely Chinese, desiring to be allowed to live their own lives with a minimum of government interference or oppression. By all that we had been attempting, by the continued presence of our Army and Navy Advisory Groups, by the hopes we inspired of further monetary aid while actually doing very little, we were in danger of getting in bad with all elements. The government leaders would charge us with desertion, the Communists with partisanship, and the highly intelligent but discontented intellectuals, speaking for the helpless masses, with imperialistic intrusion. The argument in favor of professional military advice should be explained. Since about the beginning of this century, China has been passing through multiform revolutionary changes in ideas, knowledge, political structure, technological methods and social patterns, while fighting off foreign aggression culminating in the Japanese invasion. It is not surprising that in this ferment of new forces upon an ancient culture, military science was burdened by a heritage of obsolete features and slow in assimilating modern techniques. Even when these were mastered, it was not easy for the Chinese leaders to break away from the old personal or political relationships or the ingrained habits and to hold rigidly to impersonal, objective standards of fighting efficiency. It happens that we Americans have at this crucial period of human history a fortunate combination of enormous natural resources, new technological inventions and the human capacities for utilizing these, stimulated and improved in military affairs by the exigencies of the last war. Chinese are slowly becoming machine-conscious, capable of corporate action in hitherto unknown patterns or of putting the cause above the older loyalties of family or "face" or friendly social amenities. The science of logistics, almost as new as the word itself to us, is even more novel to Chinese strategy. For reasons such as these it was in no sense derogatory to Chinese nor supercilious on our part to emphasize their need of the kind of advice we were fortunately able by force of circumstances to give them.

In reply to the objection that they often seemed reluctant to take such advice or even to resent it, two comments are pertinent. Among a people to whom good manners are a part of morality, the tact and courtesy with which advice is given are of primary importance. Mencius commends the starving beggar who refused a crust of bread insultingly offered. The other is that military advisers contributed by and accountable to our government, with the prospect of material aid conditioned on the quality of Chinese performance, were not apt to be ignored.

Parenthetically, I am perhaps incurably an educationalist. To my mind all American aid to China could and should have been an educational process, helping to train this nation to adjust itself to its modern, international environment in the spirit of neighbors who for historical reasons had learned some things only slightly earlier and under less turbulent conditions. From the experience of a lifetime I can testify that Chinese are capable of learning anything and that there are few more satisfying joys than their eager appreciation of the effort to teach them when this is done humbly and with the desire to be helpful.

4

All through the year 1947 American policy toward China was hesitant or wavering, perhaps for reasons such as these:

1) Postwar developments in Europe had become incredibly alarming. The demand for action was urgent and engrossing. In a global strategy for peace it was inevitable, and to the ultimate advantage even of China, that America consider Europe first.

2) It might seem to some Americans that there would be a real danger that any effective assistance to China, especially when this took the form of advice affecting issues of national policy or procedure, would lead America to become inextricably involved in her internal affairs and with ever-deepening commitments. This would be resented by some, if not all, elements in the country and merely add to the confusion. It might also provoke the hostility or retaliatory action of other powers, or even imperil our ability to meet obligations elsewhere in the world.

3) The American Government and people had been urging reform measures upon the Kuomintang Government and implying that our assistance was waiting for more reassuring signs that these were being undertaken or even wanted. They questioned whether a government incapable of progressive improve-

ments would be able to use our aid in ways that benefited the nation as a whole.

These were all valid considerations. None the less I waited expectantly for a more positive American policy in the belief that the objections deriving from conditions within China were in no sense insuperable. In other words, we should always have followed our faith rather than our fears.

All through the year following General Marshall's departure, I had Chinese visitors who hoped to learn from me about American China policy or through me to influence it. Members of the government and its supporters hoped that there would be prompt and adequate aid, by which they usually meant monetary loans or grants. For the first few months whenever I saw the Generalissimo, almost invariably his first eager question was as to news from Washington. It was hard to explain why consistently I had nothing definite to report.

Another very vocal non-Communist group wanted to protest against any further aid to so disreputable a government. These were as a rule entirely ignorant of the very little aid we were then actually supplying and were misled by radical propaganda as well as by constant rumors in the newspapers of projected large-scale assistance. But the most pathetic groups were those liberals who asserted themselves against the extremists in both of the warring parties and demanded that some better solution be found. Some were representatives of various unregistered political parties, of which there were said to be over seventy. Some were college professors or others of that general type, intelligent, patriotic, but woefully impractical in comparison with the skilled politicians, and apparently unable to coalesce into a large body with the solidarity that they must have to exert any influence. Someone has answered the query why Chinese liberals cannot organize themselves by pointing out that it is precisely because they are Chinese liberals. In other words, there seems to be something about their social heritage and intellectual characteristics that makes them so individualistic, so suspicious or jealous of one another, so timid, that they lack the capacity for cohesion and action. Another deterrent was their lack of funds and of a constituency from which these might be obtained without vitiating their objective. Even more potent than this was their fear of the ubiquitous secret police of the two warring parties. The government frowned upon independent political activities and tended to brand all such as of an unhealthy pinkish color, if not communistic in disguise.

The trend became steadily more unfavorable for the government in military, economic and psychological aspects, all of these factors interacting.

5

In the summer of 1947 the Wedemeyer mission arrived, spending a month in China and two weeks in Korea. General Albert C. Wedemeyer was appointed Special Envoy with ambassadorial rank and brought with him a corps of experts and secretaries. He himself, following General Stilwell's recall from China, had served as Chief of Staff for the Generalissimo with rare tact and understanding as well as professional competence, and was therefore admirably fitted for such a mission. But the news came as a sudden and almost entirely unexplained announcement. Except for a terse message for me to give the Generalissimo, shortly before their actual departure, asking for the approval of the Chinese Government, there had been no consultation. This episode is of interest because of the assumption on our part that such a mission to another sovereign nation could be decided upon unilaterally by us, and because of its acceptance by the Chinese as part of our implied intention to assist them in their internal difficulties. It could have been bitterly resented by them and was of course denounced by the Communists with a logic not easy to refute. It was only possible because of the long record of friendliness between the two countries, their trust in our motives, our immense expenditures in helping them defeat the Japanese, and the personality of General Wedemeyer. No one could have met the delicate situation better than he.

The mission arrived on about the hottest day of an exceptionally hot Nanking summer, and through that heat or traveling elsewhere they worked tirelessly in an effort to collect and then, at a quiet spot in Hawaii, to evaluate the facts called for in their directive. The mass of data was enormous. There was something peculiarly American in the earnestness and efficiency with which they compiled their exhaustive report. This has never been completely published, and the recommendations could only be surmised by noting General Wedemeyer's testimony later on before Congress. Nor was there any evidence in subsequent changes of American policy toward China that the mission had accomplished anything. There was also a typical contrast in Chinese and American attitudes in what occurred at the conclusion of the mission. The Generalissimo, with characteristic Chinese courtesy, wished to entertain the mission on the eve of its departure, but the Envoy countered by proposing that instead of a dinner, he might have a chance to address the leading members of the government. This was arranged to include about forty of them at the Generalissimo's residence. General Wedemeyer conscientiously prepared a typewritten statement with great care in which he spoke frankly of the evils within the government. This was with an American sense of duty and in the hope that it would stimulate them to effect reform and thus assist China to secure the aid which he confidently expected as a result of his report.

But the Chinese reaction was also typical. This public criticism by a guest was against all their canons of decency. It would have been all right to have said such things in a very small and intimate circle. But to do so in a mixed gathering, with the consequent publicity, simply was not done. One dignified old Confucian scholar literally wept afterward. No one questioned the truth of what had been said nor the good intentions of the speaker, and in time these considerations neutralized the earlier, instinctive indignation. This was helped by the later statement intended for publication which seemed to them much milder.

For myself, I shared the hopes and the disappointments which the mission aroused among the Chinese, but I greatly enjoyed the deepening of the friendship with "Al" Wedemeyer. In his own splendid qualities and in his genuine friendliness for China and her people, he was in the finest sense an American envoy of good will. This kindly and constructive spirit was shared by the members of his team. They made it amply clear that theirs was a purely fact-finding mission. But the puzzled Chinese could very well wonder for what purpose the facts were wanted and by what right they were so officiously sought. We of the Embassy were also puzzled as to why the systematic reporting of facts about China by ourselves and our consular network needed to be supplemented by experts from Washington moving at such speed. And the American public was puzzled because the contents of the report of so costly and spectacular a mission were never completely disclosed.

Mr. William C. Bullitt arrived during the visit of the Wedemeyer mission, and his views advocating large amounts of military and other forms of financial aid were widely publicized in China even before they appeared in _Life_ magazine. Dr. Walter Judd followed soon after in an effort to reorient himself as to Chinese affairs. His ideas were so stimulating and so eloquently expressed that most of his time was actually spent in making speeches in essential accord with Bullitt.

6

Although a coalition with the Communists had failed, the government tried to respond to General Marshall's urging that its base be broadened. In the spring after much bargaining two of the minor parties were given certain ministries. There was, however, no corresponding benefit. Not unlike our own discredited practise of spoils of office, these minor parties wanted jobs for their members, nor were the new ministers and their subordinates any improvement over the displaced Kuomintang officials. It was an instance of what often happened when Chinese reluctantly yielded to well-meant American pressure, as well as one more evidence of the private economic considerations which underlie almost all Chinese seemingly political issues.

The government continued to pass reform measures which were but rarely carried out. But it was too much weakened in material resources and too depressed in spirit to do much more than keep going. The combination of economic, military and psychological deterioration was causing a creeping paralysis. The patient was too ill to recover without the administration of a strong tonic. If nothing succeeds like success, nothing fails like failure. Public confidence in the government was waning steadily, and this mood was permeating its own officials of all ranks. Student strikes and demonstrations, many of them Communist instigated, became more frequent and these, as always, were symptoms of swelling discontent. Anti-American feeling was deepening, due chiefly to the belief that we were delaying the Communist party's overthrow of a rotten government. This was revealed in the violent student agitations over any minor incident that would otherwise pass unnoticed.

In China, even more perhaps than elsewhere, the students serve as an excellent barometer of popular trends. They are the most highly sensitized element. Their reactions are more intelligent and spontaneous, and they have fewer inhibitions. Chinese students are as a class passionately patriotic. Their good motives can be cleverly utilized for political purposes. With the rapidly spiraling inflation and the increased cost of living there was all through 1947 and 1948 growing student unrest due latterly to economic as well as political causes. Food riots dramatized this. During the Japanese war the government had wisely subsidized students in exile colleges in the far interior. Even so, their hardships and discomforts were acute, but they willingly endured these. The practise of subsidies for food and for almost everything else continued after V-J Day in the government institutions. But as the food became scarcer and less palatable they found fault with a government which could not give them peace and better living conditions. Fighting against Communists, who were also Chinese after all, failed to arouse the same patriotic loyalty as when the enemies were Japanese. Student sympathy was also more with radical, socialistic movements than with a government which most of them regarded as hopelessly reactionary. Dejection, even despair, was prevalent among all student groups. It was not only that the food was bad. Clothing, warmth, textbooks, laboratory equipment, the quality of classroom instruction, employment after graduation—everything in short that touched their lives was as wrong as the food. The teachers and all professional classes, including notably government employees of all grades were suffering even greater distress. Coolies and artisans could command wages at least sufficient to give them food for the strength they needed. They were in many cases actually better off than the intellectuals. Their subsistence level more or less set the standard for all.

Even with students, therefore, mere bodily existence bulked larger in their thinking than national problems or ideological arguments. In September, 1947, it was estimated that in Tsinghua and Yenching Universities about ninety to ninety-five percent did not want China to become communized. But a year later, this figure had dropped to sixty to seventy percent. They felt so disconsolate that they believed that even Communist domination could not be worse. It would at any rate bring peace and a better livelihood. To those who were not responding to the appeal of communism, what would happen if the National Government collapsed did not matter. They were not looking that far ahead.

Unfortunately, the Communist propaganda was exceedingly skillful and the Kuomintang propaganda incredibly stupid.

7

A diverting and pleasant experience at this difficult time was an invitation from the Mayor of Hangchow to visit the city of my birth. I was given an official reception and the customary feasts but more than that a very real and hearty welcome by government, civic and educational organizations and also by many old friends. I accepted all this not as a tribute to me personally but rather as an evidence of deep and sincere friendship for the American people, a friendship which I am sure will not be destroyed through this period of misunderstanding and estrangement in official Sino-American relations. I was greatly touched at the end of the visit to be given honorary citizenship of Hangchow by the Mayor.

8

The prospect of American aid was kept alive by frequent news items. The controversy in America over this issue became violent after the meeting of Congress and continued during the first months of 1948. This was all fully reported in the Chinese press, often with unfounded rumors, and was eagerly read and discussed. When finally the amount of $400,000,000 was approved, the news was received with varying emotions. The government and its friends were grateful but feared that the amount was not enough to insure their triumph. The Communists lengthened the time schedule for their victory. The intellectuals sighed with despondent apathy; this merely meant the aggravation of their misery and the postponement of peace.

The appointment of Roger Lapham as Deputy Director for the Economic Co-operation Administration in China proved to be a happy one. His genial manner and friendly chattiness sheathed a shrewd competence which those who dealt with him learned to respect. His associate, Allen Griffin, was a fine combination of American practicality and idealism. His reconstruction projects were admirably selected and planned for. The rest of their co-workers were also well chosen. The Chinese matched them with a committee composed of men of unquestionable integrity and capacity. The item of $125,000,000 was for the Chinese Government to use entirely without restrictions, but was intended for military aid and was so understood by them. It might have accomplished more for that purpose if the customary E.C.A. procedure had been employed but this would have involved us in the Chinese civil war. Actually, our Army and Navy representatives were constantly consulted by the Chinese and exerted no slight influence in the apportionment.

The feature of the American aid which had the most personal interest for me was the one for rural reconstruction. Virtually everyone agrees that the Communist issue in China will never be settled by military means. The natural corollary to this is that it can only be settled by giving the rural masses a better local government than that of the Communists. The nature of this is fully expounded in the "Third Principle" of Sun Yat-sen, the Lincolnian "Government for the People," but its neglect was one of the greatest weaknesses of Kuomintang rule. With all this in mind my thoughts turned to Dr. James Yen and his Mass Education Movement. I had known "Jimmy" practically from the beginning of his effort to teach illiterates one thousand ideographs and to prepare suitable literature for them within this range. For many years I had been a member of his advisory council. Numerous Yenching students had worked in the Movement. He had for over twenty years dedicated himself to this cause with selfless devotion. After the Japanese had driven him from his experimental center near Peiping, he had transferred to his native province of Chungking.

Shortly before General Marshall's departure I talked with T. V. Soong, then the Premier, about asking Dr. Yen to undertake a special project in training for citizenship in a certain area which had just been recovered from the Communists. We sent him a joint telegram asking him to come to Nanking for conference. Our thought was that before the typical Kuomintang control could be re-established in that area or the Communists be able to retake it, the Mass Education Movement should employ its trained personnel to organize the populace for self-defense against any form of oppression or misrule and to teach them the rudiments of the rights and responsibilities of citizens—even the humblest—in a democracy. When he arrived he grasped the idea at once but disagreed with us as to the scope. He had a vision of training hundreds, even thousands, of students eager to do something for their country but with no outlet, and of starting a movement that aimed at covering the entire country. Instead of depending on inflationary Chinese currency, which would have lost much of its value after all the bureaucratic red tape and political obstruction had been overcome, he argued that he would accomplish more in the long run and be less hampered by soliciting American funds as he had most successfully done more than once in the past. Familiar with the almost invariable Chinese desire to appeal to American generosity, I at first objected but became reluctantly convinced that he was right. It was several months before he could finish his arrangements for the trip and he was in the States for over a year. But the time was used to good advantage and the provisions for expending this relatively large amount were wisely drawn. The three Chinese and two American members of the commission were selected with great care. Unfortunately, the commission had hardly begun its real work before the Communists took over.

9

During the year 1948 the Chinese Government achieved two really notable reforms which partially disproved the charges that it could not help itself.

One was the meeting of the new National Assembly, postponed from the previous December, and the presidential elections. There were irregularities in the election of delegates and controversies over their status. In the Assembly itself there were disorderly shoutings and many crudities. None the less, the first step had been taken in representative government by popular election and in public exposure of the attendant abuses. There was real freedom of debate including open criticism of the government. The actual balloting for President and Vice-President was carried through with meticulous care and literally glaring publicity under powerful searchlights. There could not have been any violations and apparently none were attempted. As always, the Generalissimo's personality was the dominant feature, but there was conscious restraint on his part as he tried to discipline himself to observe constitutional procedure. His worst problem was in the election of the Vice-President. According to the Chinese constitution, the President is an honored but rather inactive figure, as in France. The Generalissimo did not fancy any such role for himself but neither did he wish to ask for extraordinary war powers, especially at the very inception of constitutional rule. In this dilemma he really did not want to assume this title, and would have preferred to be the Premier.

The Generalissimo did his best to persuade Dr. Hu Shih to be the candidate. Failing in this and unable to find anyone else who seemed to him suitable, he reluctantly agreed to be nominated. But meanwhile he had advised two military candidates for the other office to withdraw on the ground that he was doing the same since no military officer should fill either position. One of these docilely retired, but the other one indignantly complained that he should have been given this advice earlier because he had long since publicly announced his candidacy and had been working hard for it.

The other reform was in currency. Inflation was reaching fantastic figures. The volume and weight of paper money required even for minor transactions was burdensome. Everyone was trying to get rid of it before it became completely valueless, and speculation was rife as to when and how this point would be reached. Obviously something had to be done. The government leaders studied the problem and on August 19, 1948, issued a new currency known as the "Gold Yuan" to be pegged at four to one United States dollar, to be guaranteed by actual government assets, and to be kept within the amount of these with the assistance of a committee of competent and highly respected Shanghai citizens who would publish a monthly statement of accounts. There would be rigid price and exchange control. One Gold Yuan was estimated at 3,000,000 of the old *fapi* dollars. Patriotic citizens were urged to exchange their gold or silver holdings for the new notes. Strict regulations were announced governing export, import and other trading activities. The whole scheme had been kept secret, which alone was a notable achievement in China. The Premier had confided it to me a few days before, and I was greatly pleased. As I pointed out to him and others the scheme would only succeed if rigidly enforced, if it won popular support, and if military victories could recover the lost confidence of the people in their government. He acknowledged that this was their last chance. If it failed, they had in mind no other conceivable device.

For the first month or so the plan went well. The government had shown vision, courage and determination. The monetary measures, while not wholly satisfactory, were perhaps about as effective as could have been designed. The people of moderate means responded nobly and the government soon collected over $200,000,000 from this source, although the really wealthy were conspicuous by their avoidance of the opportunity. We advised all Americans to co-operate with the Chinese Government in its brave efforts, and this was generally done although some of the new regulations were quite harmful to our business interests. All American Government agencies were required to play the game with scrupulous fidelity. There was a new spirit of hope and endeavor among the Chinese.

Slowly at first, then more rapidly, things began to go wrong. About the middle of September the loss of the strategic city of Tsinan to the Communists had a most depressing effect on public morale. Then the loss of Hsuchow—the only remaining stronghold in the advance against Nanking—was exposed, and this resulted also in the capture by the Communists of extensive military stores and the obliteration of virtually all the government troops. Inexorable economic laws were already making themselves felt in the exchange rate and rising commodity prices, and this latest military debacle sent these spiralling into a new inflation. This would have come sooner or later in any case, for when the government income was less than fifteen percent of its expenditures, it could not have been otherwise. The economic hardships of the populace became more acute, especially those of the salaried classes. The discontent sank deeper and was more openly expressed.

10

For long months the situation in Manchuria, or the "Northeast" as Chinese prefer to designate it, had been heading toward its inevitable crisis. Nowhere else had the Generalissimo's policy been more inept. Despite General Marshall's repeated advice, he had kept a notoriously incompetent military commander there and had appointed another one as his personal representative to check on all others. When at last conditions became almost intolerable he sent his then Chief of Staff to take sole control. General Chen Cheng was personally free from all suspicion of graft and began at once to clean up the scandalous practises which had alienated the whole population. But he did so without building up a new force of competent officers to take over, with the result that the ever-vigilant Communists made full use of the opportunity. General Chen was suffering from stomach ulcers which were not helped by the strain and directed affairs largely from his sickbed. Before long the outlook worsened alarmingly, as did his health, and he was replaced by a capable officer of the Sino-Japanese War with orders to retrieve a desperate situation.

The city of Changchun, the capital of the Japanese Manchoukuo, had been besieged by the Communists for months. The Generalissimo had been repeatedly advised to order the beleaguered garrison to fight its way south to Mukden while this was still possible, and he was warned that they could not survive after the approach of cold weather which comes early in that climate. But he none the less left them there. The city had no slight strategic value, but it was more probably pride and a fallacious idea that by defending cities he might someday recover the area. In course of time supplies were airlifted, but done so inaccurately that an unknown but considerable proportion benefited the Communists surrounding the city. The Premier told me that one-third of the whole national expenditure was being used for this purpose and insisted on this ratio when I questioned whether I had heard him correctly. In any case at least this proportion was being used for supplying the two Manchurian cities. And yet a few weeks after the fall of Tsinan, Changchun surrendered to the Communists as predicted, with the loss of all its military supplies and of all its troops. The attempt to hold it had been as costly as it was futile. Meanwhile, Mukden was being encircled in the same manner, and again it was pointed out that it could only be held if its well-trained and equipped troops fought their way so as to effect a juncture with those within the Great Wall, and then to clear the area of Communists and restore rail communication. They had been inactive in Mukden while the populace fled if they could, or starved, and while the Communists strengthened their encircling positions.

Immediately after the fall of Tsinan, I called on the Generalissimo, and as I walked in, he asked what I thought about this news. I replied that this was what I had come to talk about and raised the question whether in the light of this serious misfortune, he might not cease to direct the campaign alone and leave this to a carefully chosen Board of Strategy, both for the planning and, after securing his approval, for the operation. I said that he might let those now holding important posts remain nominally in charge but depend on competent and preferably younger men to do the real work. He replied that he would give this his careful consideration and actually did take steps to this effect. But shortly after he suddenly went to Peiping to direct personally the crucial battle for Mukden and the Northeast. He stayed there until the troops, which finally withdrew from the city as ordered, were annihilated and the last vestige of National control of the Northeast disappeared.

This worst disaster of the civil war played havoc of course with the currency reform and convinced even its best friends that it was doomed. The Generalissimo's elder son, with the best of motives for helping his father, had been enforcing the fiscal regulations in Shanghai with determined courage and energy. But what had begun as a controlled currency program became an attempt to repress economic laws by police state methods, popularly known as "the seventy-day terror." The disruption of all trade, the injustice and suffering, the evasions and threatening outbreaks, became so serious that the Generalissimo finally called him off. Improved regulations were announced, but the economic disease had reached a point which required something more than palliatives. Meanwhile, as one consequence of the new measures, the middle-class people who had trustingly exchanged their metal for notes had their savings practically wiped out and naturally felt very bitter toward the government.

During these autumn months, the E.C.A. as conducted by Roger Lapham and his capable staff was doing much to alleviate the distress of the population in the big coastal cities. Food was rationed on what was agreed on as a joint arrangement with the

Chinese authorities, but as the military and financial deterioration grew worse, it became mainly an American enterprise. Rice riots in Shanghai and Nanking were stopped by prompt measures for supplying the market. In Peiping and Tientsin, the problems of General Fu Tso-yi were greatly lessened by providing food for their civilian populations, immensely swollen as they were by destitute refugees. In view of Communist gains, the reconstruction projects were largely kept in abeyance except for preliminary engineering studies. The Rural Reconstruction Commission, after having been inexcusably delayed in the appointment of both Chinese and American members, consumed long weeks in reconciling conflicting opinions and in otherwise getting organized.

Thus the potentially most effective feature of American aid for fighting communism at the grass roots frittered away months in getting into action. Until peace had been attained economic aid could accomplish little more than supply for a brief period a fraction of the sorely needed relief and serve as a humanitarian gesture. But this was largely neutralized by the animosity aroused by the actual or apparent assistance it gave to a government in waging a war which it could not win. In so far, therefore, as the intention of Congress in voting $400,000,000 for China aid was concerned it had achieved nothing and might better not have been spent. We should either have done *more* to stop the Communist advance and *then* carry out economic measures in a securely non-Communist section or refrained from all active participation in Chinese affairs until the Chinese had found a solution which would have made our assistance worthwhile and wanted by the people.

II

The loss of Manchuria released a potential 300,000 soldiers under Lin Piao, one of the ablest Communist strategists, to reenter the Great Wall and capture Peiping and Tientsin. Their

valiant defender, Fu Tso-yi, would have been entirely outnum-
bered. With this threatening danger to American nationals in
that area, the question of advising their evacuation became acute.
The Embassy had no authority to order them to leave, but only
to advise. Frequently before during the recurrent internal disturbances beginning in 1911, I had been one of the civilians so
advised to leave by our consular authorities, who always seemed
to us to be overcautious or to be primarily interested in clearing
off their responsibilities rather than concerned with ours. Now
I had the ordeal of viewing this from the other side. There were
roughly 650 Americans in Peiping and over 200 in Tientsin. It
meant a serious disruption of the life-long interests of many of
them to abandon their work. I had my beloved Yenching colleagues poignantly in mind, and I knew that they were counting
on me to counsel them as though I were still one of them. On the
other hand, no one could predict what outrages the Communists
might perpetrate—or be powerless in the transition period to
prevent. When the emergency actually occurred, it might be
too late. The attackers would be sure to put the airfield out of
commission at once and to cut the railway.

But apart from this dilemma, was the almost more distressing
one of my Chinese relationships. The government was struggling desperately to survive, and for the Embassy to issue such a
warning would have had a very harmful effect on the popular
morale. It would seem inconsiderate and unkind, almost a deliberate blow. In China the claims of friendship are paramount, and
my country was the friend of theirs; I the personal friend of most
of the higher officials and of the Chinese people. An ambassador
whose ties with them were not so close might have been excused.
He would have been performing his normal duty. But they would
expect something more sympathetic from me. I persuaded my
Embassy colleagues to defer action until even I felt it would be
remiss to do so longer.

According to custom the Foreign Office was notified and they at once reported this to the Generalissimo in Peiping. He sent me a long telegram asking me not to issue the warning (in any case not to publish it) and giving assurance of the ability of his government to protect all our nationals. When the head of a state makes such a plea it cannot be ignored. I promised that the notice would be delayed a few days. It seemed to us to be to the advantage of the Chinese Government to have the text of our notice published rather than the distorted rumors which were certain otherwise to appear. We postponed the notice about four days, and it created quite a flurry when it became known. Actually, the substance of what we said was that those who were not ready to remain after whatever political changes might occur should plan to depart while communications were still open. We soon issued a stronger warning to those in north China definitely advising all who had no "compelling reason" for staying to avail themselves of our facilities for immediate evacuation, especially women and children or those in bad health. It was not long before we had issued similar warnings to all consular districts. All this caused great perturbation among Chinese. We were supposed to have special sources of information as to impending events, and all our movements were—as always—carefully watched. We were also blamed by the government leaders for starting the panic, and we undoubtedly did increase the wild tendency toward flight. But this had already begun and would have happened regardless of the behavior of foreigners.

Following his capture of Tsinan, the Communist commander, Chen Yi, started moving southward toward Hsuchow, some 200 miles north of Nanking. This is an important railway junction and had the largest concentration of national forces and army supplies. The Nationalist officers and men were in a pitifully defeatist mood, and it was generally supposed that the Communists could either disperse them or by-pass Hsuchow and make straight for the capital. But the indefatigable Generalissimo somehow galvanized them into a fighting mood, and they were at last persuaded to abandon Hsuchow, taking all the equipment they could carry and attempting to destroy the rest. Chen Yi was apparently caught off guard, but with the help of his one-eyed colleague, Liu Po-cheng, his columns soon encircled the armies which had started out from Hsuchow. The whole region from Hsuchow south became a battlefield in which many more than 500,000 soldiers were involved. The fighting lasted several weeks with steady attrition of the government forces and their dispersal or retreat southward. But the Communists also suffered heavily in casualties and in supplies. Although it was generally accepted that the Communists would sooner or later reach Nanking and Shanghai, there was much anxious speculation as to when this would happen and as to whether there would be a negotiated settlement to spare these cities the horrors of battle.

12

The last quarter of the year 1948 had something of the quality of Greek tragedy. The lone figure of the Generalissimo stood out sharply defined against the fateful background of military defeat, fiscal devaluation and popular disapproval, serenely imperturbable among irresolute and baffled colleagues. He was as conscious of the ominous trends as any of them. Yet more than once before in his hazardous career, all the odds had been against him, but a combination of indomitable will and a fortunate turn of events had always brought him through shattering disasters to victory. He was fighting the world-wide menace of communism. So was his powerful and sympathetic ally across the Pacific. Once again the United States—if only the right person could be found to awaken her to the imminent danger—would come to his rescue. He must meanwhile hold grimly on.

Beginning in September, he urged me to make a trip to Washington for this purpose. In October, Dr. Wang Shih-chieh, the Foreign Minister, attended the United Nations meeting in Paris and had long conversations with Mr. Marshall on the subject. In the course of these, the Secretary of State asked about former Premier Chang Ch'un in such a friendly fashion that after Dr. Wang had reported to the Generalissimo the substance of the talks, the latter decided to send Mr. Chang to Washington. Fortunately, Mr. Chang asked my advice and was convinced by it of the futility of the mission. This ought already to have been apparent from what Dr. Wang himself had been told by Secretary Marshall and by a courteously worded reply from President Truman to an urgent appeal cabled to him by the Generalissimo. In delivering this, I asked the young Chinese secretary who would translate it to bring out in unmistakable language the inability of the American President, despite the friendly language, to accede to the request for prompt and ample military aid. Chinese are so averse to offending social amenities by baldly stating unpalatable facts that they are in the habit of mentioning these in euphemistic circumlocutions, with the result that when Americans try to be equally polite they—knowing our more direct speech—draw more comfort from what we say than was perhaps intended.

This is probably what happened to Dr. Wang's report of his conversations with Mr. Marshall in Paris, further aggravated both by his understandable desire to demonstrate the success of his mission and by the readiness of the newspapers to play up any ray of hope for their despondent public. But the most important factor was the confidence of the Generalissimo in the rightness of his course and in his star, and his almost mystical belief in his power to will into existence American aid to fight against world-wide communism.

13

Shortly after noon on Thanksgiving Day, 1948, Madame Chiang Kai-shek telephoned me in excitement asking me to come to see her at once. On arrival, she told me that she had just been talking by Pacific telephone with Mr. Marshall who had reached

Leesburg from Washington late the evening before (U. S. Eastern time), regarding a visit to the States. I was sorely tempted to advise her against making a trip which was almost certain to prove fruitless, but I confined myself to assisting her in the practical arrangements for enabling her party to depart as promptly as possible. Later on when the Generalissimo asked if she had sought my advice, he remarked that he rather wished she had, and he added that he himself was quite dubious about the adventure.

My own experience during these months was harrowing in the extreme. My heart ached for the nation in the exhaustion of this gigantic struggle and for the people of all classes who were suffering the consequences and yet powerless to avert them. It is impossible to give statistics as to the swelling numbers of those brutally slaughtered or no less callously allowed to perish from neglect, of those rendered destitute or who fled as refugees before the Communist terror, or of those shamelessly plundered by government troops or exploited by their officers. Scarcely less pathetic was the spiritual despondency. The dislike and fear of communism was very general, but the government's officials and military forces showed up none too favorably by comparison. In any case, the people reasoned that nothing could be worse than their present plight.

My sympathy with the Generalissimo sprang from long acquaintance and high admiration for his many sterling qualities. I had seen him supported with enthusiasm by the whole nation when he incarnated their will to resist Japan. Their spontaneous loyalty and their willingness to share in all the hardships involved then was in painful contrast to their sullen apathy or their increasingly unrestrained denunciation as he now found no alternative but to go on in a war that they felt was already lost.

In November Dr. Wong Wen-hao resigned as Premier. The Generalissimo tried without success to get another outstanding scholar, Dr. Hu Shih, to form a new cabinet. No one wanted the job, but Dr. Sun Fo was finally persuaded to undertake it. It was hoped that his symbolic value, as being Sun Yat-sen's son, might at least heal some of the widening rifts within the party. Actually, the prevailing reaction was one of mild dismay. However, he boldly determined to demand that his cabinet have its rightful authority especially in the crucial issue of peace or war, he himself being for peace. He had accepted the post just before going into a Shanghai hospital for an operation, thus prolonging the period when the nation in so grave an emergency had no functioning cabinet.

Toward the middle of December, he returned to the capital and began his rather futile efforts to form a cabinet. No one cared to join it unless he knew what its policy would be. It was a comical perfomance against the dark background of danger and distress. He asked me one morning to call on him and probed again the possibilities of American aid or at least of our opinions. He inquired as to whether I was in direct touch with the Communists, and when I replied in the negative, he wondered how contact could be made with them. After the interview, he fumed openly against American neglect. In the midst of all this, the Generalissimo summoned Wu Tieh-cheng, a faithful party member who had been among those hesitating to join the cabinet but sympathizing with Sun Fo in attempting a change. He was ordered to become Vice-Premier and really take control.

14

Meanwhile, however, hard facts were forcing themselves even upon the Generalissimo's unfailing will. The fighting in the wide battlefield extending from 100 to 200 miles north of the capital, into which almost all available reserves had been flung, was already virtually a defeat for the government with the usual loss of troops. From the end of September the Gold Yuan had lost ninety-eight percent of its value. The public outcry for peace was becoming more insistent. One of the highest-ranking officers,

General Pai Chung-hsi, had actually sent him a telegram from
Hankow advising the Generalissimo to retire in order to attain
this. In the beautiful but never occupied official residence near
the Sun Yat-sen Mausoleum which Madame Chiang and he
had converted into a "Song of Victory" church, especially for
Christians in the government, he attended carol singing Christmas Eve. On Christmas Day, the twelfth anniversary of his
release from Sian, the second from the adoption of the constitution he had advocated, he made his decision to resign and
announce that the Vice-President would take over with full
authority to determine whatever course of action was for the
national welfare. He summarily dismissed the dignified Secretary
of the President's Office and appointed another one—also named
Wu—to work out in orderly procedure all the details for this
momentous decision. Mr. Wu enlisted the help of Chang Ch'un
and Chang Chih-chung, and together they called on Vice-
President Li. The President would announce his resignation,
and this would be followed immediately by a carefully worded
proclamation by the Vice-President calling for a negotiated peace
and a cease-fire order.

The former document was actually being drafted and preparations seemed to be proceeding smoothly, when the Communists
broadcast a list of about forty-five "war criminals" headed by
the Generalissimo and his wife, which made him furious. The
planners feared that he would change his mind, as indeed he did.
He hastily summoned the chief military commanders over the
country for a conference. It was a hectic week for him and for
all concerned. I was being kept informed but tried to be prudent.
Rumors began to spread and everyone was anxiously awaiting
authentic news. It had been his custom to issue a New Year's
message to the nation, the text of which was usually released
about a week in advance. But this year it was the afternoon of
New Year's Eve before the draft was made available for translation and distribution, and with instructions not to release it

until final word was received. That evening the Kuomintang inmost circle literally saw the old year out in the Generalissimo's residence in animated discussion, but this resulted in no change in the message which was in all the papers the next morning. It had cancelled the others. On the whole, it was a dignified and noble statement. But it had the fatal flaw of assuming the gracious attitude of a powerful ruler in dealing with troublesome rebels and of ignoring the desperate plight of his government. It thus officially opened the way to peace but contained nothing decisive as to how to go about attaining it.

15

The military history of those last two years before the Communist victory was the determinative factor and there is not much in it to the credit of either the United States or China. When it seemed that the Marshall negotiations would result in a coalition in which American officers would be responsible for reorganizing the troops of both the warring parties into a single, efficient but greatly reduced National Army, an elaborate structure was created consisting of army, navy and air officers, with all the necessary services and equipment. This came to be known as JUSMAG (Joint United States Military Advisory Group). It consisted normally of some 500 officers and about as many more enlisted men. The great majority, especially of the officers, had their families with them. An agreement was entered into by which the Chinese Government provided what might be described as local expenses, but as that government became more impoverished and its currency decreased in value, this became a very heavy drain upon its dwindling resources. The original concept was splendidly idealistic as a program for modernizing the Chinese military forces according to the best western standards, and in the process for serving as a guarantee that internecine fighting would not break out again.

During the lengthy discussions which occupied most of the

year 1946, JUSMAG was kept intact and busy in reshaping the National military system or in training tasks, on the theory that peace would again be attained. When the negotiations were finally broken off toward the end of that year, JUSMAG was still retained in the hope, no doubt, that a reconciliation might even yet be effected and its intended contribution to China's peace and progress might be realized. To have dismantled it and have nothing else to take its place would have symbolized America's abandonment of any such hope as well as of further aid to the National Government itself. But its retention seemed to the Communists to be giving much more assistance to their enemy than was really the case, and it intensified their bitter anti-American feeling.

Actually, JUSMAG was permitted only to give advice in theoretical reconstruction of the Chinese military system and in the training of officers or new recruits, except that when Major General David G. Barr was put in charge in January, 1948, he was allowed to give informal and confidential advice to the Generalissimo on combat operations. General Barr was the finest type of American military officer and did his best in a difficult situation. But to have been effective, his advice should have been reinforced by subordinates in direct contact with Chinese regional commanders and junior officers as well as with the services of supply and the financial administration. There should have been the assurance of sufficient materiel to enable the Chinese to carry out the advice given and to make it worth their while to do so. The Generalissimo had a high regard for General Barr and always listened attentively to his advice. But instead of planning his operations according to purely military factors and the new science of logistics, he was too much of a Chinese not to be governed primarily by personal or political considerations.

The presence of this unit with all the accessories and with outlying stations elsewhere was of course very conspicuous and inevitably convinced the Communists that we were fighting against them, whereas the government benefited very slightly by all the notoriety and expenditure. As its fortunes declined, it became increasingly apparent that all the activities of JUSMAG were in training a hypothetical armed force that would never come into existence.

The sociological aspects were also suggestive. The officers were in general competent, fine-spirited and anxious to do a good job. In order to keep them contented, it was reasonable to have their families join them. But this involved the pre-empting by the Chinese authorities of buildings sorely needed for other purposes in the acute housing problems of the capital and the construction of apartments on a scale never seen there before, together with all the appurtenances necessary to satisfy those accustomed to American standards of decency and comfort. But these were luxurious in comparison with the Chinese of corresponding social positions, and as living conditions became harder were in glaring contrast with the resources of all but the highest officials. These delightful American wives in entirely innocent efforts to escape the boredom of their exile unwittingly flaunted their economic superiority. JUSMAG motor vehicles of every description seemed painfully abundant on the Nanking streets. The enlisted men occasionally had clashes with Chinese or played drunken pranks upon them, but discipline was severe, and these occurrences were rare though when they happened there was always a flaring out of latent anti-American sentiment. Had the officers been occupied in combat operations, there would have been less reason for the presence of their families, and in the grim realities of warfare, these social comparisons would have been largely overlooked. Nor would the Communist denunciations have been more violent.

Military aid approved by Congress to the amount of $125,000,-000 had no restrictions whatever on its use, although the Chinese were scrupulous in consulting with General Barr and his staff in making their purchases. However, it was late in the year 1948 before much of what had been ordered began to arrive, and by that time the National forces had deteriorated to a point where American equipment only delayed the final outcome. We incurred the animosity not only of the Communists but of a number of Chinese intellectuals who had lost respect for their government and longed for the peace which was supposedly hindered chiefly because of our aid. The government itself complained because it was "too little and too late." We were criticized by Chinese of every type of political opinion. This was to some extent neutralized by E.C.A. economic assistance and relief, but this had little if any effect in stopping communism.

The failure of American military aid to contribute toward ending the civil war provokes the question: Why? When the Marshall negotiations were abruptly broken off by the Communists late in 1946, the government had every advantage. It was, first of all, the legally recognized government of China with all of the prestige and the material resources which this implied. It had more territory and larger armies, far better equipped, and that was supplemented by a navy and an air force which, however inferior, were lacking to the other side. We had since V-J Day given well over two billion dollars worth of supplies and financial aid, most of which directly benefited the government.

The Kuomintang had come into power largely on the negative urge of overthrowing an effete and alien imperial dynasty and then of doing the same to regional war lords, rather than on the more positive aims of democracy and social reform. These were all stressed in the "Three Principles" and in official phraseology, but the pressing demands of military conquest and, later, of resistance to Japan, and the Communist conflict were too engrossing. Along with these preoccupations there had been an unconscious reversal to the age-long failings of Chinese officialdom—profiteering from public funds, primary concern over the welfare of family or friends or faction rather than the cause of the country, the pressure to maintain appearances, bureaucratic red tape, and incompetence.

These evils were especially prevalent perhaps among army officers. Common soldiers were as much neglected as in the past and were in the main forcibly impressed into service with but little idea as to why or whom they were fighting and with the barest provision for their existence. Reliance was placed on modern equipment with no corresponding moral discipline or motivation, with the result that costly and delicate weapons or instruments were carelessly misused and then discarded when damaged. Although there were many officers who had excellent technical training and were highly proficient, there was too much individualism and very little cohesion or team spirit among them. Commanding officers had too much control of money allocated to their units and too little discretion in military operations. All of this would have been worse if it had not been for the Generalissimo's constant efforts. The morale became rapidly worse during the latter half of 1948.

Troops were transferred long distances by sea or air—mainly in ships or airplanes contributed by the United States—only to be removed again elsewhere at great cost or to be dispersed by the Communists. The embryo navy was far more costly than could have been justified by its usefulness for this kind of war. So also were fortifications and moats for the defense of cities— which were invariably lost—when the troops should have been busily assaulting, encircling and annihilating Communist columns. All this extravagance was against the background of an impoverished populace and of the skillful use of slender resources by the Communists. The aviation, shipping, trucks, etc. which we had generously provided had the unforeseen effect of sapping Chinese initiative and ingenuity and of causing them to depend too much on mechanized devices which—except in a narrowly technical sense—they lacked the experience to use wisely and on money which again they had learned to look for from us.

16

This narrative of Chinese-American co-operation while I was Ambassador is not written in criticism so much as to furnish a guide for the future from these failures.

The Chinese people ardently desired independence, unity, peace, economic recovery and democratic government. These things the American Government and people also desired for China. With my dual attachment there could, therefore, be no slightest conflict of loyalties for me as to the objectives. The Chinese knew of my love for their country, my concern for their welfare, my liberal attitude and my convictions as to a peaceful solution of their internal strife through inclusive and untrammeled co-operation. I had therefore the full advantage of their trust.

But I failed them. I did not succeed in helping General Marshall to persuade either side to concede the points that might have brought agreement nor to allay the fears and suspicions that I was convinced were then the principal obstacles. After these negotiations had finally broken off, I was unable to influence those who controlled either American or Chinese political action to the point where this might have had some constructive result.

Meanwhile American policy reversed itself completely as to our participation in effecting a coalition which included Communists and implicitly as to the desirability of this even if the Chinese proved able to achieve it by themselves. We had of course been learning during those two unpleasantly eventful years a great deal about the global aspects of communism, which doubtless explains our contradictory attitude toward its Chinese variety. But within China itself the issue remained essentially as it was when we took it upon ourselves to urge both sides to unite in such a coalition despite all of their own misgivings, except that it would now be much more difficult for each of them.

Were we too naive and unsuspecting as to the true nature of communism wherever found? Were we too hopeful of drastic and dramatic reforms within the Kuomintang? And what, if anything, were we going to do about it?

My dream of China peaceful, united and progressive, helped in this by American technical advice and financial grants or loans, failed. But I still believe that it was right and could have been realized. I base this partly upon the sterling qualities of the Chinese people as I have come to know them and their history and partly upon my unwavering faith in democracy when practised in a free society.

China is after all a single cultural entity with deeply entrenched family, historical, economic and other ties. It has been amply demonstrated of late in more than one country that the dangers from Communist tactics are very real. But the surest method of thwarting these is by ample and free publicity, an aroused political consciousness and new standards of devotion to the public welfare among democratic leaders. A one-party system cannot but be vitiated by the faults for which the Kuomintang was denounced. Democracy will always be as bad as its people let it be. The only corrective is in more democracy in which the people are determined to assert themselves. The Communists' insidious penetration, their whole totalitarian philosophy, their unscrupulous use of any methods, can only be guarded against by a populace convinced that their way of life has other values which they will defend at any cost. If China, with her traditional reliance on compromise or the avoidance of extremes in the finding of a middle way, can demonstrate the feasibility of such a solution it may not be without benefit in the larger aspects of this problem. And because these principles are eternal and the spiritual forces within and around mankind are the most potent of all, I believe that my dream for China will yet come true.

11

Mounting Perplexities

The end of the year 1948 was also in effect the end of a system and of a tradition in Chinese politics. None the less the Generalissimo was superb in his serene courage and inflexible will power during these last weeks when his world was cracking up around him, and he remained imperturbable as he quietly made his plans.

On Christmas Day he reached the decision to retire. He appointed certain trusted associates to work out the procedure in detail and to arrange for Vice-President Li Tsung-jen to take over as Acting President. He wanted an orderly transfer of authority and continuity in anti-Communist resistance. In his New Year message he made references to his desire for peace and his readiness to retire. But he specified five conditions for the Communists to accept, as prerequisite to his retirement.

A week passed with no Communist rejoinder except for a few sarcastic references in their broadcasts. The government concluded that the peace approach had been definitely rejected and plans were taking form both for defending the capital and for removing it to Canton. At the end of another week, Mao Tse-tung broadcast a blistering reply concluding with his own eight conditions and ordering his armies meanwhile to continue their advance. This threw the government leaders into even greater confusion. The eight conditions were exceedingly harsh and amounted almost to unconditional surrender, the first one calling for the handing over of the "war criminals."

The Communist troops advanced in three lines practically without opposition toward the north bank of the Yangtze directly across from Nanking and to convenient crossings east and west of the city. In a foolish and futile attempt at checking them, four armies were sent across the river only to be recalled as the Communists approached. Money and toil were further wasted in trenches and concrete "pill boxes" over the nearby hills on the south bank. The responsible leaders all realized the hopelessness of continuing the war as it was being conducted, but it was a bitter humiliation to surrender. They had been the unchallenged National Government of China since its establishment through their efforts, victorious in the Japanese war and with the heightened prestige of being one of the "Big Five" in the United Nations.

In desperation the government tried various expedients. I was consulted as to a *démarche* to the other four nations of the "Big Five," and although I pointed out the improbability of relief from this source, it was none the less attempted. These governments were requested, either singly or in unison, to exert their good offices merely in bringing the two opponents together. Each one promptly but politely refused, explaining in effect that this was an issue which Chinese had best solve by themselves. Anywhere in the world it would have been a mortifying predicament for those in power, but in China this loss of personal as well as party "face" and the inability any longer to keep up appearances was almost more unendurable than the hard realities themselves. A month or so earlier, the removal of the capital to Canton had been hastily decided on and as hastily abandoned; but as there seemed no other way of escape, the decision to move was again reached after lengthy debate. The events that followed were in effect the instantaneous disclosure to all the world of the inner contradictions among the Kuomintang leaders and within many of them as individuals. This was apparent to me in many a personal conversation which almost without exception revealed also the desire to ascertain American policy or to influence it to come promptly to their rescue.

All I could do was to express a vapid sympathy and to discourage any reliance on American succor in the role of *deus ex machina.*

2

The government naturally wanted the Diplomatic Body to remove to Canton and thus help to maintain its own prestige. Technically we all were accredited to it and properly should follow it to the "temporary capital." My counselor, who also had the rank of Minister, Lewis Clark, was ordered to proceed to Canton with a working staff. The ambassadors of those countries belonging to the North Atlantic Group had been meeting informally during these puzzling weeks for conference. All were of the same opinion—to stay temporarily in Nanking—and were similarly supported by their governments. I was forcibly reminded of our new position in the world not only by the attitude of the members of that Group but by the deference shown by all the others to the American decision. Several of the smaller countries had instructed their representatives to do whatever we did. There was an ironic humor in the fact that, as it turned out, the Soviet Ambassador was the only Chief of Mission who made the move. He explained to one of us that his government had ordered him to do so to avoid rumors and speculations if he remained in Nanking. The Soviets seem rather careful about doing the correct thing according to protocol.

The government, meanwhile, was having its own troubles. There was the underlying disagreement about where the capital really was and even Sun Fo admitted after his safe arrival in Canton that it was still Nanking. It had been decided that the heads of all sections should remain there, but most of them loitered in Shanghai or found their way to Canton. The hardships of the wretched minor officers may be illustrated by a group of 200 of these belonging to the Ministry of Foreign Affairs who with their 400 dependents began their trek by spending about three days in the densely crowded railway station with train service all badly disorganized. When finally on board they and all other passengers were ejected somewhere on the way to Shanghai to make way for troops and when last heard of were still waiting a week or more later at Woosung for a steamer to take them south. Another group of eighty members of the Ministry of Health waited forty days in Shanghai. The delay and disorder in performing official business can be imagined.

3

One week after the Communist retort to his New Year message had been broadcast, the Generalissimo quietly flew away to his picturesque native home in a hilly region near the Chekiang coast. On January 22, 1949, Vice-President Li Tsung-jen became Acting President. But the Generalissimo's loyal subordinates in the ground, air and sea forces respectively still wanted him and obeyed only his orders. It was a striking evidence of his masterful personality and of the depth of the noble Chinese virtue of loyalty. He hated communism so much that he simply could not conscientiously be either inactive or indifferent.

Acting President Li Tsung-jen was in an almost impossible position. Li was a realist and felt strongly that there should be a negotiated peace if at all possible. The Generalissimo had opened the way for this, and the government had officially approved. But it had also left him in the lurch almost alone in the capital. The Communist vanguards were directly across the river. Their daily broadcasts were taunting the government with its palpable irresolution and disintegration and were adding unreasonable and irrelevant demands. What National troops remained were commanded by officers who still took orders from the Generalissimo. The currency was becoming daily more valueless, and what metal or other liquid assets the government possessed had been taken to

Formosa under the Generalissimo's orders. This was to show his determination to fight the Communists to the end. The populace wanted peace and generally inclined to the Communists as the winners. Li himself was on the list of war criminals, and there was a sardonic humor in the Communist demand that the others be handed over as a preliminary to talking peace. Left alone, therefore, in the deserted capital, undermined by the bickerings of his own absentee colleagues, excoriated by the Communists, Li bravely continued his endeavors for peace. Unofficial delegations journeying to Peiping to open the way were treated by the Communists with studied indifference.

4

For me personally, the last month or two of 1948 and the first ones of 1949 were a period of absorbing interest but with an overwhelming sense of impotence. I was reminded of what my old friend, Nelson Johnson, at that time the American Ambassador, had said to me soon after the Japanese invasion of China, to the effect that we were watching one of the most fateful dramas of history, with seats in the front row but powerless to do anything but look on and interpret. I remember wondering at the time whether the representative of the United States need be only a spectator. Yet, here was I sitting luxuriously in a private box watching an even more heartrending performance.

The earlier one had at least had the splendidly heroic quality of a clearly defined and united resistance to a vastly more efficient foreign aggressor, whereas this one had become a gigantic struggle between two political ideologies with the overtones of democratic idealism perverted by bureaucratic incompetence on the one side, succumbing to a dynamic socialized reform vitiated by Communist dogma, intolerance and ruthlessness on the other. And the great mass of suffering inarticulate victims cared for neither but were powerless to do anything about it.

I had vainly hoped to go as usual to Yenching for the Christmas holidays, but the fighting had by that time enveloped the Peiping area, and, in any case, my appearing there would have caused undesirable publicity. I had already learned to take this into calculation in any projected trip, and it had become especially true as the intense desire for peace began to be articulate. For many years I had celebrated Christmas at Yenching by having an afternoon party for faculty children under a certain age. What began with a few, chiefly American, youngsters of whom I was especially fond was rapidly enlarged to include all those eligible, and in recent years the number had reached some two hundred, overwhelmingly Chinese. Supplies were not to be purchased in Peiping so I had sent from our commissary the customary amounts of cocoa, candy, etc. and learned that these got out to the campus the day before the closing of the city gates against the Communist advance. The campus soon came under their control but all the usual Christmas festivities and religious services were carried on without interference.

Despite my disappointment over not being able to spend that holiday season where I felt myself to belong more than anywhere else in the world, I was glad in the end that I was compelled to stay in Nanking. For almost all of our Embassy "dependents" and others not regarded as essential had been sent away for precautionary safety. It was a pleasure, therefore, to help maintain the Christmas spirit among the members of my new family and, in their loneliness, to get to know them better. Twice before I had planned a pre-Christmas gala party for Yenching graduates then in Nanking, but it was felt that even so intimate a reunion would seem to be in offensive bad taste at a time of national distress, so I had a dinner one evening for some twenty of their leading spirits. With an elaborately decorated tree and several suitable functions, my home contributed something of Christmas cheer in the gathering gloom.

5

During these months of rapidly advancing trends, events important to China and to me had also been taking place in the States. The Generalissimo and his comrades had been led to believe that the election of Thomas E. Dewey was practically assured and that this would mean prompt and powerful military aid to China instead of the Truman-Marshall hesitations. Whether this form of intervention would have been feasible or desirable became a completely academic issue with the amazing outcome of the presidential election. The one thing certain was that the Generalissimo would have welcomed it with almost any conditions we imposed.

The serious operation performed on Secretary Marshall early in December and his subsequent resignation stirred me deeply. For, as was doubtless true of everyone else who had been closely associated with him, I felt an esteem for him which his great qualities compelled. Since I had been chosen by him for this post and had agreed to serve in it as long as he seemed to need me, to say nothing of my being well beyond any proper age for retirement, I should naturally have gone out with my chief. Mr. Acheson was Undersecretary at the time of my appointment and continued in that position during the first months of Mr. Marshall's incumbency. I had, therefore, a certain acquaintance with him at long range. I tried to make it easy for the President and him to get rid of me, but they wished me to stay on until the confusion in China had somewhat cleared.

6

This leads naturally to the very complex and controversial issue of the real nature of Chinese communism and of my relation to it. General Marshall had originally brought me into his efforts to form a coalition government because of my reputation as a liberal American friendly to the Chinese people as a whole and with no pronounced sympathy for any one faction or school of thought. This included the Communists, several of whose leaders I had known fairly well. Many Yenching students had "gone over the hills," and as those whom I met later were apt to assure me, they believed themselves to be living up to the Yenching motto: "Freedom through Truth for Service." This was the idealistic phase of the movement. With my own passionate insistence on freedom, I could not but apply this to their right to choose their own experience. During the Marshall negotiations, I did my best to remove the mutual suspicions and misunderstandings which were then perhaps not the chief hindrance to the coalition rather than irreconcilable ideologies.

But during the years 1947-8, Secretary Marshall's experiences with Soviet Russia, as shared by the entire American nation and supported largely by the opinion of the western world, led to a radical change of attitude toward the whole subject. It came to be assumed that the Communist party in every country was controlled from the Kremlin in the interest of world revolution by violence, that it would dominate any coalition and utilize its power for enforcing all the evils of a totalitarian system, and that communism was, in short, a sinister menace to free institutions, unscrupulous in the employment of any means to attain its ends, to be feared and fought on all fronts.

In course of time I received the most explicit instructions not to encourage or in any way assist in the formation of a coalition which included Communists. American official policy had seemingly therefore completely reversed itself. Chinese communism was undoubtedly in the orthodox Marxist-Leninist tradition, but would it be transformed by historical, demographic and other factors inherent in the Chinese environment, by the impossibility of enforcing totalitarian techniques in so vast and amorphous a population, or even by an ineradicable nationalistic consciousness among the leaders? During this time of rapid Communist gains American editorial opinion reflected the prev-

alent dismay and contained much caustic criticism of the State
Department. How baffled were even supposed authorities on
China was epitomized by the report of a public debate held in
New York City in February by two good friends of mine, Stanley Hornbeck and Nathaniel Peffer, the former of whom argued
fatuously that it was still not impossible to help retrieve the
military potential of the Chiang armies, while the latter held
consistently to his advocacy of our complete withdrawal from
every form of interference with Chinese internal affairs. Was
there not something between these two extremes that we could
do, wholeheartedly, constructively, useful to the Chinese people,
neutralizing those features in European communism which we
had learned to dread? In all this welter of perplexity certain
guiding principles were crystal clear. The Chinese people were
desperately anxious for peace.

It was an ironical situation. The United States had come into
existence through a revolutionary struggle for freedom, and had
led the world in establishing a truly republican form of government which had in successive tests demonstrated and improved
upon its feasibility. Our history and our well-known friendly
helpfulness to China had been the inspiration of its reforming
spirits. Sun Yet-sen's "Three Principles" were a felicitous translation of Lincoln's deathless description of democracy. Communism
as standarized in the Soviet Union had degenerated into the
only remaining form of totalitarianism with all its evils. Yet in
China we were being accused of imperialistic assistance to the
forces of reaction and corrupt bureaucracy by those who were
leading in a victorious revolution based on slogans of liberation
and democracy.

7

The swelling desire for peace finally crystallized in a "people's
delegation" led by the distinguished diplomat, Dr. W. W. Yen,
and including Mr. Shao Li-tse, a prominent Kuomintang official

unscathed by Communist attacks. Dr. Yen had once been Ambassador to Moscow. I recall his telling me after his return how dull it had been there. No Russian dared to have any social relations with foreigners, so the little circle of diplomats entertained one another in turn, always meeting the same people, eating the same food, with no other diversions. He commented humorously to me on the brusque or even offensive speech of contemporary diplomacy in contrast with the formal language and etiquette when he had gained his experience in European capitals. The members of this peace party were all highly respected citizens of Shanghai except Mr. Shao who represented the National Government. After repeated delays, causing apprehension as to the Communist attitude, they finally took off on February 14, 1945. It was the first airplane trip for Dr. Yen, and he took with him a physician because of the possible effect on his heart. They were received by the Communist leaders and brought back a hopeful belief in their desire for peace. It was not to be expected that details would be taken up on this exploratory mission, but they were promised that delegates would be invited to a peace conference in Peiping as soon as practicable after March 15. Dr. Yen and Mr. Shao traveled from Peiping on to Shihchiachuang where Mao Tse-tung and Chou En-lai were staying. But on arrival they learned that it would be necessary to go thirty miles into the country in a jeep over country roads. At the end of the journey they were too tired for anything but bed and arose the next morning stiff and sore. It was another first experience for Dr. Yen, and he had a glimpse into the austere simplicity of Communist living even at the top level. But Dr. Yen was surprised to find the famous Communist ruler a genial, at times even jovial, and affable host instead of the stern ascetic he had visualized.

The optimism created by the return of this mission on February 27 greatly strengthened the position of the Acting President. He had meanwhile flown to Canton to invite the Premier to return to Nanking, a gracious act which immensely increased his popularity as being willing to go to any length in his desire to unite his government and work for peace. Such condescension by the head of the state counts for more in China than it would have in America. Sun Fo soon found himself in the dilemma of refusing to comply—which would have ended his career—or of going to Nanking where the Legislative Yuan had mustered a quorum and was denouncing him for the move to Canton. He finally came.

8

I have wanted somewhere in these memoirs to pay a tribute to those officers in the American armed services whom I have come to know throughout my life in China and especially in my more recent official relations with them. This seems to be an appropriate place because the theme throughout has been interaction between these two nations, and because these Americans also are what they are because of the tradition and environment which have helped to make them. In Peking I had known more or less casually those serving as naval or military attachés in our Embassy, the fine succession of Commandants of Marine Guards and occasional visiting officers. After my release from the Japanese I met more of them as they came into Peiping, or when I traveled to Kunming, Chungking or Shanghai.

It was in this last place just before taking off for the States that I made the acquaintance of General A. C. Wedemeyer and in an intimate conversation had my first personal appreciation of his splendid qualities. But this generally favorable impression of American military personnel was strongly confirmed by the close association when we were all officially representing our country's interests in China. Even a layman could recognize their professional attainments and their high standards of duty. They were men of whom I learned as a fellow American to feel proud and whose friendship I deeply valued. First in time and in quality of my high esteem was General George C. Marshall. Others who stand out similarly in my memory chiefly because I saw more of them are Major General David G. Barr, Vice Admiral Oscar C. Badger, Rear Admiral Francis P. Old, Admiral Stuart S. Murray and without exception my own military, naval and air attachés. As far as it was possible to know them, I felt the same way toward petty officers and enlisted men, but among these my opportunities were more limited.

I realize of course that there is another side. But my primary interest is not unqualified praise of the American armed forces so much as my desire to see their superior qualities reproduced in their Chinese counterparts, as I am confident would take place given the same opportunity. Ours are what they are not only because of well-conceived technical training and treatment, but also because of our national culture. And as I have watched them at close quarters it is quite apparent that our Christian faith has been an important ingredient in this culture as it has influenced their characters. The plight of China today is largely due to the twin deficiencies of scientific training and ethical standards for her officers in a superficially modernized military system. Whatever we may think of the horror and hatefulness of war, we can rejoice for the sake of America, and of all mankind, that at this supreme crisis of history we have produced a splendid system for the training of those to whom we can confidently entrust the responsibilities of national defense.

9

In the midst of deepening political anxieties, there was a pleasant interlude one rainy Saturday afternoon in March. It was the engagement party in my home of Philip Fugh's second daughter to the son of Dr. Handel Lee, once a student of mine in Nanking Seminary, and afterward its President. Nanking Seminary and Yenching were thus blended in this attractive young couple, my spiritual grandchildren. Mrs. Fugh and John Fugh had come from Shanghai. My reception rooms were almost

literally banked with floral baskets from the Acting President
and other Chinese friends. I conducted a simple ceremony in
two languages, Richard and Dorothy exchanged rings, after
which the guests mingled freely as refreshments were served.
It was an unusual gathering of missionaries and Chinese church-
men, government officials, Yenching graduates and members
of the Embassy staff including naval and military attachés in
uniform. It was symbolic of the various phases of my life in
China, and it all aroused in me quite a sentimental strain.

10

Apart from this little romance, the day was an eventful one.
We had news of the exact terms of the Atlantic Pact, and the
North Shensi Communist broadcast contained the most explicit
declaration yet made of the alignment of Chinese Communists
with the Soviet Union. This broadcast was obviously provoked
by the formation of the Atlantic Pact and presumably on instructions from Moscow. It grossly misrepresented the Soviet
efforts for peace in the United Nations, thwarted allegedly by
the "warmongers" led by the United States. It glorified Stalin.
The whole statement breathed hate, intolerance and fidelity to
the cause of world communism. In this and other broadcasts,
due doubtless to Russian influence, they also denounced American imperialism with a virulence almost more than they used
against the Kuomintang. They began to mention me as "still
(under Li Tsung-jen as previously under the Generalissimo)
the overlord of Nanking," thus implying that these men listened to my advice as puppets of American imperialism. They
urged Li to disassociate himself from Chiang Kai-shek and me.

The currency problem was rapidly becoming more serious
than even the military one and was damaging this as well as the
public morale. Toward the end of February the entire Gold
Yuan circulation could have been bought up by 20,000,000
U. S. dollars, so rapid was the inflationary process. But a month

later this could have been done for one half that amount. At the earlier date, the note issue amounted to about thirty billion Gold Yuan, but a month later this had increased 150 percent. The rate of exchange with the American dollar was increasing about ten percent daily, and the cost of commodities was keeping in general the same pace. The situation became grimly comical as the printing presses were unable to issue new notes fast enough for use, and in consequence, interest rates assumed fantastic figures. In April the government had an income of five percent of its expenditures, but more than this amount was expended in its collection. Despite all these fiscal difficulties the government continued to meet all of its foreign obligations.

This was greatly in its favor, but it was offset by anomalies like the airlift of food for the troops from Tsingtao to Taiyuan. The resolute old Governor of Shansi, Yen Hsi-shan, had long been beleaguered in his capital and to hold this there had to be a continuous food supply. Taiyuan kept immobilized Communist forces which could otherwise have been released to attack elsewhere. But after the loss of Peiping and Tientsin, the military importance of holding Taiyuan dwindled. Arsenals, however, were producing munitions which would all fall into Communist possession with the loss of the city. Efforts were made to airlift some of these to needy places like Hankow, but anti-aircraft firing made this too dangerous. The utmost that could be gained was delay in capitulation. Yet the impoverished government voted to squander over 300,000 U. S. dollars daily in this costly parallel to the Berlin airlift. It illustrated the extent to which personal relations count in China, and how political arguments everywhere defy common sense. Meanwhile citizens of the beleaguered city were starving by thousands.

11

Acting President Li spent these early months of 1949 in coping with colossal problems with a skill and courage which won great admiration and sympathy. We kept assuring him of this, although there was little else we could do to help him. Finally, General Ho Ying-ch'in agreed to serve as Premier, apparently from worthy motives. It was extremely difficult to form a cabinet, but after many efforts a group of younger men was secured, not of first rank either in prominence or ability but clean and public-spirited. The time had come in Chinese affairs when there could no longer be any other motive. Mr. S. Y. Liu (Liu Kung-yun) illustrated this spirit as Minister of Finance which, as I told him, called for more heroism than fighting in the front line. Two Yenching boys who had been serving with unsullied reputation in various financial posts were named as the Vice-Ministers. I advised them both to accept as about the most useful form of patriotic duty. It was no slight handicap to have the "seat of the Government" in faraway Canton, but these administrative difficulties were accentuated by political tensions. In general the National Government in Canton was more opposed to any attempts to secure peace through negotiation, and it was suspicious of Li as being ready to yield too much.

At the same time the Generalissimo in his native village had secretaries, guards, long distance telephones and all the apparatus for the conduct of affairs. There were constant visitors. He was described in idyllic terms as relaxing among familiar scenes and friendly neighbors, watching his grandchildren at play, and in general following the classic pattern of a retired official enjoying bucolic leisure. Actually, he was active in military and all other planning. He kept sending messages to the Acting President and Premier that he was backing them up to the limit, and he was undoubtedly sincere. He knew the peace talks would fail and that the fighting would be resumed. He counted on American aid when at last we would become aroused to the Communist menace.

The old Chinese relationship of master and pupil cut across all abstract claims. The chiefs of the air force and navy, the high-ranking generals were loyal to him rather than to any titular leader, or still less to the impersonal state itself. The modern-minded younger officers in the Ministry of National Defense felt that if they could have a unified command and coordination of air, water and ground forces they could make it extremely hazardous for the Communists to cross the Yangtze. But more crucial than strategy were silver coins with which to pay the troops. They did not want Gold Yuan, but four silver dollars per month apiece (two U. S. dollars) or even two of these would sustain their morale. Otherwise Communist agents could buy them off with hard money or with mere promises. The government had nearly 300,000,000 U. S. dollars in gold and silver bullion, but most of this was safely in Taiwan as were the ample stocks of munitions.

12

The preparations for the peace talks dragged slowly on through the first three months of 1949, but as what proved to be a ghastly April Fool's joke, the official peace delegation of six members headed by General Chang Chih-chung left on that day for Peiping. Then followed two more weeks of informal consultations, during which public suspense was relieved or increased by reports from Peiping or by the wildest rumors. Currency fluctuations reflected these. Li Tsung-jen showed courage in his efforts to secure the peace for which all the people yearned by dealing with the Communists, arrogant in their military success. He grew steadily in public opinion as he modestly and patiently parried Communist insolence or pled for solidarity within his own group.

The Communists chose to be haughty conquerors, uncompromising one-party dictators. Their pose of naming delegates for peaceful negotiations was—to use one of their own favorite words —entirely "insincere." They had drafted a lengthy document which the government leaders would be ordered to sign on the dotted line. According to an already familiar pattern, these latter were to confess their crimes and humbly ask as individuals for reinstatement. They were to transfer all assets and to perform their usual duties until relieved of these, at which time the Kuomintang administration would by its own action go out of existence. All that the government delegates had achieved by their two weeks of patient discussion was the softening of a few phrases.

I was keenly disappointed for I had been hoping that their Chinese heritage and the finer qualities which I knew many among their leaders had possessed would prevent such unreasonable excesses. How much of this was due to the overweening pride of victory—intensified in their case by long years of bitter struggle and swelling personal animosities—and how much to distinctive Communist ideology, is an interesting speculation. But in any case the fateful decision had been made. In their order to all field commanders to cross the Yangtze and "liberate" the southern provinces, they used language about the rejection of so "generous and reasonable" an offer as they had made which causes one to wonder anew about the peculiarities of Communist thinking. Does their discipline do something to the mind which prevents them from forming the same judgments as would all others? Is it possible that they really believed that the tone and terms of the document containing their dictated peace were generous and reasonable? From time immemorial the Chinese have observed their spring festival *Chingming*, "Clear Radiance," by visiting ancestral graves, somewhat in the spirit of our Easter which usually occurs about the same time. I had planned to make a trip to Hangchow early in April for this purpose and to take with me a few of the Embassy staff to enjoy the vernal beauty of the scenery. The Premier had informed the Governor and Mayor which meant that despite my request there would be at least a Chinese minimum of official entertaining. I had sent word that there would be no public speeches but had suggested meetings with the foreign community—perhaps entirely missionary—with Chinese Christian workers, and with Yenching graduates. But a day or two before the time of departure, the Communists startled the Acting President by making peremptory demands which if not agreed to within five days would be the signal for them to cross the Yangtze River. Li was palpably relieved when I told him that I had cancelled my trip.

The following week was the one before Easter, but its sacred memories were largely blotted out for me by day-to-day happenings and by anxious speculations as to what would be revealed of the Communist intentions in the Peiping conference. In a sense the fate of mankind was involved in whether they wanted a truly representative or a totalitarian type of government. Beginning with Palm Sunday, I had the usual numbers of callers but all with a sense of impending crisis. There were government officials of various ranks, liberals caught between the hopeless outlook for democracy and their dislike of communism now almost at the city gates, American correspondents seeking my off-the-record explanation of what was really happening, Embassy officers dealing with matters on the borderline between routine and emergency. Almost every day the harassed young Minister of Finance or some friend of his called to inquire as to any possible help from America in the fiscal confusion and the need for paying the troops in silver, at least during the peace talks.

One morning I was called on by appointment by Ma Hungk'uei, Mohammedan Governor of Ninghsia, who had flown to the capital for conference and was hoping to go to America for medical treatment. We met, however, in the home of a missionary friend to avoid attracting attention, the Governor's secretary having been a student of our host. The northwest is largely populated by adherents of the Moslem creed, and for this as well as other reasons there is strong anti-Communist sentiment. What attitude would the United States take toward their determined resistance? The usual question was adumbrated in this case by the proximity of that region to Siberia. The papers had been describing this picturesque chieftain as weighing 300 pounds, but he protested that it was only 240. I invited him and his wife to dinner in the evening when his coming would be less conspicuous, and I charged the cook to serve no pork.

The next day was again a mingling of hectic politics and a charming romance. An American army officer and a girl from the French Embassy were married that afternoon in my home. When a month or so earlier they had asked if I would perform the wedding ceremony—as had been happening in a surprising number of cases—I commented on their adventurous courage in expecting that this would be possible. My reception rooms were attractively decorated with spring flowers, my French colleagues gave the bride away, and the whole event was a delightful interlude in the gathering gloom.

The weather on Easter Day reflected this mood, and much of the day was occupied by me in trying to comfort my sorely harassed Chinese friends. But I had promised to preach at a union service in English, and although no other preacher is apt to have made his homiletic preparation in the midst of similar distractions, yet it was inspiring to speak of undying Christian hope in the midst of so much frustration and fear.

It had been arranged that the Acting President should come to my home that evening and that the British, Australian and Canadian Ambassadors should also be present. The last named had been caught in Shanghai and learned afterward with disgust of what he had missed. "Tommy" Davis was a full-blooded man and a very good friend of mine. President Li's secretary had brought with him a translation of the Communist ultimatum. It was even more haughtily uncompromising than the worst I had feared. We listened with amazed indignation. We could not of course advise Li when he told us that he and his colleagues could not sign any such document, but we assured him of our heartfelt sympathy. So Easter Day ended on this grim note.

13

All hopes for a negotiated peace were now finished. How rapidly would the River crossing take place and what would be the fate of Nanking? Monday morning began for me with a visit from Li's intimate colleague of many years, General Pai Ch'ung-hsi. He told me that in this crisis Li had decided to insist that the Generalissimo either resume office and take full control or leave the country. That afternoon Li sent for Philip Fugh and said that, while he himself would stay in the capital to the last moment, he urged me and all the Chiefs of Missions to remove promptly to Canton.

A platoon of marines had been guarding the Embassy for over two months in anticipation of the time when the government troops would be leaving and the Communists had not taken over. This period might involve serious fighting or more probably looting by deserting or defeated soldiery and by the more lawless type of civilians. The original plan had been to have a naval vessel stationed here continuously to take the marines on board as soon as order had been restored and to evacuate me and others if this became necessary. But action by Congress slashing naval appropriations had made it impossible for the commanding officer in Shanghai to spare a vessel for Nanking. He assured me, however, that whenever I asked for one it would be there in three days. I had accordingly sent a request ten days or more earlier, but there were delays and, fortunately for us, Admiral Badger finally stopped the sailing unless I overruled him. The British had been following the same practise in co-operation with Canada and Australia, partly for security but also to bring needed supplies.

The Communist ultimatum expired on Wednesday, April 20, after which they might be expected to begin crossing the river.

The British Ambassador, Sir Ralph Stevenson, had therefore pushed up the routine exchange of vessels so as to have it safely over by that date. But Wednesday morning he called to tell me that *H.M.S. Amethyst* coming upstream had been fired upon and grounded with heavy casualties some miles down river, according to the ship's final radio. Ralph and I had taken office about the same time and had at once become close friends. I listened with a sympathy tinged by a sense of relief at what might so easily have happened to me. The *Consort* which was to have been relieved had started for the scene at once moving rapidly under constant fire from north shore artillery which its return fire partially silenced. But the shelling was too severe to enable it to stand by for rescue so it continued down stream. Meanwhile the *Black Swan* and the flagship *London* steamed rapidly from Shanghai only to have the same experience. Some of the *Amethyst* wounded men and others swam to the south bank and eventually reached Shanghai by railway in a pitiful condition. Others were carried off with great difficulty by a seaplane.

On all the ships there was a total of over one hundred casualties, almost one-half fatal. The *Amethyst* was a total loss, and all the others were badly damaged. It seemed unbelievable that Communist troops would have fired without warning on neutral vessels and continued this so deliberately, especially as it had long been a routine procedure for humanitarian reasons. The British officers first thought that the Communists may have been too ignorant to recognize the foreign flags flying and pointed conspicuously on the hulls and the white flags which were promptly hoisted. They had probably received orders to prepare for a crossing already actually in process, unfortunately at the very point where the *Amethyst* was first disabled. They brazenly defended their conduct by charging that these British warships were helping their enemies and had fired the first shots.

Indefensible and callous as this was in not even permitting

the rescue of dead and wounded seamen, yet I could sense an undertone of national pride among other Chinese in this achievement. Commercial and naval ships of foreign countries, principally British, had long sailed up and down this mighty river at their own unbridled will, but now at last they had been bravely challenged and routed. From the broader standpoint it was lucky after all that it was the British rather than American Navy in view of the way we had been singled out for Communist vituperation. Incidentally their land battery marksmanship was excellent.

14

The next afternoon Roger Lapham was arriving in Shanghai from Washington where he had been arguing before Congress regarding the unspent balance of E.C.A. amounting to some $54,000,000. It had seemed to him and me and to our respective associates that from the standpoint of American national interest this could be most usefully employed to stabilize the currency and enable the government to pay its troops on the Yangtze frontier in silver, rather than to carry on relief or reconstruction projects. At the best it would meet only a fraction of the need, and at the worst would be wasted in the war or supply unwanted assistance to the Communists. Roger had brought back with him Mrs. Lapham and the wife of his colleague, Allen Griffin, both of whom had returned with him to the States for safety. The movements of these ladies will illustrate the uncertainties and shifting opinions of this period. I wanted both men to come from Shanghai on Friday with two others directly concerned in order to learn what had happened in Washington and see what, if anything, could be done to help the distracted Chinese officials avoid a fiscal and military collapse while still attempting to protect the Yangtze frontier. They telephoned that they would all come together on one of our Embassy airplanes, returning the next day, and that the two ladies would accompany them.

The two delightful ladies had often come with their husbands on previous trips, but I called back that I was very dubious about the advisability of their doing so this time and that it would be safer if the men could come in the morning prepared to return the same afternoon. Premier Ho Ying-ch'in had invited the group to dinner that evening and had wanted to have a private chat with Roger and me before the others were due, but had telephoned early that morning cancelling the invitation. These details will help to make graphic some of the incongruities of life in China at that time. We who lived in China long recurrently faced the inevitable catastrophe which somehow did not happen; we grew callous to the ghastly welter of human misery around us; we were not surprised at the inverted sense of values as when, with victorious enemies actually crossing the River, the Premier—concurrently Commander in Chief of all armed forces—planned to entertain foreign guests, instinctively maintaining these social courtesies but not without the fatuous hope that American dollars might miraculously halt the advancing foe.

If the government intended to continue its military resistance the Yangtze was the natural barrier. As one of the highly competent younger men in the Ministry of National Defense had described it to me, it was worth 3,000,000 soldiers. He and others of his kind were endorsed by my military and naval attachés in the opinion that with the co-ordination of ground, naval and air forces and unified command in their Ministry, together with payment of the troops in silver and decent care of them, they could have at least held the river for several months and quite possibly have led the Communists to change their overall policy.

The whole Kuomintang military system was at last revealing with stark realism the shocking consequence of its disregard of its soldiers. They had always been shamelessly neglected alike as to physical needs or comforts and indoctrination as to why they were fighting. This had been the traditional treatment of soldiers. During the Japanese war every private had his own reasons for resisting the foreign invaders. Even then the graft among their officers had been rampant. This continued as the national resources became depleted and the outlook desperate. After having done my best to devise ways in which we could divert unspent E.C.A. funds to help pay the troops, it was sickening to learn from Paul Parker, our competent young treasury representative, that for several months the top ranking generals had been holding 30,000,000 silver dollars. They remonstrated with a wry grimace, when questioned, that some of it had actually gotten to the private soldiers at last. It was easy to understand why they had no will to fight. But the mere instinct for survival might have been expected to cause the civil and military authorities to correct such abuses.

After the Lapham party had left on that eventful Friday afternoon, we had a meeting of our whole Diplomatic Body to discuss again whether we should follow the government to Canton. The government's representatives were getting away as fast as they could, and several of them had asked that we do the same. But the opinion of our government was the same as before. However, the next afternon I received instructions to return to Washington for consultation. Subsequent exchange of messages made it clear that this need not be at once and would not be until I had received more specific orders or—if communications were severed—I myself felt it advisable. I wanted very much to stay long enough to observe Communist intentions and to give them the opportunity to discuss relationships with the United States. If they were unwilling to do this with me, it would be quite clear that they were averse to doing so with any American official, and we could form our policy accordingly. I was also very anxious to have all the diplomats continue to act together, and I asked for another meeting of the North Atlantic Group for the following Monday. They all strongly

Mr. Chou En-lai, Chinese Communist leader (now Premier and
Foreign Minister) conferring with Ambassador Stuart in the
American Embassy grounds, 1946.

Ambassador Stuart in a sedan-chair ascending Kuling, summer
resort, 1946, for a conference with Generalissimo Chiang
Kai-shek

shared my sentiments and messages to this effect were sent to all the capitals represented, including Washington.

15

The National Government officials remaining in the capital all hurriedly departed on Saturday morning, the police disappeared, and there was no control. As always, looting began and soon became more unrestrained. The night was one of horror with shooting, robbing and fear of the unknown. All except six of our marines had been flown to Shanghai to avoid misunderstanding with the Communists. Several of the Embassy young men patrolled in turn the compound in which I lived.

Early Sunday morning, April 24, the Communist vanguards entered the city. There was a marked contrast between the Communist efficiency in crossing the river and in quietly taking over the capital, their disciplined behavior and high morale, and the apathetic appearance and disorderly conduct of the government troops. The people were unresponsive to their latest conquerors but fearful of offending them.

In a previous paragraph I described my disappointment over the failure of the Communists in their hour of triumph to be more generously tolerant, or—more correctly perhaps—over the convincing evidence of their inflexible adherence to the party line. I was no less disappointed in the incapacity of the Kuomintang to arouse itself in its extremity to a spirited resistance. I felt an agonized sympathy for the many capable and patriotic young men and women, who had done their best in National service against frightful odds, and for the helpless masses than whom there are none kindlier nor more tractable, more deserving of decent government.

We Americans mainly saw the good things about the Chinese Communists, while not noticing carefully the intolerance, bigotry, deception, disregard for human life and other evils which seem to be inherent in any totalitarian system. We kept

Communist meanings for such objectives as progressive, democratic, liberal, also bourgeois, reactionary, imperialist, as they intended we should do. We failed to realize fully the achievements to date and the potentialities of Chinese democracy. Therefore, we cannot escape a part of the responsibility of the great catastrophe—not only for China but also for America and the free world—the loss of the Chinese mainland.

12 Behind the Bamboo Curtain

This began for me with literally a rude awakening. The Communist troops had been crossing the river with virtually no opposition, and they entered the city early Sunday morning, April 24, the last Nationalist officials having flown out just in time. The next morning shortly after half-past six o'clock I was aroused by hearing my bedroom door opened, and I saw several armed soldiers entering. I shouted at them asking what they were doing, and they withdrew, one or two muttering angrily. I jumped out of bed to see what it was all about when the whole group, some ten or twelve, returned and the spokesman quite politely explained that they were only looking around for fun and meant no harm, asking me if I understood. When I said yes, he repeated his assurance and finding me none too cordial led the others out.

Meanwhile, Ed Anderberg, a young Embassy attaché who was serving as my household manager, had also been awakened and rushed over to rescue me. He was roughly forced back into his room. The frightened servants had also appeared and ushered the visitors out.

In itself the incident had a very simple explanation. The soldiers were nothing more than country boys impressed into service and carefully indoctrinated. They had come with an easy victory to the great capital and were out seeing the sights. When they arrived at my front gate the terrified gateman on night duty lost his head and instead of reporting to the house as was the rule yielded to the threats and admitted the intruders. The same thing happened in the kitchen. Still less did these rustics know anything about diplomatic immunity. They had been dosed with unassimilated notions as shown in the comment one of them made to a servant to the effect that all of this belonged to the people of China anyhow and would soon be coming back to them.

But the State Department took it very seriously and instructed me to make an emphatic protest both in Peiping and in Nanking. This incidentally was not easy to do since there were no diplomatic relations, and the higher Communist officials were entirely inaccessible. Word reached us indirectly, however, that the authorities in both cities were very much annoyed and mortified over the occurrence. This was also borne out by the lack of any reference to it in their publicity which as a rule unscrupulously denounces the other side as the best defense. It was apparently widely publicized in the States because for several days I had to listen to references to it over the radio. We learned later that the culprits had been traced and placed in custody for a period of further education. Similar intrusions took place at the British and the French Embassies.

2

By a curious circumstance on the day before the turnover a summons came to me from the Department to return to Washington. This would have been the normal procedure since there was no longer any recognized government in Nanking and my counselor, Lewis Clark, was representing the Embassy, with the rank of Minister, in Canton. But the Diplomatic Body, especially those accredited from nations in the North Atlantic Pact, had all agreed both that we would recommend to our respective governments that we ourselves not be ordered to follow the Chinese Government to Canton and that we ask to be permitted to remain in Nanking for an indefinite period after the Communists had established themselves there. The Department authorized me to remain until I was satisfied that our consulates

and our nationals in Communist-controlled areas were satisfactorily cared for.

On receiving these instructions I promptly asked for a meeting
of the representatives of the North Atlantic Pact nations, which
was held as usual at the French Ambassador's home, he being
doyen of the Corps *Diplomatique,* on the afternoon of the day
of the intrusion into my bedroom. The news had spread and they
were all at once amused, sympathetic and worried. No one knew
to what lengths the Communist scorn for all non-Soviet countries might extend, nor to what unwarranted behavior the
ignorance of those in the lower echelons might lead them. There
had already been a few minor incidents. As to the primary purpose of the meeting, it was already too late for any of us to get
away. National Government officials had urged us to do so,
especially me. Their attitude and that of my colleagues was a
fresh reminder of the new position of the United States in the
world. But we were all trapped now in Nanking at least until
the "liberation" of Shanghai, followed by restored communications with that city.

None of us was interfered with as we went to or from that
meeting. But for the days following all foreigners were more or
less prevented from leaving their homes. This was said to be
purely precautionary. The Communists were particularly concerned about me, so I made no attempt to leave my residence.
The State Department raised questions about my freedom of
movement but I preferred not to force the issue. It reminded me
faintly of my sequestration by the Japanese. One of the Embassy staff kept me informed as to radio messages and what
other business there was. After a week or so these restrictions
were removed. But my normal routine had suddenly ceased.
There were almost no appointments or social functions. All mail
had been stopped, except an occasional letter from Peiping
which took two weeks or more in transit. The local Chinese
papers were immediately metamorphosed into party propagandist

organs with almost no general news and with what there was slanted to the party line. Very fortunately we were allowed to continue our Embassy radio network and to listen to current broadcasts.

3

Meanwhile an internal conflict of which I had long been conscious was becoming more acute. This was in my personal sentiments regarding the two parties. In the Kuomintang were many friends of long standing, for not a few of whom as individuals I had hearty admiration. I knew them to be men of integrity and public spirit as well as with trained intelligence. And yet this party almost from the time it came into power had tolerated among its officials of all grades graft and greed, idleness and inefficiency, nepotism and factional rivalries—all the evils in short of the corrupt bureaucracy it had overthrown. These evils had become more pronounced after V-J Day in the attempts to crush communism by a combination of military strength and secret police. The government had been steadily losing popular support and even respect. As the Communist forces advanced in a victorious march toward the Yangtze River, the grandiose plans for defense crumbled amid political bickering, desertions or betrayals, disorderly retreats. Yet this was the government which had been benefiting from substantial American aid in many forms, and in whose principles and aims, as sincerely formulated and as expressed in numerous individual lives, we thoroughly believed.

In painful contrast the Communist party was free from private graft, officers and men lived very much together, simply and industriously, severely disciplined, thoroughly indoctrinated. All of this was evident as they came into Nanking. There was almost no mistreatment of the populace. They borrowed extensively but generally returned these articles or made restitution. Their broadcasts boasted of the smooth efficiency of their long southward march, the supplies and attendants sent long in advance by stages, the arrangements for transport and shelter, etc. They had in short perfected their own logistics. Their morale was excellent. The daily drills and lectures went on all around our Embassy property so we had visual and almost too much audible proof of it. The Communist party was thus giving the appearance of being a dynamic movement fostering among millions those qualities of which China had stood so palpably in need, qualities which Christian missions and other cultural forces had been slowly inculcating among so pitifully few. These gains included capacity for organization, strict but largely voluntary discipline, putting the cause above all personal or family considerations, unselfish service to the underprivileged, the enthusiastic loyalty of idealistic youth. This was no mean achievement, especially in the perspective of Kuomintang shortcomings.

Unfortunately, there was another side less apparent to disillusioned youth and to a populace so afflicted by misrule and the economic hardships of civil strife that any change seemed preferable to them. The Communist party had all of the harsh intolerance inherent in the orthodox Marxian-Leninist tradition, all of its repressive techniques for absolute control of thought and action, all of its callous disregard for individual human rights and for principles or beliefs other than its own. I shuddered to think of the inescapable consequences to the Christian movement which had been exerting an influence for good in China's national life far in excess of its numbers, to educational institutions like Yenching and to all of the fruitful cultural relations which had obtained with my own and other democratic countries.

My sympathies went out most of all to the large numbers of younger men and women who if they were in the Kuomintang at all were there because it seemed to stand for what they wanted for their country and who had no other outlet for their patriotic urge or their own self-expression which they could endorse, who had striven to bring about the reforms or accomplish the objectives desired by public-spirited citizens. There were many others like them, belonging to some minor party, or to none, who shared in the shattering of eager hopes and in all of the physical and economic sufferings, the disruption of family and social life, the misfortunes of fugitives seeking a sheltered haven. Not only were they miserable in body and spirit, but China was losing one of her greatest assets in the constructive services such people should be rendering.

The spiritual consequences to me were not so very different. What I had feared most in American policy had happened. As described in the account of my last conversation with General Marshall before his departure from China, I had felt that we should then have either given sufficient aid to the National Government together with the requisite advice and controls in order to enable it to defeat the Communists, or we should have withdrawn completely from all intervention in Chinese affairs; that either would have been better than a hesitating, half-hearted form of continuing assistance. I had long been observing the unfortunate results of this third course and had myself become a helpless target for the vicious anti-American denunciation this had provoked. But with the Communist triumphs, all of this became much more pronounced.

The most bitter invectives were against the $125,000,000 voted by Congress in the spring of 1948 for the Chinese Government to use in any way it wished. The government had at once allocated the entire amount for military, naval and air force supplies. Either because of intentional delays by American officials or priorities in placing orders with manufacturers this materiel was extremely slow in delivery. We thus became targets of criticism for all classes of Chinese. The National Government blamed us because it was "too little and too late." The*General-issimo and later on Li Tsung-jen had repeatedly urged me to speed up the shipments and increase the quantities. The Communists were embittered and in their virulent diatribes exaggerated the amount of our aid to their enemies. Actually they benefited greatly from captured booty or the equipment of the constantly deserting Kuomintang soldiers, and their taunts to this effect had a sting. On the other hand, the Kuomintang air raids on towns taken by the Communists and the faulty marksmanship led to pathetic civilian casualties which the Communist party cleverly utilized by pointing out that they were caused by bombs from American planes manned by American-trained pilots.

Even the E.C.A. grant of $275,000,000 was of doubtful value. In this connection there could be nothing but praise for the work of Roger Lapham and his staff whose energy, efficiency and nobility of spirit were in the best American tradition. While it brought some humanitarian relief, yet from the standpoint of American national interests this had to be estimated against the political ill will it helped to aggravate. Furthermore, the economic misery of the Chinese masses had become so vast that this amelioration was relatively slight and of brief duration.

The item for rural reconstruction was a partial exception to these strictures. It had been my own special enthusiasm. But for various reasons it was about two years after the idea had been first conceived before it began to function properly. With the southern and threatened western advance of the Communists the earliest results would soon be in areas under their control and thus violate the intention of Congress. In the face of the volume of Communist organization and experience this project appeared rather small-scale and amateurish. And yet it had sprung from the finest ideals and was in charge of a commission of three Chinese and two Americans than whom none could have been found more hard-working and highly qualified. Perhaps a somewhat cynical moral might be drawn about the futility of mixing philanthropy with politics.

There was an ironic humor in my own predicament. Having

been regarded as an exponent of American liberalism and friendly good will for the Chinese nation, I was now maligned as the official representative of "the imperialistic American Government and its chief agent for aiding and abetting the reactionary and hopelessly feudalistic regime of Chiang Kai-shek." Yenching graduates in all walks of life were grieved that I had not continued as University President. There was a measure of warrant in much of this. But the first lesson I had learned as a diplomat—and one of the hardest—was not to talk too much. I could only hope that before the end it would somehow be made clear that I had consistently remained the same sort of person throughout.

It was ironical also that the Chinese Communist party with its crassly materialistic dialectics was producing some spiritual values. Its success was in large part due to the differential between the spirit of unselfish devotion to a cause which it managed to engender and the woeful lack of this among some Kuomintang members. It was sobering to reflect that Christian influence had penetrated Kuomintang circles much deeper and that Christian sympathies were almost entirely on that side. I had often speculated as to whether the moral and social fervor of the Communists could be preserved without the bigotry of the dogmas of the necessity of world revolution by violence and of overthrowing the governments of capitalist nations by surreptitious or armed aggression, without the motivation of hate, the reliance on rigidly controlled propaganda, and all the evils of a police state. As long as its socialized program was vitiated by these, there could be no hope for the two things for which I cared most; the Christian movement in China and mutually beneficial Chinese-American relationships. Any appearances or adjustments to the contrary could only be temporary and tactical. What then should the new American policy be if it was not to be merely negative?

4

It happened that shortly after the Communist party had taken over in Nanking, Huang Hua was sent there to assume control of its Bureau of Foreign Affairs. Wang Ju-mei had been one of the earliest of Yenching graduates to join the Communist party and had promptly changed his name—as was commonly done in such cases—to Huang Hua. He had been active in the "Executive Headquarters" set up in Peiping by General Marshall as one feature of the General's mission. I saw him there at that time and found him both friendly to me personally and thoroughly communized. In view of his position, the Communist anti-American line and their repeated assertions that all diplomatic officials were to them merely private citizens, I wondered what his attitude to me would be.

A few days after he had taken office he telephoned Philip Fugh for an appointment and spent about an hour with him in very cordial conversation. In departing he suggested that Huang call on his old President. Huang replied that it could of course only be on that basis, but he would consult with others and would let Philip know. A few days later he called and spent nearly two hours in his usual friendly manner. Since the Communist party had been making such a point of not recognizing "imperialistic" countries too closely allied with the Kuomintang, I took the cue of being an ordinary American citizen following the lead of the representative of the *de facto* regional authority. He soon broached this question (of "recognition"), which gave me an opportunity to explain first that foreign countries could not do otherwise than continue to recognize the existent National Government as the Communist party itself had done; that when there emerged a new government which obviously had the support or at least the acceptance of the Chinese people, and gave evidence of its willingness and ability to maintain relations with other nations according to international standards, then the matter

would naturally be discussed; but that until then we outsiders
could only passively wait. In other words, it was they rather than
the foreign countries who were on trial. He had undoubtedly both
secured approval for this visit from Peiping and reported back
what transpired.

The interest of this episode lies in the way it illustrates what
must be done in countless contacts if there is to be any mutual
penetration of the barrier separating two violently antagonistic
ideologies, each claiming to be a democratic and liberating force
while regarding the other as hostile and aggressive. Even though
these opinions have been created among their followers by Communist indoctrination, the resulting state of mind is none the less a
factor with which we of the contrary way of life must reckon.
Huang Hua was an example of this as well as of the substratum
of normal human sentiments which are fortunately just as real.

5

Nanking having fallen quickly to the Communists, they were
virtually compelled to follow on at once to Shanghai. They were
well aware of course of the international, economic, administrative and other problems focusing in that swollen Eurasian
metropolis. It is quite possible that they would have preferred to
by-pass it until they could arrange a peaceful transfer. But the
Generalissimo had ordered the withdrawal from the Yangtze and
resistance at Shanghai. So his subordinates improvised measures
for defense of the Shanghai area. The physical efforts were
fatuously conceived and wastefully executed. But the treatment
of Shanghai residents and its psychological consequences were
even worse. Secret service agents hounded down persons suspected of leftist leanings. Prominent citizens thought of as ready
to negotiate with the Communists for a peaceful turnover were
forced to withdraw to Hongkong or fled there for safety. Special
"contributions" for defense measures were extracted from all
according to ability to pay, and this became a form of private

extortion as well. Vessels and vehicles were commandeered. A "scorched earth" policy—which had been marvelously effective against the Japanese and cheerfully agreed to by the public—merely increased a now sullen resentment. Houses were razed, trees cut down, thoroughfares barricaded, posters and parades enforced in order to win popular support. Silver dollars were paid and movie tickets and other special privileges were given or promised to the soldiers for the same purpose. Communist agents were meanwhile active underground. The Generalissimo's hold upon his followers was, however, strong enough to galvanize the defense forces into some measure of co-ordination and to inspire in them more of the will to fight than had been shown in previous battles where it would have been worth-while. Within a few weeks, however, the Communists were able to claim Shanghai.

6

My diplomatic colleagues, stranded in Nanking, ignored by the new authorities, confined within the city walls for alleged precautionary reasons, most of them prevented even from communicating in code with their home governments, were getting very bored and restive. We and the British had our own radio equipment, as did the French to a more limited extent. But cipher messages were not permitted over commercial lines, on the understandable ground of military necessity. This illustrates one of the many anomalies of the situation. The authorities never missed a chance to remind us that to them we were merely private citizens of our respective countries. Yet they allowed some of us to function as usual. When the chiefs of the smaller missions came to me for news or advice, as I liked them to feel free to do, it was brought home to me how completely isolated they were both as to news and contact with Chinese affairs. With some of them this was also true of social life and recreation, more especially and quite ironically the Asiatic countries. For myself,

I was in no sense busy but never lacked for something to do. The mere reading of and dealing with the daily messages took some time. The American Embassy was a big and friendly family, which with diplomatic intercourse, missionaries and a few Chinese, provided ample social diversion. There was always what Longfellow described as "the sweet serenity of books." But the combination of representing the American Government and of having lived so long in China meant that even in this period of voluntary sequestration I was constantly in touch with the situation.

7

I wanted to see Shanghai under the new control and especially to confer with American nationals. For some days after the take-over the railways and other means of communication would naturally be in confusion. Allowing enough time for this, I asked Huang Hua to indicate the procedure necessary for me to visit Shanghai. He again commented that I was now only a private American national but that it would be, of course, "a special case." Having put me in my proper place, he took over all the arrangements for my Embassy escort, Philip and myself, and one of the Embassy staff and three of Huang Hua's special service men. We were met in Shanghai by his agents, and wherever I went I was accompanied by two carloads of these plain-clothes guards. The reason seemed to be their fear that Kuomintang agents, whom they believed to be still swarming in the city, would embarrass their new authority by doing something sensational to me. The consequence was that instead of moving around freely as usual, I stayed in the Consul General's residence, refusing social invitations and expecting people to visit me. I would not only have felt conspicuous but might have attracted the unwelcomed attention of secret service agents to the people visited, especially Chinese. The impression of Shanghai during these first days of Communist rule was that they had taken control with vigor, competence and incorruptibility, but that their propaganda against American imperialism and on behalf of the less privileged masses would provoke labor disturbances that might become very serious, and that their combination of both nationalistic and Marxist fanaticism clashing against the economic structure of this cosmopolitan city and the practical exigencies of keeping five million people fed and protected would make of Shanghai a very significant experimental laboratory.

My diplomatic colleagues were all anxious to observe how I fared, for several of them were planning to follow me. I had determined, therefore, to make an issue of the internationally accorded rights of diplomatic immunity in such matters as not having baggage searched. The Communist official position was that we had no such rights, being only ordinary citizens, so this might well be a test of conflicting principles. Fortunately the issue did not arise. But my special pass described me as "Formerly American Ambassador" which amused me and others to whom I showed it, although one of my European colleagues became furious when a similar designation was applied to him.

While in Shanghai I had an illustration of a characteristic difference between the British and the American approaches to Chinese issues as well as perhaps their changing relative status. There were two foreign-owned English-language newspapers in Shanghai which survived the Communist "liberation" and which were determined to carry on tentatively under the new regime, the *North China Daily News* (British) and the *Shanghai Evening Post* (American). The name of the former perpetuates the record of the British advance northward from Canton and Hongkong to a city which in that pioneering stage seemed to them to be in the far North. My father subscribed to it when my brothers and I were little boys in Hangchow. It had then the subtitle *And Supreme Court and Consular Gazette*, the whole sonorous phrase instilling into my childish mind an increased awe for the wonders of that already imposing outpost of Empire.

The *Daily News* had long occupied one of the buildings in the line of those belonging to official or semipublic British enterprises facing the Bund or waterfront, and in more recent years had been irreverently dubbed "The Old Lady of the Bund" because of its typically British editorial restraint.

While I was on this trip, it had inadvertently publicized a rumor about mines laid by the Nationalist Navy in the Yangtze estuary, thus endangering the approach to the port of Shanghai. The immediate result was that all shipping was paralyzed and that fears became rife in a city dependent for its very existence upon this approach. The new authorities, skilled in military and ideological conflict, were entirely inexperienced in coping with this type of problem, and for over a week nothing was done. Finally with British guidance two improvised mine-sweepers cleared the channel and restored public confidence. The incident had been due either to a hoax or a chance remark. But a scapegoat had to be found and the Chinese-Communist-controlled press blamed it all on the *North China Daily News* with a vituperative fury, which was in part the standard Communist technique and in part a vent for long festering anti-foreign grievances or jealousies. How would the organ for decades of unassailable British semicolonial domination take this affront? It published on its front page a letter in English, with a translation of it in Chinese, addressed to the Military Control Commission, expressing its sincere and humble apologies for its fault in causing harm to the city by spreading an unverified report. Making full allowance for the ability of the Chinese to stop the publication of the paper and for the enormous British investments in Shanghai, this action revealed certain qualities which are helping the British people to adjust themselves to the shrinking of their former grandeur. The paper had at least a reprieve during changing conditions.

Meanwhile, the editor of the American daily, Randall Gould, had a telephone call from his business manager that he was then locked up on their premises by the employees who were demanding a wage increase. This had become a by no means uncommon experience for Chinese as well as foreign employers, due of course to the radical propaganda of the latest conquerors. Gould, with a fine sense of his duty to his American colleague and to the newspaper, went at once to the office, knowing that he would share the same fate. The argument continued until trade union delegates came and advised a more reasonable settlement. Curiously when the Americans proposed that the matter be referred to the municipal authorities all the Chinese objected. Toward midnight an agreement was reached. But when the typesetters discovered that a purely factual narrative of the occurrence had been prepared by the editor for the next issue they went on strike again. To Gould this was an interference with editorial prerogatives which could not be tolerated and he preferred to close down the enterprise rather than make any such concession. But to even these humble Chinese operatives it was a public loss of face. Whether the new authorities would later on have made it unendurable to maintain as free and frank, even though essentially friendly, a newspaper such as this one had always been was at least an easy possibility in the light of the usual Communist practice. But Gould's decision was as unalterably American as that of his contemporary was realistically British.

The harm done to Shanghai by the mere rumor that its Yangtze estuary had been mined may have led the defeated Nationalist leaders to announce the closure of all Communist-held ports. They sedulously avoided the use of the word "blockade" and were too desperate to pay serious attention to British and American protests of its illegality. But it had the desired effect of still further strangling the economic arteries of the city's life.

The incidents involving British, American and other foreigners in Shanghai became exceedingly troublesome. These were usually provoked by the general labor unrest, sometimes by an inadvertent violation of new regulations. The sudden insistence on the use of the Chinese language only in what began as a foreign settlement where English had been almost indispensable was disconcerting to what remained of the foreign population. The victims were subject to rough manhandling and abusive tirades which were insulting and humiliating in the extreme. They were forced to sign statements and make apologies which were gloatingly published in the local press together with obscene distortions of the facts. All this may be regarded as a bit of sociological case-study. The British chiefly had affected an attitude of contemptuous racial superiority, quite in the Kipling tradition, toward Chinese people and their civilization. The "Shanghai mind" had become notorious. With the rapid growth of the port and of Chinese nationalism, this treatment was increasingly, though from necessity silently, resented. Although modified by the Japanese occupation and by the transfer of municipal authority to China following V-J Day, yet the old atmosphere lingered and the sullen animosities festered. During this last period, the Kuomintang had been so anxious for American aid that instructions from the top had resulted in Americans having preferential treatment which many of them innocently took for granted and in the process gave additional cause for the smoldering sense of racial discrimination.

In addition to all this was the unceasing Communist anti-foreign, notably anti-American, propaganda, describing us all as grasping imperialists. The foreigners who had stayed on in Shanghai rather than respond to arrangements for evacuation had done so in the main because of their friendly feelings for the Chinese and with a full realization of the disagreeable or even dangerous possibilities. But they were the luckless victims of the cumulative effects of past hatreds and of the recent Communist indoctrination which had released a new nationalistic spirit of self-assertion feeding upon the old animosities.

8

Toward the end of June I began to plan seriously for my departure. There were several unsettled issues such as the withdrawal of our consular staff from Mukden. I was waiting for the return from Peiping of a leading spirit of the Kuomintang party who was anxious to co-operate with the Communist party on a liberal and international program. He had been urged by Mao Tse-tung and his associates to visit Peiping, and I believed that he would give me reliable first-hand information as to their intentions. In order to ensure ample time for his arrival under uncertain conditions of travel, July 18 was fixed as my target date. The waiting airplane had been repaired and had shown up satisfactorily in a test flight. Permission for this was clear evidence of the willingness of the Communists to facilitate my departure. But there had already been ominous hints of trouble. The local Bureau of Public Safety (police) had prepared exit-permit blanks which included at the end a "shop guarantee" in the event of the person concerned leaving with unpaid debts or unsettled legal claims. Thus began a conflict in ideas over an issue trivial enough in itself but which had all the appearance of becoming irreconcilable. The Communists had arbitrarily determined to treat all foreign diplomatic personnel merely as citizens of their respective countries. They had intended that these exit-permit blanks should apply alike to all foreigners, not having thought—or perhaps known—of the right of diplomatic personnel to leave a country with the usual immunities. But having issued such regulations it would be not only a loss of face to back down but also an acknowledgment of error by a fanatical system that maintains its morale partly by unquestioning belief in its own dogmas.

The State Department took, however, an extremely serious view of the matter on grounds of principle, prestige and precedent. Huang Hua and Chang Han-fu kept in contact with their superiors in Peiping and tried to influence their local associates. Huang Hua being always on guard of course against seeming to sacrifice party interests for sentimental attachment to his former University President. He secured a number of important concessions. I was exempted from the objectionable "guarantee" and from baggage inspection. I could take the three-month accumulation of highly confidential official documents as well as personal mail for the whole staff without any search. He felt that the original permission to leave China in an Embassy airplane was also quite exceptional. It was here when they took over, and as long as the coastal blockade lasted, it was my only method of egress.

There were four members of the crew including my Air Attaché, Colonel John Dunning, and his copilot. The other passengers were Mr. John M. Cabot, Consul General at Shanghai, Mr. Henry Hinderer of the Embassy staff, Mr. and Mrs. William Olive and Mr. Philip Fugh, all of whom were leaving on medical advice. Mr. Olive had been subjected to physical violence by the Shanghai police and had been ordered home for that reason and its psychological consequences. We had tentatively explored the possibilities of securing guarantees from two Chinese private banks and one or two other firms, only to learn that they would not dare to take the risk in view of their distrust of Communist methods. On reporting this, we were told that an American firm would be satisfactory, although it would have been ridiculous from our standpoint to have any of our citizens guaranteeing their own foreign service officers. The Department had given instructions that no American in the party was to accept any guarantor, not even that of the Embassy itself. So the days slipped by in the Nanking summer heat and in maddening suspense. It was mortifying to meet one's diplomatic colleagues and other friends or to turn up once more at church or some other gathering, when I was supposed to be speeding homeward through the air.

To complicate matters further, the Department had decided to issue a "White Paper" reviewing the whole story of its recent China policy as a reply to its critics in Congress and elsewhere. This was evidently going to be very critical of both the National Government and the Communists, for the Department wanted to have me safely out of China before its release. This release was to have been on July 23, which seemed at first to give me ample leeway, but printing delays led to a postponement till August 2. As the exchanges between Washington and me or between Huang Hua and Peiping dragged slowly on, it seemed as though even this accidental reprieve would not save me from whatever it was that the Department feared from its publication. My own concern was that this might anger the Communists and upset the delicate negotiations for my departure.

While impatiently waiting for action in my own case, the trends in Communist policy led me to recommend to the Department that plans be made to evacuate Americans from Communist-controlled areas, especially Shanghai. The anti-American propaganda was becoming more vitriolic, the allegiance to the Soviet Union more frank, the discrimination against foreign and indeed all private business more flagrant, the techniques of police-state repression and of state-operated trade more true to form. Missionaries who had not already left China were in general ready to face the unknown in the spirit which had originally led them to this career and with the hope that the very fact of staying on under unpromising conditions might itself be an effective form of witness-bearing. But for businessmen the outlook was bleak indeed, unrelieved by any idealistic aims. There was also a difference between the circumstances of American and British merchants. Many of the latter had invested all that they possessed in Shanghai and other China ports and would be ruined by withdrawal. It was also of far greater importance to the British nation to retain what was possible of this lucrative trade. Fortunately our own trade with China was only two or three percent of the total volume of U. S. foreign exports and imports. Americans, even those most seriously harmed by abandonment of their China interests, could probably start business again elsewhere without excessive hardships.

Underlying such considerations was the bluntly stated Communist sentiment that foreigners should let China alone. This was primarily political resentment against our annoying aid to their opponents. But there was more than a modicum of truth in what Huang Hua said to me to the effect that any peasant or merchant or student would agree with his comrades and himself in the hope that we quit intruding into Chinese affairs. There was, however, another side to all of this. Their leaders knew of all the material benefits China had received from us in the past and of their own desperate need of economic and industrial recovery in which neither the Soviet Union nor any other nation could be of adequate assistance. But there could be no deviation from their doctrinaire orthodoxy despite these practical exigencies.

After what must have involved spirited discussions, the Communists finally agreed to allow the other members of my party to have the Embassy sign the required guarantee. This was done with great reluctance, and I was instructed to lodge a vigorous protest setting forth in detail how rudely their regulations contravened all hitherto universally accepted international diplomatic courtesies. Since they were brusquely unyielding in not recognizing our official status they consistently refused to receive the protests we were repeatedly instructed to present because of recurrent issues affecting ourselves or our nationals. In this again Huang Hua relaxed his other loyalties sufficiently to let me say as to a former student what he could not listen to from the American Ambassador. *Apropos* of this rather silly attitude, my Canadian colleague enjoyed telling the story that when he arrived in Shanghai shortly after I had made that trip and his escort remonstrated over a certain requirement which had not been demanded of the American Ambassador, the retort was that no American Ambassador had come that way. When my name was mentioned the functionary blandly remarked that a well-known educator of that name had recently been seen.

It looked at last as though we were able to take off and the date was again fixed for August 1, exactly two weeks after the date earlier set and just before the scheduled appearance of the "White Paper."

13 To Washington and in Washington

I finally left Nanking, bound for the United States, in the older and smaller of the Embassy's two planes, on August 2, 1949. With me were Philip Fugh, John Cabot, Mr. and Mrs. Olive, and Henry Hinderer; the plane had a crew of three and was piloted by Colonel John Dunning, Air Attaché of the Embassy. I did not know then, but was informed later that with this number of persons and a considerable amount of baggage the plane, none too airworthy at best, was overloaded. Whatever may have been the hazard, we were glad to be on our way. The last weeks in China had been weeks of discomfort, uncertainty, vexations, frustrations and even apprehension.

After an easy flight under a clear sky and over a calm sea we reached Okinawa where we were cordially greeted and well looked after by the United States military personnel. The next day we were transferred to the larger Embassy plane, a new and well-equipped B-27 that had been sent to China for use of the Ambassador. Before leaving Okinawa I had the pleasure of a good swim in the surf.

The B-27, with its ample accommodations and minimum of hazard, was ours for the remainder of the flight. On it we reached Guam. There again we received a cordial and efficient welcome, and I enjoyed another swim—from a beautiful beach.

We arrived at the Honolulu airport at two o'clock on the morning of August 5. At that early hour we were greeted by Admiral and Mrs. Stuart S. Murray and their charming daughter Suzanne. Throughout two delightful days I was the recipient of most gracious hospitality from the Murray family. A dinner was given in my honor by Admiral Radford, Commander in Chief of the Pacific Fleet, and Mrs. Radford; and I was welcomed at a reception by the Yenching Alumni Association of Honolulu. I found time to swim twice and revelled in the warm sunlight on one of Oahu's superb beaches.

When in Honolulu I received two copies of the "White Paper," the volume prepared and just released by the Department of State under the title, *United States Relations with China— with Special Reference to the Periods 1944-1949.*

We left Honolulu, exchanging *Alohas* with the Murrays and others on the evening of August 6, and arrived in San Francisco on the 7th. We were greeted by government officials and, among others, Dr. William B. Pettus, my old friend of Mobile childhood and long-time colleague in Peking and my cousin Warren McBryde. There I stayed overnight with Mr. and Mrs. McBryde. We then flew to Washington, landing at the airport there at four in the afternoon on the 10th. In the welcoming group were many friends—both American and Chinese, relatives, official associates, members of the press and photographers. I was especially glad to see my brother Warren and his wife Annie; Dean Rusk, Walton Butterworth, Philip Sprouse and officers who had been with me at Nanking, from the Department of State; Dr. Shaohwa Tan and others from the Chinese Embassy.

2

From the Washington airport I was whisked to the Department of State. In the course of my first conversation there, with Walton Butterworth, I was advised to avoid interviews, to receive no callers whom I had no good reason to see and, in fact, to keep under cover for a few days. It was even suggested that I might go away from Washington for ten days or two weeks. I was then driven, with Philip Fugh, to the Carleton Hotel.

Two days later I called on the Secretary of State, Dean Acheson, and on the third day, accompanied by Mr. Acheson, I had my first interview with President Truman. My first conversation in Washington with General Marshall took place some weeks later. On the personal side, I enjoyed the friendliness of these conversations, but the substance of what was imparted to me intensified the great misgivings regarding policy toward China to which my perusal of the White Paper had given rise.

3

On the plane, after Honolulu, I had had opportunity to examine the Department of State's volume on *United States Relations with China*. Since then I have had ample opportunity not only to study its contents but also to observe and reflect upon its character and to note its influence and some of its effects.

In that book there is presented—with some narrative and many documents or excerpts from documents—an account of relations past and contemporary between the United States and China, with special attention to conditions in China and to the United States' policy during the five years 1944-1949. The "White Paper" begins with a "Letter of Transmittal" dated "Department of State, Washington, July 30, 1949 (pp. III-XVII), signed by the Secretary of State, Dean Acheson. In this there is indication of the genesis of this "report" and the purposes to which it was to be put. The opening paragraph reads:

"The President: In accordance with your wish, I have had compiled a record of our relations with China, special emphasis being placed on the last five years. This record is being published and will therefore be available to the Congress and the people of the United States."

In the next paragraph it is stated: ". . . I instructed those charged with the compilation of this document to present a record which would reveal the salient facts which determined our policy toward China during this period and which reflect the execution of that policy. This is a frank record of a great country to which the United States has long been attached by ties of closest friendship. No available item has been omitted because it contains statements critical of our policy or might be the basis of future criticism."

In the third paragraph, after references to the traditionally friendly interest of the people and the Government of the United States in China, it is affirmed, with an expression of regret, that "respect for the truth in the compilation of this record makes it necessary to publish an account of facts which reveal the distressing situation in that country. I have not felt, however, that publication could be withheld for that reason."

"Two factors," the letter goes on to say, "have played a major role in shaping the destiny of modern China": one, the growth of population, "creating an unbearable pressure on the land"; the other, "the impact of the West and of Western ideas," which "played an important part in stimulating ferment and unrest."

There follow references to the Chinese revolution, to the Kuomintang and its principal leaders, to the Chinese Communist party, and to the break in 1927. Then: "To a large extent the history of the period between 1927 and 1937 can be written in terms of the struggle for power between the Kuomintang and the Chinese Communists, with the latter apparently fighting a losing battle. During this period the Kuomintang made considerable progress in its efforts to unify the country and to build up the nation's financial and economic strength. Somewhere during this decade, however, the Kuomintang began to lose the dynamism and revolutionary fervor which had created it, while in the Chinese Communists the fervor became fanaticism."

Neither in that account nor in what closely follows is there any mention of the coming to power of the Nationalists in 1928, of the setting up of the National Government of the Republic of China or of the world-wide recognition of that government as the government of China. The "civil conflict" or "strife" in China from 1927 to the present day is portrayed as simply a struggle between two political parties. There do, however, appear later in the narrative references to "the Government," "the Government and the Kuomintang," "the Government of China," and "the National Government."

Of the Japanese assault, begun in 1937, and its consequences: "The tragedy of these years of war was that physical and human devastation to a large extent destroyed the emerging middle class which historically has been the backbone and heart of liberalism and democracy."

There then comes an account of developments in China and of interpretation thereof by responsible United States officials in consequence of which "traditional concepts of [United States] policy had to be adapted to a new and unprecedented situation"; an account of General Hurley's mission; and accounts of the making of the Yalta Agreement and of matters related thereto, of the conclusion of the treaty signed between the National Government of China and the Soviet Union on August 14, 1945, and of American official advice before and American warning after that signing.

The subject of United States policy after the defeat of Japan is introduced with the statement: "When peace came, the United States was confronted with three possible courses in China: (1) it could have pulled out lock, stock and barrel; (2) it could have intervened militarily on a major scale to assist the Nationalists to destroy the Communists; (3) it could, while assisting the Nationalists to assert their authority over as much of China as possible, endeavor to avoid a civil war by working for a compromise between the two sides."

There follows an account of the reasoning which led to the adoption of the "third policy whereunder we faced the facts of the situation and attempted to assist in working out a *modus vivendi* which would avert civil war but nevertheless preserve and even increase the influence of the National Government."

Both General Hurley and, after him, General Marshall endeavored to effect the "working out" of "a *modus vivendi*," but,

"As the event proved, the first objective was unrealizable because neither side [neither the Government nor the Communist leaders] desired it to succeed . . . The second objective of assisting the National Government, however, we pursued vigorously from 1945 to 1949. The National Government was the recognized government of a friendly power. . . . By the time General Marshall left China at the beginning of 1947, the Nationalists were apparently at the very peak of their military successes and territorial expansion. The following year and a half revealed, however, that their seeming strength was illusory and that their victories were built on sand."

The next several paragraphs of the letter as printed deal further with the Marshall mission and then with the Wedemeyer mission. And then:

"The reasons for the failure of the Chinese National Government appear in some detail in the attached record. They do not stem from any inadequacy of American aid. Our military observers on the spot have reported that the Nationalist armies did not lose a single battle during the crucial year of 1948 through lack of arms and ammunition. The fact was that the decay which our observers had detected in Chungking early in the war had fatally sapped the powers of resistance of the Kuomintang. . . .

"The Nationalist armies did not have to be defeated; they disintegrated. . . .

"Fully recognizing that the heads of the Chinese Communist party were ideologically affiliated with Moscow, our Government nevertheless took the view, in the light of the existing balance of forces in China, that peace could be established only if certain conditions were met. The Kuomintang would have to set its own house in order and both sides would have to make concessions so that the Government of all China might become, in fact as well as in name, the Government of all China and so that all parties might function within the constitutional system of the Government.

"None of these conditions had been realized." Furthermore, the Nationalists disregarded General Marshall's military advice and invited the military disasters which accrued to them. Nevertheless, "The historic policy of the United States of friendship and aid toward the people of China was, however, maintained in both peace and war.

We gave "aid to Nationalist China in the form of grants and credits"; we "sold the Chinese Government large quantities of military and civilian war surplus property." Of the military supplies, a "large proportion" has "fallen into the hands of the Chinese Communists through the military ineptitude of the Nationalist leaders, their defections and surrenders, and the absence among their forces of the will to fight.

"A realistic appraisal of conditions in China, past and present, leads to the conclusion that the only alternative open to the United States was full-scale intervention in behalf of a Government which had lost the confidence of its own troops and its own people. Such intervention would have required the expenditure of even greater sums than have been fruitlessly spent thus far, the command of Nationalist armies by American officers, and the probable participation of American armed forces—land, sea and air—in the resulting war. Intervention of such a scope and magnitude would have been resented by the mass of the Chinese people, and would have been condemned by the American people.

"The heart of China is in Communist hands. The Communist leaders have . . . publicly announced their subservience to a foreign power, Russia, . . . In this case, . . . the foreign domination has been masked behind the façade of a vast crusading movement which apparently has seemed to many Chinese to be wholly indigenous and national. Under these circumstances, our aid has been unavailing.

"The unfortunate but inescapable fact is that the ominous result of the civil war in China was beyond the control of the government of the United States. Nothing that this country did or could have done within the reasonable limits of its capabilities could have changed that result; nothing that was left undone by this country has contributed to it.

"We continue to believe that, however tragic may be the immediate future of China and however ruthlessly a major portion of this people may be exploited by a party in the interest of a foreign imperialism, ultimately the profound civilization and the democratic individualism of China will reassert themselves and she will throw off the foreign yoke. I consider that we should encourage all developments in China which now and in the future work toward this end.

"Should the Communist regime lend itself to the aims of Soviet Russian Imperialism and attempt to engage in aggression against China's neighbors, we and the other members of the United Nations would be confronted by a situation violative of the principles of the United Nations Charter and threatening international security.

"Meanwhile our policy will continue to be based upon our own respect for the Charter, our friendship for China, and our traditional support for the Open Door and for China's independence and administrative and territorial integrity."

4

I have felt it worth-while to make this digest of the "Letter of Transmittal" a part of my story for the reason that the Letter serves as a key to the confused thinking of the Department of State as of August, 1949, regarding the history and the actualities of United States relations with China, and is indicative of the mold in which United States official policy regarding China was at the moment of my arrival in Washington (and for many months thereafter) being shaped. I had had, when first informed that my government intended to publish such a book, grave misgivings. I found, when I read the "Letter of Transmittal," confirmation of those misgivings and more than ample reason for astonishment.

I have since been told, and I have read repeatedly, that there is absolutely no precedent for the publishing by any government, while friendly diplomatic relations still prevailed, of a portrayal of another country and its government so adversely critical as that which the Government of the United States made, in this summary, of China and its National Government.

My astonishment increased as I became acquainted with the contents of the report. I found a seventeen-page table of contents, a five-page chronology of principal events, a 409-page narrative and a 641-page exhibit of annexes. The narrative and the annexes were of course the *corpus* of the book. The narrative gave an *ex-parte* account, fortified by extensive introduction of documents or excerpts therefrom or paraphrases of United States-Chinese relations from 1844 to June 1949. All of this was, of course, of interest to me from many points of view. However, the part which held my attention most compellingly was "Chapter VI, The Ambassadorship of John Leighton Stuart, 1947-1949." Although I had been appointed Ambassador on July 11, 1946, events during and immediately following General Marshall's mission were dealt with in the preceding chapter, V, "The Mission of General George C. Marshall." In the eighty pages of Chapter VI the story was carried on from January 15, 1947, to June 2, 1949.

All through the book, there were quotations of or from documents which I had always understood were of "top secret" character. In Chapters V and VI and in the annexes thereto—the latter filling some 333 pages—I found quotations of dispatches or parts of dispatches from the Embassy in China in which the reporting of confidential conversations, of information which had been given in confidence, and of the Embassy's own interpretations, proposals and suggestions were thus made known to the world.

A delegation of Kuling Elementary Girls' School presenting flowers to Ambassador Stuart during an illness in 1946.

President Stuart in front of the Yenching University
Administration Building in Peiping, 1946.

The contents of the "Letter of Transmittal" had astonished and alarmed me. The contents of the report, with this laying bare of confidential materials, shocked me. I thought with constantly growing apprehension: what effect will all this have in and upon the United States, in and upon China, in and upon American-Chinese relations? Soon, too, I asked myself: how will this affect various Chinese whose names are given and whose statements are quoted; how will it affect various Americans—myself among them—whose observations and estimates and advice are reproduced *verbatim*; how will it affect the future reporting of United States diplomatic and consular officials?

Another disturbing feature of the "White Paper" was the inconsistency of its conclusions with previously stated policies and later stated policies of the United States Government. Two months after its publication the Department of State declared that the United States still recognized the National Government as the legal government of China. In January, 1950, the United States Government declared that no assistance would be given to the National Government of China (by then moved to Formosa), and this policy prevailed until the Communist attack upon the Republic of Korea in June, 1950, when it was suddenly changed.

I was, in fact, merely one of many persons who were perplexed and filled with apprehension by what they found in this extraordinary book. Among other things, I learned soon that the Department of State had sent copies of the book in considerable numbers to all United States diplomatic missions abroad and had instructed that it be given wide distribution and effective publicity.

The book has been both highly praised and severely criticized. I know of nothing with which to compare it, and I shall not attempt to assess its merits or its demerits. On one point, however, I feel disposed to go on record: it seems to me to have given an accurate display of the materials on which the United States Government *relied* in the making of its decisions of policy regarding China. It is clear that the purpose was not to produce a "historian's history" but to select materials which had been used in making the policy in effect at the moment. What had been omitted were materials rejected in the making of policy, materials which had *not* been relied upon.

The "White Paper" served to inform the world that the Nationalists, in the opinion of the United States Government, had lost the "civil war." Without admitting any mistakes in United States policy, it tried to place all the blame upon the National Government of China. United States policy, it claimed, had been in no way responsible for the "ominous result." By implication it announced that the United States support of the National Government and the efforts of the United States toward survival of that government were at an end.

Such was the officially declared position of my government in the summer of 1949. And such I found to be the position of the officials whom I met in Washington after my arrival there.

In Washington my principal conversations were with the Director of the Office of Far Eastern Affairs, Mr. Walton Butterworth. I found him fully committed to the position which our government had adopted and to the idea that I should think and should express myself accordingly. It was he who suggested that I avoid contact with the press and with the public, and attempt to "calm down" certain editors.

When it came to the question of public utterances I was authorized to give an address before the Hartford Seminary Foundation—on the basis of a text which I prepared with great care and which was censored and then approved by the Department of State. I delivered that address, and I repeated it, with the same text, before the Central Presbyterian Church in Rahway, New Jersey.

5

In September, 1949, the Communist victors in China organized in Peiping (whose name they now changed back to Peking) a new government, with Mao Tse-tung as Chairman. That government was modeled upon the government of the Soviet Union in its formative stages.

In October the Department of State convened a conference of "experts" on the Far East. The attendants were persons from various walks of life, assembled upon invitations issued by the Department, together with officials assigned by the Department. Accounts of what transpired, together with the names of the persons present by invitation and of several, but not all of the officials present by assignment, together with a full text of the verbatim recording of the discussions, have since been made public.

The conference was "briefed" by several officials on subjects relating to the Far Eastern situation—especially in China—and on matters of policy. Discussion was held in accordance with an agenda circulated in advance of the conference. As the meeting went on it became clear that the majority of participants, among whom several educators were the most vocal, assumed that the National Government of China was "finished." They were no longer interested in the fate of that government. The chairman, Mr. Philip Jessup, proposed that the question of recognizing the Communist regime be discussed; thereupon several participants strongly urged recognition of and assistance to the new regime. A smaller number opposed this view and urged that action be not hastily taken.

I was present during the whole period of that conference, and the effect of what I heard was disconcerting and discouraging. Notwithstanding the weaknesses and shortcomings of the National Government—which I have freely affirmed in my story— that government had after all been brought into existence through a revolutionary enthusiasm inspired by American democratic ideas. Throughout the years, it had been under attack from dissident elements in China, especially the Communists, and had been under the pressure of diplomatic and armed assaults from without, especially from Japan. There had been no period in which it could devote itself under circumstances of peace and security to problems of reform and the "people's livelihood." No wonder that when, after eight years of defensive struggle against the Japanese invaders, it was subjected to an all-out attack by the armed forces of the Communist party in China, which in turn were given encouragement and material aid by the Soviet Union, it had been unable to rally to an effective resistance a war-weary people. It had been forced to retreat from one position to another and finally to withdraw to Formosa. Yet in this conference relatively little was said about China's difficulties within and without, and all the onus for the National Government's collapse was placed upon that government itself.

The National Government had counted on assistance from the United States greater in amount and different in kind from that which it received. Some of the aid promised was so long in reaching China that it did no good. The National Government had not envisioned a Yalta Agreement turning over vital rights in Manchuria to the Soviet Union and thus also to the Chinese Communists and paving the way for Communist victory in China. Nor did that government—or others—expect that the Soviet Government would so soon repudiate its agreement of August 15, 1945, promising material and moral aid to the National Government only. The aberrant and contradictory policies of the United States Government during the period between the end of World War II and the beginning of the Communist attack in Korea in 1950 served to weaken rather than to strengthen the National Government at a time when it desperately needed sympathetic understanding and assistance.

When General Cheng Chieh-min, a confidential representative of Generalissimo Chiang, arrived in Washington on October 11, 1949, I was able to say to him only that, as the situation appeared to me, the National Government would receive no further assistance from the United States.

6

On October 1, 1949, the "Central People's Government of the People's Republic of China" was formally inaugurated, and it at once sought recognition by other governments. On the next day, October 2, the Soviet Union announced its recognition. On October 3 the National Government of China announced severance of diplomatic relations with the Soviet Union.

On October 4, as already stated, the United States Department of State reaffirmed United States' recognition of the National Government as the legal government of China.

Although I gained no impression at that time or later that my government intended to recognize the Communist "People's Government" in China, I found the attitude of the Department of State on the whole subject of China essentially one of frustrated, unsympathetic defeatism. Viewing matters in retrospect, it seems to me that the low point was reached in October 1949, when, although the National Government was still recognized, the American Government discontinued assistance to it. This attitude persisted until the Communist aggression eight months later in Korea, when it was decided that the Communist advance in the Far East was dangerous to the peace of the world and must be resisted by the United States and the United Nations.

As the Communist armies advanced southward in the fall of 1949, the National Government decided that evacuation of Canton was necessary. On October 12, Acting President Li Tsung-jen announced that the government would move to Chungking. Seven weeks later, however, Chungking fell to the Communists. Finally, the National Government, under the direction of Generalissimo Chiang Kai-shek, removed to Formosa, and on December 9 the Executive Yuan began to function in Taipeh, Formosa's capital city. Li Tsung-jen went to the United States and, on December 7, entered a hospital in New York for medical treatment.

On December 30, the Government of India accorded recognition to the Communist regime at Peiping. One week later, on January 6, the British Government announced recognition of that regime by the United Kingdom. This involved, of course, withdrawal of recognition from the National Government. There ensued, during the first six months of 1950, a series of such transfers of recognition, some by Asiatic and some by European governments. In all, some twenty-five governments thus committed themselves. Had the United States Government followed the example of the British Government, that number would probably have been increased, for many would presumably have followed the example of the United States.

The United States Government was apparently in a quandary. It seems to have been unfavorably disposed toward the National Government and favorably disposed toward the Communist regime. But abuse by the Communists of American officials and seizure by the Communists of property of the United States in Peiping produced in the United States such waves of popular resentment that official action affirmatively favorable to the Communists was precluded. The government did, however, take negative action against the Nationalists. President Truman announced on January 5, 1950, that the United States would give no military assistance, directly or indirectly, neither materials nor advisers, to the Nationalists in Formosa. On January 12, Secretary of State Acheson, in a speech at the Press Club in Washington, repeated and elaborated this statement.

After that, for several months the question of recognizing the Communist regime at Peiping was debated, in the press and on many platforms, throughout the United States and also at the

United Nations. In May, 1950, some thirty-five United States senators signed jointly and sent to President Truman letters asking for a clear assurance that the United States Government did not intend to recognize the Communist regime in China or to give support to the movement to admit that regime as representative of China in the United Nations. In reply Mr. Acheson gave an assurance that the administration would not accord recognition to the Communist regime without first having consulted with the Senate Committee on Foreign Relations.

Meanwhile, Chiang Kai-shek had on March 1 resumed office in Taipeh as President of the National Government; General Chen Cheng had been named Premier on March 8; Dr. K. C. Wu, former Mayor of Shanghai, had been appointed Governor of Taiwan; and General Sun Li-jen, Chief of Ground Forces.

7

This may be an appropriate place for me to give my final estimate of Chiang Kai-shek. During the six months of my association with the Marshall mission, the Generalissimo was always the dominant figure. It was he who made all decisions for the government or party, and it was he who was most feared or denounced by the Communist delegates. It was always interesting to watch how quickly he understood what was being said to him, how incisively he grasped its essence, and how tenaciously he held to that first reaction. He is a man of strong will power and indomitable courage. But as so often happens his failings are due to the excess of his best qualities. Any judgment of him should be formed against the background of his cultural heritage and of the precarious circumstances amid which he has carried his terrific responsibilities. With this in mind, and by comparison not only with the history of Oriental despotism but also with contemporary dictators, Chiang Kai-shek deserves credit for the restraint with which he has generally acted.

I never had any question as to the moral character of the

Generalissimo despite some of the political measures he took which might seem wrong according to our contemporary European and American standards. I am convinced that he has faithfully acted for what he believed to be the best interests of his country. It has not always been easy for him to distinguish between his personal and his country's advantages. But in contrast with the venality, avarice, indolence and cowardice of many of the traditional "Mandarins," his nobility of character stands out as exceptional.

When Chiang Kai-shek burst into prominence after the death of Sun Yat-sen, he was a popular hero. The new movement under its youthful leader had vigor and high idealism. But as he successfully pursued his efforts to unify the nation the shadow of the Japanese policy of continental expansion grew darker. Chiang seemed to be doing nothing effectual about it. Was he in sympathy with the Japanese militarists? Was he so much preoccupied with the nascent Communist uprising that he failed to sense the imminent Japanese threat? No, he knew that there must first be political and military preparedness. He had the sense to exercise restraint in order to avoid inviting—and possibly warranting—a Japanese attack.

The Japanese invasion of north China in the summer of 1937 was undoubtedly hastened by the increasing unity and strength of the National Government under Chiang's progressive planning. During the following eight years of incredible devastation and suffering for almost the entire population, of defeat and withdrawal ever further inland, he was the inspiring embodiment of the popular will. It was the essence of democracy because he ruled not by political organization, nor by military power, but by the united support of all classes of the people, to all of whom he was the symbol of their own will to resist the invader at any cost. Despite many sordid or stupid happenings in the conduct of the war, the Chinese people rose to a sublime height in their patient endurance and unflinching resistance. All this would have been ineffective, however, without the right leader.

In striking contrast with this almost universal esteem, was the steadily increasing opposition to the Generalissimo after V-J Day when his popularity was at its zenith. After three years of civil war he lost in large measure the confidence of his people. This curious phenomenon compels an attempt at explanation. First, the Kuomintang had genuinely aimed at erecting a democratic government of the western type, yet except for a limited number of idealists the actual dynamic was nationalism. The Generalissimo was anxious to effect these reforms, but while he was engrossed in pressing military or administrative problems, the ancient evils reasserted their hold. The system was not sufficiently rectified. A second factor was the steadily mounting inflation and consequent economic distress. When resisting Japan, this was loyally accepted, but in what seemed to be sense-less and inconclusive civil strife, discontent festered and deep-ened and was inflamed by clever Communist propaganda and infiltration. Not a few dissident political leaders and military commanders were actually plotting against the Generalissimo; some were in collusion with the Communists, all of them aug-menting the turmoil and the defection from Chiang. Another contributing cause to Chiang's waning popularity was that, be-cause of the suppression of Communist infiltration, the methods he adopted gave the impression to the people of what seemed to be his high-handed violation of civil rights. From his own standpoint he was fighting against an enemy utterly un-scrupulous in its methods. The only practicable defense, to him, was resort to emergency measures. He recognized the real nature of the Chinese Communists before almost any others of his fellow countrymen or of Americans or other "foreigners" living in China, and he resolutely decided to risk misunderstand-ing, unpopularity and even defeat in following out his own better comprehension of this crucial issue.

In the light of the record, any attempt to pass judgment on the Generalissimo will necessarily be influenced by one's attitude to democracy and communism. On the eve of his sixtieth birthday, I gave him my birthday wish. I said that he had already passed through two transforming experiences, each of which had made a big difference in him and in the history of his country. One was when he had joined the Kuomintang revolution, and the other was when he became a Christian. I hoped he would now have a third such experience by becoming a true democrat which would be about as difficult and as radical a change for him as had been the other two. As I spoke, his brilliant eyes—perhaps his most notable feature—were piercing me to discover what it was that I had in mind. Then he broke into his winsome smile and said that he would try his best. One of General Marshall's penetrating remarks about him was that he always did the right thing—too late. In fairness to him it should be added that he would doubtless have been more venturesome in progressive movements if he had been sure of enduring support from "democratic" quarters when asked to discard those persons or procedures which he had understood and trusted from long association.

As to his personal characteristics, he lives simply, almost abstemiously. He drinks only enough to meet the requirements of Chinese etiquette. He takes but little relaxation though he thoroughly enjoys diversions which his wife contrives for him. Until Mrs. Marshall taught him to play Chinese checkers he had no such diversions, but under her tutelage he became a devotee. It was amusing to watch them playing. Neither of the two could talk to the other, so each carried on a sort of monologue. Chiang has a keen sense of humor and all the instinctive courtesy and the gracious hospitality of a Chinese gentleman. For those who have won his confidence, he is the best of friends. Whether in serious affairs of state or on a holiday excursion in the hills, this genius for friendship is one of his outstanding qualities.

Under Chiang Kai-shek's leadership the National Government on Formosa has made remarkable recoveries from its bitter defeat on the mainland. Many political and social reforms have been carried out. Whether Chiang will again become a political force in China as a whole is problematical. But he is now as he was during the war against Japan a symbol of Free China. History will be kind to him as the criticisms of his contemporaries are forgotten and he stands out in the greatness of his qualities as a devotedly patriotic, incorruptible, resourceful leader, inflexibly determined to maintain the independence of his country from any foreign domination and to lay the foundations for her constitutional democracy.

8

On June 25, 1950, the world was startled, and the complacency of a good many optimists was shattered, by the news that armed forces of the Communist regime which the Soviet Government had established in northern Korea had crossed the 38th parallel, invaded southern Korea and were sweeping toward Seoul, the capital of the Republic of Korea. The Government of the United States and the Security Council of the United Nations promptly went into action. The Security Council declared the invasion an act of aggression in violation of provisions of the Charter of the United Nations, and called on members of the United Nations to go to the assistance of the invaded Republic.

On July 27 the President of the United States announced that he had given orders under which air and naval forces of the United States would give support to the forces of the Korean Republic and the U.S. Seventh Fleet would prevent any attack on Formosa; also that he was calling on the National Government on Taiwan to desist from military operations against mainland China, and that the United States programs of military aid to the Philippines and to Indo-China for the strengthening of resistance to Communist aggression would be stepped up.

By this resolute and comprehensive action, President Truman committed the United States to a program of positive action in opposition to Communist advance. Already military forces in several areas—in Malaya, in the Philippines and in Indo-China —were engaged in armed resistance to Communist attack. Now, United States forces became committed in Korea, and with them in a United Nations operation the forces of some fifteen other countries, including British and French contingents.

These developments brought virtually to an end the debate in the United States over recognizing the Communist People's Government on the mainland of China. The later intrusion of Chinese Communists into the armed conflict in Korea halted all serious consideration at the United Nations of admitting Communist China to that body. It did not, however, bring to an end agitation and diplomatic effort by the Soviet Government and several other governments toward effecting those steps.

A new orientation of United States policy in relation to China thus took place. When at the outset of the conflict in Korea, the National Government on Formosa offered to send to Korea some 30,000 soldiers, ready for action, the United Nations Command considered it militarily and politically inexpedient to accept that offer. It was felt that the armed forces on Formosa were most needed there for defense against a possible Communist assault from the mainland. After the entry of Chinese Communist forces into Korea in the winter of 1950-1951, the United States sent to Formosa a military mission to discuss with Nationalist military authorities plans for the defense of the island. Soon thereafter, in April 1951, the United States Government detailed to the National Government, with its full approval, a United States Military Assistance Advisory Group.

The Communists had achieved their conquest of mainland

China by skillful use of several instrumentalities chief among which were propaganda, infiltration and armed force. They exploited the continuing social revolution, the strong nationalistic feelings, and the general desire for peace. Many of the Communist leaders are, or were at some time, sincere believers in the teachings of Marx and Lenin, and the great majority of the party members, both leaders and followers, appear to have accepted wholeheartedly the gospels of Stalin and Mao Tse-tung. From 1921 to 1948 the leaders preached "liberation," liberation of the Chinese people from political tyranny and economic slavery, and from restraints and exploitation imposed by the "capitalist" practices of "imperialist" powers—meaning by these adjectives the western powers and Japan but not the Soviet Union. They still preach that gospel but now in terms of consolidation and defense rather than in terms of a political goal to be reached.

Up to the time of its victory in 1949, and for some months thereafter, the behavior of the Communist party in its public relations was such as to inspire confidence and win friends. There were some incidents to the contrary, but misconduct according to Chinese standards was seldom if ever attributed to the principal leaders. On the whole, the party was able to give the impression, both to the Chinese masses, especially the peasantry, and to foreign observers in and out of China, that it was truly devoted to the cause of the people and was truly seeking to promote in China the cause of democracy and to win for China a position of real independence and strength in the family of nations. Communist propaganda portrayed the party in China as a party intent above all upon "agrarian reform," a party essentially indigenous in motivation, a party independent of Moscow and of the Comintern and, later of the Cominform. Stalin's statement that the Chinese Communists were not really Communists at all but were merely "agrarian reformers" gained credence far and wide.

Mao Tse-tung's statements to the contrary were not publicized and made little impression abroad.

The official Communist line, describing the National Government and the Kuomintang as utterly corrupt, inefficient and
decadent, and expatiating on the honesty, the sincerity, the
incorruptibility, the democratic way of life, high thinking and
the high purposes of China's Communists, effectively prepared
the way for an easy acceptance by the Chinese people of the
turnover from Nationalist to Communist domination. It also
encouraged unsophisticated foreign observers, in China and
throughout the world, to accept the idea that this turnover would
strengthen democracy and the cause of international peace.

Strange to say—or was it strange?—the idea was seized upon
with most confidence and least skepticism by persons and groups,
both in China and abroad, who rate as intellectuals, the "in-
telligentsia." Whatever the honest historian may some day say
in explanation and in appraisal of this phenomenon, he will
have to record that in China a majority of the articulate intellectuals welcomed the advent of the Communist regime with
enthusiasm, and that outside of China the various Communist
governments recognized the regime with alacrity, while many
non-Communist governments soon followed suit and several
others were, at the outset, favorably disposed toward it.

Until they had gained nation-wide (mainland) ascendency,
the Communist authorities governed in areas that they controlled with little manifestation of totalitarian inclination; they
seemed to be benevolently disposed, tolerant and friendly, on
the principle: live, let live and help live. Their conduct as they
moved in 1947, 1948, and 1949 to victory after victory and took
control in region after region and city after city was indeed that
of well-disposed liberators. And such it continued to be until
they had established their domination over the mainland. In
those days there came from China and from various "experts"
many glowing reports regarding the Communists. A large num-

ber of foreign diplomats, businessmen and missionaries were confident that the new regime was and would be a great improvement on the old.

In power, the Communists did indeed proceed with a program of reform. They took land from the landlords and gave it to the tenants. This was pleasing to the latter, and it looked like progress toward democracy. Later, however, they took from the new owners so much in taxes that no net gain for the latter was perceptible. They soon began to subject the whole population to courses of indoctrination in Communist principles. They imposed new taxes, regulations and prohibitions in great variety and ever increasing numbers. They established a system of secret police, of informers, of people's courts, of wholesale convictions and of mass executions. They "nationalized" all education. They took over private schools and hospitals. Although proclaiming religious liberty, they placed many restrictions upon religious organizations. They accused missionaries of espionage and other crimes. They closed in on merchants and shippers, both Chinese and foreign. They abused foreign officials. They refused to do business with the diplomats of some countries, even of countries that had recognized the Communist regime, conspicuously the British. They embarked before long upon a series of violent purges which continue to this day, in the course of which they are said to have liquidated several million of their own people and more than a few foreigners. Their animus appeared at first to be directed especially against those of their people who had opposed them politically, next against those who had been "poisoned" by foreign influence, including many Christians, and finally against businessmen and missionaries, whom they suspected—or accused—of subversive activities and of being agents of western imperialism and cultural aggression.

Foreigners in China, especially those who had roots there, were loath to believe and slow to admit that the Iron Curtain was being lowered around China, that the Communists wanted none of their works inside the Curtain and meant for them to leave. They have been forced to face the hard facts. They have seen their institutions and enterprises destroyed or taken over; they have seen their Chinese associates persecuted and sometimes imprisoned; they have seen their properties confiscated and appropriated for the use of the Communist Government or pro-Communist organizations. They have found themselves mistreated, squeezed out and, in many cases, forcibly deported.

The most startling of recent developments has been the withdrawal of a majority of British businessmen and the seizure by the Communists of the products of 100 years or more of British commercial effort. One of the latest liquidations of western-created and supported cultural enterprises has been the closing of Yenching University and the merging of all its faculty, student body and facilities with those of other institutions, including Tsinghua University and Peking University, in a new national university under the direction of the Communist Ministry of Education. The foreign personnel of the Yenching faculty has been forced to leave.

It is a tragic thing for men and women who have devoted their lives to an enterprise, no matter what, to see their life's work destroyed or diverted to the service of causes which they consider evil. It is even more tragic to witness the persecution and killing of people with and for whom they have worked, and the enslavement of a people to whom they have preached the gospel of Christ and whom they have endeavored to serve in the spirit of Christ. I am one of the many who have had and are having this experience. I myself have been spared the physical sufferings, indignities and perils to which many of my life-time colleagues or associates have been subjected. But I have vivid knowledge, from reports heard and read of the havoc that has been wrought.

I have knowledge too of things that have not been destroyed, things that cannot be destroyed, things that will not be destroyed.

In the apparent darkness on the China mainland there burn many lights—lights of faith, of courage, of freedom that will not be extinguished. And among the millions of Chinese overseas, in Chinese communities in Formosa and in many places around the world, the light is shining and will help some day to rekindle the lamps of true democracy, liberty and justice for the great population of China.

9

On November 28, 1949, I left Washington for Cincinnati, to pay a visit to my old friends, Dean George Barbour of the University of Cincinnati and Mrs. Barbour, who had once been on the faculty of Yenching University.

On the evening of November 30, I boarded a train in Cincinnati for Washington, D. C. In the dining car I became ill, and I left without finishing my meal. From then on I have no recollection of what occurred until on the next morning I found myself being removed from the train and transferred to an ambulance. I was informed later that in the morning members of the train crew had found me lying unconscious in the men's room, and that I had been identified by papers on my person. I also learned that telegrams had been sent to the Department of State and that arrangements had promptly been made for me to be received at the Naval Hospital in Bethesda, Maryland. To all the many persons who came to my aid I was, and shall ever be, profoundly grateful.

I had had a severe "stroke." The doctors did not know until twelve days later whether I could live. I was given superb care in the Naval Hospital from December 1, 1949, to March 29, 1950. Philip Fugh, who had been away for some time, hurried back to Washington and was with me every day. My son Jack visited me periodically. On March 26 I left the hospital and, with Philip, took an apartment at the Hotel Fairfax in Washington. After one week I had to return to the hospital. On April

28 I rejoined Philip at the Fairfax. On the occasion of my seventy-fourth birthday, on June 24, several of our close friends dropped in on us there—a simple, but to me heart-warming "celebration." From July 4 to September 3 I was in the Presbyterian Hospital, New York, and then returned to Washington, much improved in health. In December a letter came from the Department of State informing me that I had been detailed to the Department for an indefinite period.

During the days of my twilight consciousness, I especially enjoyed and appreciated the fragrance and beauty of the flowers which came from many sources with expressions of friendly sympathy. Through the months and years since, I have been cheered and inspired by the visits of many good friends. From the first moment of my dependence, Philip Fugh has taken care of me and my needs with a completeness, efficiency and devotion that words cannot describe. Since their arrival in 1950 his family has contributed in full measure toward the comfort, tranquility and security of my life in Washington. We moved to a house on 28th Street, northwest, "out Chevy Chase way," which Philip and his wife purchased. Here we now are, here I work, and here we expect to stay.

On November 28th, 1952, I sent to President Truman a letter expressing my desire, on account of ill health, to retire from the position of United States Ambassador to China. On December 11, I received from President Truman the following letter thanking me for my services and accepting my resignation, to be effective on December 31.

THE WHITE HOUSE
Washington

December 11, 1952

Dear Mr. Ambassador:

I have received your letter of November twenty-eighth tendering your resignation as Ambassador to China. In accepting your resignation, effective December 31, 1952, I wish to express my sincere personal gratitude as well as that of our Government for the outstanding service which you have rendered in representing our country so well and faithfully under the most difficult and tragic circumstances.

You brought to your mission in China, not only an unusually intimate knowledge of the country, its people and its language, gained through a lifetime of service to the education of its youth, but also a profound devotion to China's welfare and to the cause of Sino-American friendship. Thus richly equipped in wisdom and spirit for the arduous task to which you were called, you gave to it unstintingly of both. I have no doubt that this devotion to your mission beyond the ordinary call of duty made a heavy contribution to the long illness which you have so unfortunately suffered since your return to the United States.

It is a source of deep regret to me that this illness has deprived our Government of your further service at this time. However, I sincerely hope that when your strength is recovered you will continue to devote your unique abilities to the furtherance of understanding and friendship between the American and Chinese people —a cause more urgent than ever in these days when the communist regime at Peiping is bending so much energy to the destruction of good will and the fostering of hatred.

Very sincerely yours,

(signed) Harry S. Truman

Honorable J. Leighton Stuart,
American Ambassador to China,
Department of State,
Washington, D. C.

This cleared the way for the appointment by the incoming administration of a new Ambassador to China, and made possible for me a new approach to problems of personal concern and questions of public interest.

14 Reflections in Retirement

The three external factors which have influenced the course of my life the most are religion, education and the country of China. Perhaps it would be more accurate to describe China as the setting in which the other two have found their chief expression and by which they have both been profoundly affected.

Many books about China have been written in recent decades. They deal with China's history, politics, economics, literature, art, the characteristics of the people, current internal changes and China's place in the international scene. They include serious and humorous writings, novels, translations of poetry, philosophy and other literary works, and the authors are of as varied types and attitudes as are the facets of Chinese life with which they respectively deal. A number of these writers have been acquaintances or personal friends. It is interesting to note how many among successful writers of books about China, especially novels, have been women.

To this vast and growing literature on China I have felt that my only significant contribution would be the story of my own life and experience against the background of this turbulent period in Chinese history. My sympathies were early aroused against the humiliating terms of foreign treaties and the unfair privileges that the nationals of foreign countries enjoyed—including missionaries. In sharing the rightful national aspirations of the Chinese people, I revived my own latent beliefs in democracy, personal freedom, and social progress through applied science. I was brought almost unconsciously into such an understanding of Chinese grievances and ambitions as virtually to become identified with them in these sentiments, with the result that they have become dominant elements in my own life, coloring my attitudes and controlling my activities.

Nor is this merely a sentimental emotion due to my fondness for China and its people. I long ago reached the conviction that a stable peace in the Pacific would not be possible unless China were independent, united, strong, and with no fears or festering grievances toward other countries. More constructively, this means that China could be an enormous asset in a new world order based on reason, righteousness and international good will. This broadly human outlook would be in harmony with the teachings of China's ancient sages and the best traditions of her people. The adoption of a truly republican form of government would satisfy the aspirations of young intellectuals and would give political expression to the social democracy which has always obtained among the Chinese people since their earliest recorded history. The realization of such an aim would require the maintenance of China's administrative and territorial integrity—her national independence—against aggressive threats from any direction. China is not so much a biological or racial unity as a single cultural unity. The preservation of China's national freedom and of her fine national culture is vitally related to the peace of the Pacific and the progressive welfare of all mankind. To this cause my life has been devoted.

2

The attitude one forms toward another country than his own and the influence it exerts are usually due in the last analysis to personal associations. In no other country would this be so strong a factor as in China whose very civilization, moral philosophy and ethical standards are founded on human relationships. It would almost seem at times that the Chinese have no abstract morality but are honest, truthful, kindly, and so on, only as a duty to the individuals concerned. This may be putting it too strongly, but their basic virtue is perhaps that of personal loyalty.

Bertrand Russell in *The Problem of China*, a book written in high praise of Chinese good qualities, lists avarice, cowardice and callousness as what he regards as their worst faults. I would select mutual jealousies and suspicions as more characteristically Chinese, in contrast with vices or weaknesses more or less common among all peoples, and these are directly traceable to the highly personalized element in their social structure. However, my personal relationships have revealed to me their virtues much more than their faults and have been a very important feature through which in my case Chinese culture has been appraised and appreciated. It is significant, I think, that so few personal friendships seem to exist even today between Chinese and Russian individuals in comparison with thousands of strong Chinese-American friendships. The temporary disavowals or betrayals of these friendships by some Chinese today under severe pressures are more than offset, I am sure, by the many deep personal loyalties which still exist and by innumerable spiritual bonds that are unbroken and will some day be renewed.

Chinese hearts like Chinese homes are generally closed to the outsider. The city of Peking, for instance, is full of private residences of which the passing tourist could see nothing nor even sense the existence. They are surrounded by drab walls, and the one-story structures within are completely hidden. The lacquered gate remains closely bolted and even when opened to a caller permits the view only of an ornamental wall which must be gone around before anything else becomes visible. But beyond these barriers are stately buildings in a succession of courtyards, separated by artistic gateways and covered porticos, pavilions, gardens, grottoes, lotus ponds and similarly delightful surprises. So with themselves the Chinese wear before the stranger the impassively expressionless countenance which has

proven to foreigners so baffling an "oriental mask." Entrance
to what lies behind is not lightly nor hastily permitted. But when
fears or suspicions have been removed and trusting good will
has evolved, discovery and exploration, as in the case of the
secluded Chinese homes, and experience of an abundant hospitality will certainly follow admittance to the grounds.

In these memoirs I have mentioned a number of Chinese with
whom I have formed intimate and treasured friendships through
the years, and many more would be included but for lack of
space.

The reader will have noticed again and again the name of
Philip Fugh, and I make no apology for referring further to him
as an example of beautiful and loyal Chinese-American friendship. I have told of how he helped me during my presidency
at Yenching University. When I was interned by the Japanese
he refused to leave Peiping, thinking that he might manage my
escape or that something might happen to negotiate my release.
He was virtually under surveillance and scarcely left his home
during the whole period. He was the first visitor I was permitted to see when my release seemed imminent and he stayed
with me during the subsequent weeks of excitement and nervous
exhaustion.

On my return from the United States toward the end of April,
1946, I was detained in Shanghai for some weeks. Certain matters of University business seemed to require Philip's help, so
I telegraphed for him to join me there. The only possible way
was to travel by air and this was not easy except by special favor
of the Allied military authorities. Flying over Communist territory in Shantung, something went wrong with the motors and
the pilot told Philip to throw his suitcase overboard. That,
Philip declined to do, with good reason: there were in that suitcase important Chinese papers. The pilot had a single parachute
for himself but as the danger became greater he faced the
horrible dilemma of bailing out while leaving the passenger to

his fate or of perilously staying with him. While he was debating this the motors miraculously started up again, and they landed safely in Tsingtau with nothing worse than jangled nerves. From there on Philip caught a commercial plane, but in all the excitement the suitcase was left at the airport. Fortunately, the company recovered it and sent it on to Shanghai a day or two later.

In the delicate negotiations between the National Government and the Communists, as well as in all relations with Chinese in my position as Ambassador, I knew that Philip would be extremely helpful. I asked him therefore to go to Nanking with me for the weeks or months required to complete the Marshall mission. Housing accommodations in the capital were scarce and costly. I had hitherto treated Philip, in my home and on our travels, virtually as one of my family. It seemed logical therefore to have him stay with me where he could be of use at all hours in dealing with Chinese visitors. But in this case I had my first encounter with American official procedure. To have a Chinese as a member of the American Ambassador's household was an unheard-of and dangerous precedent! There was some social prejudice—but only slight. The more serious objection was "security," about the importance of which I had to be schooled in various ways. General Marshall raised his eyebrows. My widely experienced foreign service colleagues looked askance at an innovation which might be bringing an "alien spy" into the inner sanctum of the Embassy. These fears were not only natural; they were necessary. Actually if Philip had lived elsewhere and had come to my home only during working hours his opportunity for espionage would have been about the same. As in all such issues, reliance must be based chiefly on one's moral integrity. I knew that Philip could be trusted without reserve and that he was much more interested in my success than in anything else. It was not long before my Embassy colleagues learned to appreciate Philip's worth and to treat him very much as I did.

Chinese, in striking contrast, were obviously pleased at this extension of a long-existing relationship, with which many were already familiar, into my new diplomatic function. They came to my home with a freedom and frequency much greater because they could visit with Philip if not with me, or see me for a few minutes only. He constantly called upon those with whom it was desirable for us to keep in touch when it would not have been entirely dignified, or for other reasons suitable, for me to do so. Almost invariably when calling on Chinese officials, I took him with me, and he never betrayed a confidence. All of this meant that I had far more intimate and extensive association with Chinese of all classes than would otherwise have been possible, and that *he* could represent me on most occasions without question. He could say things to them which they knew would be in accord with my ideas but might be inadvisable or embarrassing for me to say. So he became an accepted and all but indispensable feature of my diplomatic career. Although costing the American Government nothing, I am sure that it was considerably benefited by his keen understanding of Chinese politics and his wide contacts with the Chinese people. In minor matters he helped me also by suggesting fitting courtesies which I would have overlooked—or often by attending to these without my even knowing of them. This applied particularly to my heavy Chinese correspondence which he cared for with the help of a skilled Chinese letter writer.

This friendship has continued for more than thirty years and has ripened into one of perfect trust. It proves that idyllic comradeships do happen even between people of different races. Philip has been to me something of a son, a companion, a secretary and a public relations officer. What I have been able to achieve, especially in the understanding of China and the Chinese people I owe more to him than perhaps even I realize.

My illness, which began more than four years ago, has been the most severe test of this friendship, and Philip has responded with the utmost affection and loyalty. The doctors had ordered that no one stay with me for more than ten minutes, except members of my immediate family, who could stay at most for half an hour. But it was not long before those unsentimental men of science became aware that this visitor was different. I was able to stand hours of his companionship, which was never exciting but always comforting and relaxing. During those almost five months in the hospital Philip did not miss seeing me for a single day. Since I left the hospital, Philip, his wife Sarah, two of his children and I have lived together for over three years in what seems to me an ideal domestic arrangement. During the lengthy process of my slow improvement, they all have taken part in the care of me with the same spirit as Philip himself. He, of course, was the chief factor, but all of them followed spontaneously. It is more significant that all our Chinese friends as far as I know have commended this arrangement. Chinese take more seriously than do Americans or other western people the practical duties and loyalties of human relationships, especially those of family and friendship. The continuous care of my badly shocked body has been long and arduous, involving the greatest sympathy with my disabilities and much patience in dealing with them. In short, this peculiarly Chinese type of helpful human service, and the sentiments which go with it, seem to have been the chief factors in what doctors describe as the miracle of my considerable recovery.

3

I have twice lived through periods of sequestration, first in the three and a half years of imprisonment by the Japanese and next in my illness of these recent years. These experiences have helped me to understand and appreciate the appalling amount of suffering in the world today. I have tried to imagine the plight of the destitute, the desperate and dispirited, the bereaved, the wounded and diseased, the lonely and the imprisoned, with hardships indescribably worse than mine. Many carry nerve-wracking responsibilities or face the frightful hazards of war. Apart from all such special and temporary distress or danger, there is the ever-present proportion of those among our fellow men who are enduring some form of bodily or mental affliction. My life had been an exceedingly fortunate and happy one. I had not been unaware of human misery when my personal circumstances were more satisfactory. But this may have been touched with something of condescending pity. At best it had something of the aloofness of the onlooker. But my two great isolating experiences have given me an almost mystical sense of identity with all of suffering humanity. I have gained a glimmering insight as to the function of pain in moral growth, not only for the individual concerned but in our corporate relations. I have learned something more of the profound truth in the doctrine of vicarious suffering and of the costliness alike to God and to men of salvation from sin and its hideous consequences. Even with the optimism which had been mine by both temperament and good fortune, the tragic elements of human life are seen with stark realism when one is brought into personal contact with them or faces them unflinchingly in thought.

4

I need not repeat what has been written elsewhere in this chronicle of my passionate belief in personal freedom as the elementary right of every human being and the condition without which most, if not all, of the other benefits we seek become worthless. This is the very essence of democracy, which rests on the conviction that people can govern themselves better than even the best form of paternalistic or despotic government can, because through their own failures and blunders they will learn the obligations, the procedures and the incomparable advantages of self-government. We speak of the adventure of faith involved in the search for God by men, but we should not overlook the adventure of faith God undertook in the terrifying risk of allowing us the freedom of moral choice. It is godlike therefore to share this faith in our fellow men, in insisting upon freedom as the right of all and in believing that all have the capacity to develop in the fitness of its exercise. The fight for liberty has the highest religious sanction.

As I look upon the world in this, my seventy-eighth year, I see going on a great struggle the issues of which are of vital consequences to every human being, to every society, to all mankind. Shall an atheistic, soulless and totalitarian communism conquer and dominate the world or shall the principles and practices of political, economic and social democracy and Christian faith in God and in the dignity of man become fundamental in the way of life of all men and in the family of nations? The two ideals cannot indefinitely coexist.

The Communists have proclaimed noble social objectives but have adopted the vicious principle that the end justifies the means. They have developed deception into a fine art; they rely on force, fraud and falsehood. They presumably would not hesitate to plunge humanity into a vast welter of misery and destruction if they were convinced that such conditions suited their purpose. Years ago Chinese Communist leaders told me that they would sacrifice anything toward communization of the world. The Communists are flexible in tactics and their strategy may be changed, but their controlling purpose is immutable.

Communists have an ethic, but their beliefs are not ours. They do not reason as do most people. They have different values and different standards. They apparently regard counter-revolutionary activities as the greatest of crimes. They are fanatically convinced that they are right and invincible. Would that we of the free world were as ardent about our beliefs as they are about theirs.

I do not believe that any regime or system founded upon sheer materialism and violent suppression of all criticism and opposition can long endure. If the Communists are right, then the rest of us are hopelessly wrong. But if our finest ideals and beliefs are true we must make it our business to see that they prevail—both in theory and in practice. We should not merely be anti-Communist. We must have a positive and dynamic program of democracy, social and economic justice, and faith in moral and spiritual values, that will give new hope and power to the free world.

5

"What is the chief end of man?" is the first question in the *Westminster Shorter Catechism* which every properly brought-up Presbyterian lad in my youth was required to memorize. The answer is, "Man's chief end is to glorify God and to enjoy Him forever." This is almost an epitome of the austere Calvinistic creed which is my heritage from generations of Scotch ancestry. The influence of this sternly uncompromising and heroic faith upon political liberty and economic prosperity is well known. Confidence in the sovereignty of a righteous God and the primal duty of obedience to Him nurtured a quality of character which has been an enormous asset in all Protestant lands. But it seems to be the irony of religious idealism that its noblest advances over cruder concepts have in many situations become in turn distorted and reactionary.

An illustration of this is found in the behavior of the western residents in China—and doubtless in many other mission fields—where missionaries and their fellow countrymen engaged in secular pursuits are given to being mutually estranged and reciprocally critical, although in their homelands most of them would have doubtless found one another congenial.

Even members of the same families, and notoriously children of missionaries, have often gone to one extreme or the other. Religious consecration (without which they would never have chosen this career) combined with Anglo-Saxon glorification of efficiency and the instincts for achieving tangible results, have made missionaries appear to others as disagreeably or fanatically professional, while boredom and the release from conventional standards have tempted other westerners to practices which missionaries have found it hard to tolerate. This distressing symptom is so universal in the Orient that it cannot be entirely accounted for by charging the non-missionary element with depravity. The present world-wide cataclysm has probably shattered forever those patterns so familiar to all who have lived in mission lands, but they may still serve as a warning of the dangers lurking even in our Protestant piety and in the tendency to departmentalize life into religious and worldly behavior. Unless we can recover the concept of human life integrated by a really vital religious faith, the catastrophe in which the world seems to be involved augurs ill for the future. I am profoundly convinced that this loss of Christian faith as concerned with the whole of life and the present global struggle are more intimately related as cause and effect than would be generally conceded.

Christianity inevitably brought to China its traditional creeds and theological formulations. I have for a long time hoped that Chinese theologians might give some fresh and creative interpretations of Christian truth to their own people and to the world. It may be that the ordeal through which the Chinese Church is now passing will so enrich and deepen the religious experience of their Christian thinkers that what we have longed for may more quickly be realized, just as the most profound spiritual insights of the Old Testament came in the literature written after the Exile. China's history, philosophy, and indeed all of its best literature is primarily concerned with the moral relationships of people to one another. Certainly out of such a great tradition, challenged and sifted in the fierce overturning of these years, and vitalized by Christian truths that have taken deep root in Chinese thought should come fresh illuminations upon the meaning of Jesus Christ for our human race.

6

If I should be asked to select any single passage in the Bible as containing the essence of my religious faith it would be John 3:16. For a brief summary of this faith in practical application, I refer to the two sayings of Jesus which were woven into the Yenching motto, "Freedom through truth for service"—John 8:32, Mark 10:43-45.

My favorite hymns are Isaac Watts' "When I survey the wondrous cross," possibly the most beautiful of all English hymns, and Bernard of Clairvaux's "Jesus, the very thought of Thee." Two others would be: George Matheson's "O Love that will not let me go" and George Croly's "Spirit of God, descend upon my heart."

A poem that expresses my own prayer as nearly as any is George Eliot's:

> O may I join the Choir invisible
> Of those immortal dead who live again
> In minds made better by their presence: live
> In pulses stirred to generosity,
> In deeds of daring rectitude, in scorn
> For miserable aims that end with self,
> In thoughts sublime that pierce the night like stars,
> And with their mild persistence urge man's search
> To vaster issues. May I reach
> That purest Heaven, be to other souls
> The cup of strength in some great agony,
> Enkindle generous ardour, feed pure love,

So shall I join the choir invisible
Whose music is the gladness of the world.

Jesus Christ is as sublimely satisfying to me in my old age as he was in my youth. He has my absolute reverence and devotion. His life, teaching, death and resurrection form a harmonious whole. His crucifixion reveals the ultimate in faith and love.

It would seem that the most reasonable—shall I dare to say the most scientific—explanation of the life and death of Christ is that which gives credit to his intuitive consciousness of his own origin and nature. I believe that the more Christians there are and the more closely patterned are their lives to Christ, the better will be the world and the happier will be the lot of men, of nations and of all mankind.

The classic Christian arguments for immortality are probably as valid as ever, but the appreciation of their cogency has been dimmed by the circumstances of modern life. The natural sciences seem no more competent now in that regard than when they were less advanced. Nor have philosophy and psychology any convincing affirmations. My belief is that faith in immortality as in any other reasonable intuition of the human spirit —finds encouragement in the magnitude and mystery of the universe as further revealed in every aspect of scientific discovery. All such known and expected findings of the experimental sciences are a challenge to the belief that equally in spiritual matters the reality is apt to be splendorous beyond our highest imaginings or our most adventurous reasonings. Christian faith in immortality rests ultimately in the calm and confident awareness that the unseen power behind the confused phenomenon of the universe is such love as is supremely manifested in our Lord Jesus Christ.

The destiny of the human race, and of each individual member of it, can therefore be safely assumed to be worthy of a creative design, the amazing grandeur of which is apparent alike in our material and our spiritual experience. Recent scientific progress should be welcomed as confirming the more lofty aspiration and more profound insights of religious faith. "Eye hath not seen, nor ear heard, neither have entered into the heart of man, the things which God hath prepared for them that love Him." (I Cor. 2:9)

> *So be my passing,*
> *My task accomplished and the long day done,*
> *My wages taken and in my heart*
> *Some late lark singing;*
> *Let me be gathered to the quiet west,*
> *The sundown, splendid and serene Death.*
> (W. E. Henley, *Margaritae Sorori*)

15 The United States and China: "What Policy Now?"

I am asked over and over what policy I think the United States should pursue in regard to China—or to Chiang Kai-shek, or to Formosa, or to the Communist Government on the mainland.

"Policy" is a large word. "Now" is a constantly moving point in time, and the problems which confront the United States as a nation, and with which our government has to struggle, are constantly changing. China, although a large country with a huge population and great resources, is only one of many countries with which we have to deal. As I see it, to have a sound policy regarding any country or region we must first of all have a sound policy regarding the world as a whole. To have such a policy, we must understand ourselves and other peoples; we must see the world, its peoples, its states, in proper perspective. We must be appropriately solicitous not only regarding our own rights and obligations and interests but also regarding the rights and obligations and interests of other nations and of all mankind. In the making of such policy we should begin with and at all times be guided by fundamental principles. These should derive from and be consistent with high concepts of morality, legality and justice; and they should serve and be employed in all of our relations with all other peoples. We have such concepts—in the principles and practices of Christianity; and we should be guided by them in all of our foreign policy.

In dealing with the world's many and varying countries and regions, there must and there will, of course, be differences of method, but the fundamental and guiding principles should in all cases be the same. Likewise the ultimate major objectives,

Fundamental among our principles is that of the right of men and nations to be free. Fundamental among our objectives is that of ensuring our own existence and survival as a free nation. To be true to that principle and to serve effectively that objective, we must concern ourselves not only with our own, but with other peoples' national existence, right to freedom and right to security.

There is being waged today a world-wide conflict in which on one side a minority of men in a minority of nations is trying to impose upon all men and all nations a regime the essence of which is the total enslavement of all mankind. On the other side are men and nations—in the forefront the United States —opposed to and resisting that effort. To survive and to achieve security, our people and our government must co-operate with other peoples and governments that are, as are we, on the side of freedom. We should give support to all countries and peoples menaced, as are we, by the forces of enslavement. We— and they—should give no support to governments or regimes committed to policies of enslavement and world domination. The free nations should maintain a common front, should assist all peoples that seek to be free, in resistance to the global menace of Soviet-inspired and militant communism.

Genuine *communism* entered into by free men on a voluntary basis for agreed upon social and economic purposes would not necessarily be objectionable. But this thing now called "Communism," a system which begins with denial of the existence of God, which rules out the soul, which declares all things material and all action materialistic, which is imposed and maintained by force or falsehood or both, and which aspires to world dominion, is an evil monstrosity. It lives by devouring. It cannot be appeased. It will not be tamed by soft words and friendly gestures. It is utterly objectionable. It must be opposed.

It follows, I think, that in our relations with China, we of America, we, the people of the United States, should first of all continue to be—as we always have been—sympathetic toward the Chinese people; and that our government should firmly recommit this country to pursuit of our traditional policy regarding China, a policy expressive of the belief that China should remain a sovereign and independent state, that its territorial and administrative integrity should be respected, and that efforts by its leaders to introduce and establish principles and practices of freedom should be encouraged and supported.

Americans should study, try to understand and learn to appreciate the human qualities and capabilities of the Chinese as a people. They should grasp and ponder the fact that that people, intelligent and sturdy, numbering more than 450,000,000 constitutes one quarter of the earth's population. They should realize that the country of that people, China, embraces an area approximately 4,000,000 square miles, an area greater than that of the United States, that that country is centrally located in eastern Asia, that it has substantial material resources, and that it is capable of extensive industrial development. They should consider the significance of the fact that that China was long known to its own people and all of its neighbors as the "Middle Kingdom." They should review and study and ponder the modern history of that land, the history of United States relations—commercial, cultural and political—with it. They should view in perspective the history of its revolution, of its Nationalist movement, of the constructive efforts of its "National" Government, of that government's long and successful resistance to Japanese imperialistic aggression, of its performance as an ally, of its part and place in the creation of the United Nations, of its performance as a member of that organization with a permanent seat in the Security Council. They should ponder the effect on that government of the Yalta and the Potsdam Agreements, of the Soviet Union's betrayal of it, of the rise and the ultimate victory of the Soviet-supported Communist party in China, of the struggle which continues between the National Government now on Formosa and the Communist "People's Government" established in 1949 in Peiping. They should scrutinize, compare and contrast the attitudes and performance of those two governments respectively during the years since the latter came into existence.

There is not a great deal that the people or the Government of the United States can do at present by way of direct contact with the people of mainland China or with the government which now controls that area. It is a tragic thing that, after more than a century of friendly contact and mutually beneficial relationships, American nationals and American interests, along with those of many other countries, have been driven out of that area and now are excluded therefrom. During the century which preceded World War II, many western countries had made substantial investments—economic and cultural—in China. Foremost among the American investments had been that of cultural influence. Conspicuously, the churches of the United States, both Protestant and Catholic, had sent to China large numbers of missionaries; and various educational institutions and philanthropic enterprises in the United States had extended their work by establishing centers in China. These, in cooperation with similar undertakings by men of good will in and from other countries, had given the Chinese people the benefit of Occidental concepts and ways of life, of Christian thought and practices, of "western" education, of modern science, medical progress, mechanical arts, etc., etc. Since the advent of the Communists to power, the "People's Government" has done its utmost not only to drive out and exclude the agents and agencies of western influence but also to eradicate all evidence or effects of that influence. That government has, under Soviet influence and with Soviet support, made mainland China a part of the Communist bloc, has placed most of China and the vast majority of its people behind the Iron Curtain, is a party to Communism's "cold war" on the free world and has invaded a neighboring country as an aggressor. It has vilified, persecuted, tortured and in many cases killed missionaries and their converts. It has expelled most "foreign" businessmen, and it holds others as hostages. It denounces all non-Communist powers and peoples as "imperialists," and it declares the United States the worst of all.

The people and the Government of the United States can, however, do much for the Chinese, eight to nine million in number, on Formosa and for the more than ten million other Chinese domiciled "overseas." American missionary and philanthropic enterprises, expelled and excluded from mainland China, persist actively in educational, medical and relief work among these "free" Chinese. The American Government is assisting Chinese students in the United States and is giving economic and military assistance to the National Government on Formosa. We might, however, and we should be doing much more.

The National Government can be counted on to persevere in its resistance to communism. It keeps alive among Chinese everywhere the spirit of that resistance. It keeps Chinese Nationalism on the side of freedom in the global struggle. It sparks the spirit of resistance among the peoples of eastern Asia. It thus makes common cause with the United States. Through it and through Chinese organizations and individuals in many places throughout the world contact can be and is being maintained with the Chinese on the mainland. Yes, we still can do much for the Chinese, many of them—to their advantage, to China's advantage, to our advantage and to the advantage of the whole of the free world.

When the Communists in North Korea launched their attack on the Republic of Korea (in South Korea) in June, 1950, United States policy-makers quickly decided that positive action must be taken by way of collective resistance to Communist aggression. The United States proposed in the United Nations collective armed support to the South Koreans, and the United

Nations decided to give such support. The United States Government went, however, still further. It formulated a strategy which meant support by the United States to resistance not only in Korea but also at other points in eastern Asia: support to resistance by the Chinese Nationalists in defense of Formosa, to resistance in the Philippines and to resistance in Indo-China. With regard to the Chinese Nationalists on Formosa in particular, President Truman announced that he had ordered the U.S. Seventh Fleet to prevent attack on Formosa by the Communists, from the mainland, and that he had asked the National Government to desist from attacks on the mainland, from Formosa. That order has since, in 1953, been modified by President Eisenhower, to the effect that the Seventh Fleet is not to stand in the way of operations on the part of the Nationalists, from Formosa, against the Communists on the mainland. Also, the United States Government has since June, 1950 pursued a course regarding the Nationalists in which it has increased the amount of its economic assistance and has given and is giving military assistance in the form of materials and advice.

This change of attitude and practise on the part of the United States Government, its return to the policy of support of the Chinese Nationalists, is in my opinion a sound development. Not only are the Nationalists aligned on the side of the free world in the fight against communism but, in their resistance, they are setting an example and pattern which are being watched throughout eastern Asia. It is very important to the security of the free world that the advance of communism in eastern Asia be halted. It is very important to the United States both politically and strategically that Formosa not be taken over by Communists. In those respects and in various others the United States and China's Nationalists have common interests. Wise safeguarding of its own interests, together with service of the real interests of the whole of the free world, calls for reasoned, consistent and continuing support by the United States of China's National Government.

That brings us to two questions which keep coming up and which are again (in 1954) being actively forced—by Communist importunities and by representations of some of our allies—upon the attention of the Government and people of the United States: (1) should not the United States "recognize" Communist China? (2) should not Communist China be admitted to the United Nations?

Those questions relate not to recognition and admission of the country, China, but to action regarding a new government, the "People's Government of the People's Republic of China," a government which, Communist in origin, in support, in composition, in methods and in purposes, now exercises authority over most but by no means all of the territory and population of China. The United States long ago recognized China, and it, in 1928, accorded recognition—as did then and thereafter most other countries—to the National Government of the Republic of China. Under the National Government, China became in 1942 one of the original signers of the Declaration of United Nations and became in 1945 a founder member of the United Nations. In the United Nations, China is a permanent member of the Security Council, and China's National Government represents China, speaks for China and casts China's votes.

So, the issues now are not that of recognizing China, not that of admitting China to the United Nations: they are that of withdrawing recognition from the National Government and giving recognition to the Communist Government, and that of taking China's seats in the United Nations from the National Government and giving those seats to the—Communist— "People's Government." There is, of course, conceivable a procedure the essence of which would, if agreed upon, involve a separation and division from which there would emerge two Chinas, one Nationalist and the other Communist; but in my opinion this is so little practicable that it need not be considered here. The United States has always stood for the principle of a united and independent China, and has opposed efforts in conflict with that principle; and any proposals for a division would probably be opposed by the Chinese people everywhere and by both of the competing governments.

As matters stand, some twenty-five countries have transferred their recognition from the National Government to the "People's Government," but a larger number have not done so; several of those that have done so are supporting the demands of the "People's Government" and the Communist bloc that the United States do likewise; and the "People's Government" and the Communist world and several non-Communist countries are pressing for transfer of China's seats in the United Nations to the "People's Government."

In this situation what should the United States do? What position should we take and maintain? What efforts should we make? These questions should be considered by the people and the Government of the United States with a view to best safeguarding and serving the legitimate interests and objectives of our own country, with due respect, of course, for the legitimate interests and objectives of other countries and peoples. It happens that, with developments in world affairs, the United States has in recent years become—by virtue of many factors—the most powerful and most influential country in the free world. In this moment of history in which the whole of the free world is endangered by the Soviet-Communist program of conquest, the most vital of the many interests of the United States are those of national and international security. The people and the Government of the United States are concerned with the problem of world peace because, first, they believe in peace, second, they believe in freedom and, third, they have come to the conclusion that only in a world at peace can their country and others have security and enjoy freedom. By virtue of its power and its championing of the cause of freedom and security

the United States is the leader of the free nations in resistance
to the Communist menace. The major concern, then, of the
United States, that of security, is identical with the major concern of each and of all of the free nations.

The United States cannot afford to take any action which
would result in the strengthening of the Communist world;
and it cannot afford to take action which would diminish the
strength of the free world. Recognition by the United States
of China's Communist Government would, on the one hand,
be very helpful to the Communist world and, on the other hand,
be very damaging to the free world. It would remove from the
pathway of the Communists the greatest of the obstacles to the
consolidation of their position in China. It would lead to liquidation of China's National Government and of Chinese
resistance to communism. It would make for an early transfer of
China's representation in the United Nations from the National
Government—which speaks and votes on the side of the free
world—to the Communist Government, which would speak
and vote on the side of the Communist world. Thus subtracting
from the voting strength of the free world and adding to the
voting strength of the Communist bloc, it would greatly augment
the Communist influence in the United States and the other
free nations. It would dishearten and demoralize those of the
peoples of Asia who are resisting the Communist advance and,
causing them and others to doubt the reliability of United States
support, it would diminish the capacity and weaken the will of
many nations to persevere in that resistance.

The world has long had reason to know, from the statements
of the principal Communist leaders and from the action of the
Communist authorities wherever they gain control, that every
Communist regime seeks to destroy the principles and practices
of human freedom, makes war on religion, and is employing
every conceivable device of persuasion and coercion for the
consolidation and extension of the atheistic and materialistic

system which the Communist leaders intend to impose upon the world. No action helpful to the Communist cause can be other than harmful to the interests of the free world. With those facts and that conclusion in mind, I devoutly hope that, both on moral grounds and on political grounds, both for its own good and for the good of all mankind, the United States will continue in its refusal to recognize China's "People's Government," will continue to oppose admission of that government to China's place in the United Nations, will be firm in its opposition to action calculated to strengthen that government, and will consistently support and give aid to movements and efforts calculated to prevent consolidation and extension of the authority of that government and the Communist coalition.

The United States should, I believe, persevere in its policy of opposition to trading with Communist China. Commodities, even those of nonstrategic quality, supplied by the outside world have contributed to the economic upbuilding and the military capabilities of Communist China and thus have facilitated action by the "People's Government" such as it has taken in Korea. The free world should in no part and in no way aid and abet aggression in terms of armed attack upon forces operating under the flag of the United Nations and on behalf of the principle of collective security. It would be difficult to say, and I would not try to say, to what extent the United States should exert pressure upon other countries in regard to this matter of trade; but it seems clear to me, and easy to say, that the less there is of trading with Communist China the better will be served the real, long swing interests of the free world.

In summation: I believe that the United States should pursue a foreign policy firmly based on principles well established and generally prevailing in what we call our "way of life." Regardless of creed or sect, we are a Christian people, our culture is a Christian culture, our country is a Christian state. Generally speaking, we order our lives individually and collectively, locally and nationally, in accordance with various commonly accepted concepts of morality, of legality, of propriety and of practicability. We should, I believe, in our relations with other peoples and governments, conduct ourselves in accordance with those same concepts.

We are a free people. But we now are menaced, as are others, by forces which have enslaved many nations and are eager to enslave all. The Chinese are a people who, while struggling to become free, have fallen a victim to those forces. Most of them are now behind the Iron Curtain, are being regimented, and are being taught that we and other free peoples are their enemies and must be destroyed. Some of them, however, are so located that they can continue to aspire to and fight for freedom and security. With these we have contact, and with them we can, as with other free peoples, have mutually advantageous relations.

We should think and act regarding the Chinese and their country in terms of the Golden Rule. We should *do* regarding them as we wish that they do regarding us, and we should *not* *do* regarding them what we would wish that they not do regarding us. We should favor with moral support and material aid those of them, wherever they may be, whose purposes and efforts are on the side of freedom and security. We should refrain from any action the result of which would be to increase the prestige and strength of those of them whose purposes and efforts are to subjugate and enslave others. We should make friends with, and try to be good neighbors to those of them who are disposed to appreciate and reciprocate manifestations of good will. There are many such, not alone on Formosa and in southeastern Asia but also nearer to us and among us. We should persevere in our support of the National Government and its followers, and we should make it a fixed premise of our policy that we cannot and will not tolerate conquest of Formosa by the Communists. We should decline to consider any proposals which would involve impairment or disregard by us of our existing commitments to the National Government. Likewise, we should refuse to be moved by the demands of the Communist "People's Government" and the importunities from various quarters in its support that we accord that government our recognition. We should, moreover, firmly and consistently oppose every effort and device directed toward effecting admission of that government to China's place in the United Nations. We should refrain from and we should discourage, within reason, trading with areas and people under that government's domination.

Finally, we should keep constantly in mind the fact that compromises wherein the United States has on several occasions in the past allowed itself to become involved regarding China have in no instance profited the United States and have in every instance proved harmful to China. I have in mind as clear examples the Lansing-Ishii Agreement, with a secret commitment on the side, in 1917; the concessions to Japan regarding Shantung, at Paris in 1919; and the "Agreement on the Far East," at Yalta in 1945. Disregard of principle, abandonment of sound tradition, decisions based on considerations of fancied expediency, courses of opportunism, "robbing Peter to pay Paul" —such procedures are not in the "American way." We should in our relations with China and her people conform our plans and our conduct to the same high standards that we apply at home and in our relations with countries nearer to ours and peoples more like ourselves.

Above all, we should make sure that our decisions and action regarding China are consistent with the purposes of our foreign policy as a whole. We seek peace and security. These are objectives common to all peoples not intent upon conquest. In order to have security for ourselves, we must co-operate with all other of such peoples. Our policies and our procedures must be based, not on the sands of alluring "deals" and glittering promises but on the solid rock of sound principles, consistent honesty and enduring reliability.

Appendix

I. DIRECTIVES OF GENERAL MARSHALL'S MISSION IN CHINA

*1. President Truman to the
Special Representative of the President to China (Marshall)*

WASHINGTON, *December 15, 1945*

My Dear General Marshall: On the eve of your departure for China I want to repeat to you my appreciation of your willingness to undertake this difficult mission.

I have the utmost confidence in your ability to handle the task before you but, to guide you in so far as you may find it helpful, I will give you some of the thoughts, ideas, and objectives which Secretary Byrnes and I have in mind with regard to your mission.

I attach several documents which I desire should be considered as part of this letter. One is a statement of U. S. policy towards China which was, I understand, prepared after consultation with you and with officials of the Department. The second is a memorandum from the Secretary of State to the War Department in regard to China. And the third is a copy of my press release on policy in China. I understand that these documents have been shown to you and received your approval.

The fact that I have asked you to go to China is the clearest evidence of my very real concern with regard to the situation there. Secretary Byrnes and I are both anxious that the unification of China by peaceful, democratic methods be achieved as soon as possible. It is my desire that you, as my Special Representative, bring to bear in an appropriate and practicable manner the influence of the United States to this end.

Specifically, I desire that you endeavor to persuade the Chinese Government to call a national conference of representatives of the major political elements to bring about the unification of China and, concurrently, to effect a cessation of hostilities, particularly in north China.

It is my understanding that there is now in session in Chungking a Peoples' Consultative Council made up of representatives of the various political elements, including the Chinese Communists. The meeting of this Council should furnish you with a convenient opportunity for discussions with the various political leaders.

Upon the success of your efforts, as outlined above, will depend largely, of course, the success of our plans for evacuating Japanese troops from China, particularly north China, and for the subsequent withdrawal of our own armed forces from China. I am particularly desirous that both be accomplished as soon as possible.

In your conversations with Chiang Kai-shek and other Chinese leaders you are authorized to speak with the utmost frankness. Particularly, you may state, in connection with the Chinese desire for credits, technical assistance in the economic field, and military assistance (I have in mind the proposed U. S. military advisory group which I have approved in principle), that a China disunited and torn by civil strife could not be considered realistically as a proper place for American assistance along the lines enumerated.

I am anxious that you keep Secretary Byrnes and me currently informed of the progress of your negotiations and of obstacles you may encounter. You will have our full support and we shall endeavor at all times to be as helpful to you as possible.

> Sincerely yours,
>
> HARRY TRUMAN
>
> [Enclosure]

2. Memorandum by Secretary Byrnes

[WASHINGTON,] *December 9, 1945*

For the War Department

The President and the Secretary of State are both anxious that the unification of China by peaceful democratic methods be achieved as soon as possible.

At a public hearing before the Foreign Relations Committee of the Senate on December 7, the Secretary of State said:

"During the war the immediate goal of the United States in China was to promote a military union of the several political factions in order to bring their combined power to bear upon our common enemy, Japan. Our longer-range goal, then as now, and a goal of at least equal importance, is the development of a strong, united, and democratic China.

"To achieve this longer-range goal, it is essential that the Central Government of China as well as the various dissident elements approach the settlement of their differences with a genuine willingness to compromise. We believe, as we have long believed and consistently demonstrated, that the government of Generalissimo Chiang Kai-shek affords the most satisfactory base for a developing democracy. But we also believe that it must be broadened to include the representatives of those large and well organized groups who are now without any voice in the government of China.

"This problem is not an easy one. It requires tact and discretion, patience and restraint. It will not be solved by the Chinese leaders themselves. To the extent that our influence is a factor, success will depend upon our capacity to exercise that influence in the light of shifting conditions in such a way as to encourage concessions by the Central Government, by the so-called Communists, and by the other factions."

The President has asked General Marshal to go to China as his Special Representative for the purpose of bringing to bear in an appropriate and practicable manner the influence of the United States for the achievement of the ends set forth above. Specifically, General Marshall will endeavor to influence the Chinese Government to call a national conference of representatives of the major political elements to bring about the unification of China and, concurrently, effect a cessation of hostilities, particularly in north China.

In response to General Wedemeyer's recent messages, the State Department requests the War Department to arrange for directions to him stipulating that:

(1) He may put into effect the arrangements to assist the Chinese National Government in transporting Chineses troops to Manchurian ports, including the logistical support of such troops;

(2) He may also proceed to put into effect the stepped-up arrangements for the evacuation of Japanese troops from the China theater;

(3) Pending the outcome of General Marshall's discussions with Chinese leaders in Chungking for the purpose of arranging a national conference of representatives of the major political elements and for a cessation of hostilities, further transportation of Chinese troops to north China, except as north China ports may be necessary for the movement of troops and supplies into Manchuria, will be held in abeyance;

(4) Arrangements for transportation of Chinese troops into north China may be immediately perfected, but not communicated to the Chinese Government. Such arrangements will be executed when General Marshall determines either (a) that the movement of Chinese troops to north China can be carried out consistently with his negotiations, or (b) that the negotiations between the Chinese groups have failed or show no prospect of success and that the circumstances are such as to make the movement necessary to effectuate the surrender terms and to secure the long-term interests of the United States in the maintenance of international peace.

3. Statement by President Truman on United States Policy Toward China, December 15, 1945

The Government of the United States holds that peace and prosperity of the world in this new and unexplored era ahead depend upon the ability of the sovereign nations to combine for collective security in the United Nations organization.

It is the firm belief of this Government that a strong, united and democratic China is of the utmost importance to the success of this United Nations organization and for world peace. A China disorganized and divided either by foreign aggression, such as that undertaken by the Japanese, or by violent internal strife, is an undermining influence to world stability and peace, now and in the future. The United States Government has long subscribed to the principle that the management of internal affairs is the responsibility of the peoples of the sovereign nations. Events of this century, however, would indicate that a breach of peace anywhere in the world threatens the peace of the entire world. It is thus in the most vital interest of the United States and all the United Nations that the people of China overlook no opportunity to adjust their internal differences promptly by means of peaceful negotiation.

The Government of the United States believes it essential:

(1) That a cessation of hostilities be arranged between the armies of the National Government and the Chinese Communists and other dissident Chinese armed forces for the purpose of completing the return of all China to effective Chinese control, including the immediate evacuation of the Japanese forces.

(2) That a national conference of representatives of major political elements be arranged to develop an early solution to the present internal strife —a solution which will bring about the unification of China.

The United States and the other United Nations have recognized the present National Government of the Republic of China as the only legal government in China. It is the proper instrument to achieve the objective of a unified China.

The United States and the United Kingdom by the Cairo Declaration in 1943 and the Union of Soviet Socialist Republics by adhering to the Potsdam Declaration of last July and by the Sino-Soviet Treaty and Agreements of August 1945, are all committed to the liberation of China, including the return of Manchuria to Chinese control. These agreements were made with the National Government of the Republic of China.

In continuation of the constant and close collaboration with the National Government of the Republic of China in the prosecution of this war, in consonance with the Potsdam Declaration, and to remove possibility of Japanese influence remaining in China, the United States has assumed a definite obligation in the disarmament and evacuation of the Japanese troops. Accordingly the United States has been assisting and will continue to assist the National Government of the Republic of China in effecting the disarmament and evacuation of Japanese troops in the liberated areas. The United States Marines are in North China for that purpose.

The United States recognizes and will continue to recognize the National Government of China and cooperate with it in international affairs and specifically in eliminating Japanese influence from China. The United States is convinced that a prompt arrangement for a cessation of hostilities is essential to the effective achievement of this end. United States support will not extend to United States military intervention to influence the course of any Chinese internal strife.

The United States has already been compelled to pay a great price to restore the peace which was first broken by Japanese aggression in Manchuria. The maintenance of peace in the Pacific may be jeopardized, if not frustrated, unless Japanese influence in China is wholly removed and unless China takes her place as a unified, democratic and peaceful nation. This is the purpose of the maintenance for the time being of United States military and naval forces in China.

The United States is cognizant that the present National Government of China is a "one-party government" and believes that peace, unity and democratic reform in China will be furthered if the basis of this Government is broadened to include other political elements in the country. Hence, the United States strongly advocates that the national conference of representatives of major political elements in the country agree upon arrangements which would give those elements a fair and effective representation in the Chinese National Government. It is recognized that this would require modification of the one-party "political tutelage" established as an interim arrangement in the progress of the nation toward democracy by the father of the Chinese Republic, Doctor Sun Yat-sen.

The existence of autonomous armies such as that of the Communist army is inconsistent with, and actually makes impossible, political unity in China. With the instituton of a broadly representative government, autonomous armies should be eliminated as such and all armed forces in China integrated effectively into the Chinese National Army.

In line with its often expressed views regarding self-determination, the United States Government considers that the detailed steps necessary to the achievement of political unity in China must be worked out by the Chinese themselves and that intervention by any foreign government in these matters would be inappropriate. The United States Government feels, however, that China has a clear responsibility to the other United Nations to eliminate armed conflict within its territory as constituting a threat to world stability and peace—a responsibility which is shared by the National Government and all Chinese political and military groups.

As China moves toward peace and unity along the lines described above, the United States would be prepared to assist the National Government in every reasonable way to rehabilitate the country, improve the agrarian and industrial economy, and establish a military organization capable of discharging China's national and international responsibilites for the maintenance of peace and order. In furtherance of such assistance, it would be prepared to give favorable consideration to Chinese requests for credits and loans under reasonable conditions for projects which would contribute toward the development of a healthy economy throughout China and healthy trade relations between China and the United States.

II. THE FIVE PROPOSITIONS ADOPTED BY THE POLITICAL CONSULTATIVE CONFERENCE (JANUARY 6-31, 1946).

1. Resolution on Government Organization adopted by the Political Consultative Conference, January 1946

I. Concerning the State Council: Pending the convocation of the National Assembly, the Kuomintang, as a preliminary measure preparatory to the actual inauguration of constitutionalism, will revise the Organic Law of the National Government in order to expand the State Council. The following are the salient points of the revision under contemplation:

1. There will be forty (40) State Councillors, of whom the Presidents of the Executive, Legislative, Judicial, Examination, and Control Yuan will be ex-officio members.

2. The State Councillors will be chosen by the President of the National Government from among the Kuomintang members as well as non-members of the Kuomintang.

3. The State Council is the supreme organ of the Government in charge of national affairs.

4. The State Council will be competent to discuss and decide on:
A. Legislative principles.
B. Administrative policy.
C. Important military measures.
D. Financial schemes and the budget.
E. The appointment and dismissal of Ministers of State with or without portfolios, and the appointment of members of the Legislative and Control Yuan.
F. Matters submitted by the President of the National Government for consideration.
G. Proposals submitted by three or more State Councillors.

5. If the President of the National Government is of opinion that any decision of the State Council is difficult to be carried out, he may submit it for reconsideration. In case three-fifths of the State Councillors, upon reconsideration, uphold the original decision, it shall be carried out accordingly.

6. General resolutions before the State Council are to be passed by a majority vote of the State Councillors present. If a resolution before the State Council should involve changes in administrative policy, it must be passed by a two-thirds vote of the State Councillors present. Whether a given resolution involves changes in administrative policy or not is to be decided by a majority vote of the State Councillors present.

7. The State Council meets every two weeks. The President of the National Government may call emergency meetings, if necessary.

II. Concerning the Executive Yuan.

1. All Ministers of the Executive Yuan are ipso facto Ministers of State. There may be three to five Ministers of State without portfolios.

2. Members of all political parties as well as individuals with no party affiliations may become Ministers of State with or without portfolios.

III. Concerning miscellaneous matters.

1. Whether the membership of the People's Political Council should be increased and its powers raised, pending the inauguration of the Constitution, will be left to the Government to decide in the light of the circumstances of the time.

2. All Government employees, whether of the Central Government or of the local Governments, should be selected on the basis of merit. No discriminations on account of party affiliations should be allowed.

NOTE: A. The appointment of State Councillors by the President of the National Government will be made on the nomination of the different parties concerned. In case he does not consent to the candidature of any given individual, the party concerned may nominate another one for the office.

B. When the President of the National Government nominates any individual with no party affiliations as State Councillor whose candidature is opposed by one-third of the other nominees, he must reconsider the matter and make a different nomination.

C. Half of the State Councillors will be Kuomintang members and the other half will be members of other political parties and prominent social leaders. The exact number of members of other political parties and prominent social leaders who are to serve as State Councillors will form the subject of separate discussions.

D. Of the existing Ministers under the Executive Yuan and the proposed Ministers of State without portfolios, seven or eight will be appointed from among non-Kuomintang members.

E. The number of Ministries to be assigned to non-Kuomintang members will form the subject of separate discussions after the PCC has closed.

2. Resolution on Program for Peaceful National Reconstruction Adopted by the Political Consultative Conference, January 1946

Now that the war of resistance against Japan has ended and peaceful reconstruction should begin, the National Government has invited representatives of the different political parties and prominent social leaders to the Political Consultative Conference to discuss national problems with the double objective of putting an end to the period of political tutelage and inaugurating constitutionalism at an early date. The present program is drawn up to serve as a guide for the Government, pending the actual inauguration of constitutionalism. Representatives of the different political parties and prominent social leaders will be invited to take part in the Government. It is to be hoped that one and all will give first consideration to the needs of the nation and the demands of the people, and that they will cooperate wholeheartedly and work for the realization of the program, whose main features are as follows:

I. GENERAL PRINCIPLES

1. The principles of the San Min Chu I will be regarded as the highest guiding principles for national reconstruction.
2. All forces of the nation will unite under the guidance of President Chiang Kai-shek in order to construct a new China, unified, free, and democratic.
3. It is recognized that the democratization of politics, the nationalization of troops, and the equality and legality of all political parties, as advocated by President Chiang, are necessary paths leading to peaceful national reconstruction.
4. Political disputes must be settled by political means in order to maintain peaceful national development.

II. THE RIGHTS OF THE PEOPLE

1. The freedoms of person, thought, religion, belief, speech, the press, assembly, association, residence, removal, and correspondence should be guaranteed to the people. Any existing laws that contravene these freedoms should be either revised or repealed.
2. Any organization or individual other than judicial organs and the police should be strictly forbidden to arrest, try, and punish the people. Anyone who violates this rule shall be punished. The Habeas Corpus Law which has already been promulgated by the Government should be put into practical operation by Government decree at an early date.
3. The political, social, educational, and economic equality of women should be guaranteed.

III. POLITICAL PROBLEMS

1. All national measures of the moment should take into consideration the proper interests of the people of all localities, classes, and professions, and allow for their equitable development.
2. In order to increase administrative efficiency, the different grades of

administrative machinery should be revamped, their rights and duties should be unified and clearly delimited, all unnecessary Governmental agencies should be abolished, the administrative procedure should be simplified, and the principle of individual responsibility each for his own section of the work should be introduced.

3. A sound system of civil service should be established: competent individuals should be protected; Government employees should be appointed not on the basis of personal or party allegiance, but on that of ability and past experience; no one should be allowed to hold concurrent jobs or to be drawn into Government service through the exertion of purely personal influence.

4. The unity and independence of the judicial power should be guaranteed, precluding it from political interference. The personnel in the courts of law should be increased, their salaries and positions should be raised, the judicial procedure should be simplified, and prisons should be reformed.

5. The supervisory system should be strictly enforced; corruption should be severely punished; facilities should be given to the people to accuse corrupt officials.

6. Local self-government should be actively pushed forth, and popular elections beginning from the lower administrative units and gradually ascending to the highest unit should be carried out. Provincial, District, and Municipal Councils should be established throughout the country at an early date, and District Magistrates should be elected by the people.

In frontier provinces and districts where minority peoples live, the number of Provincial or District Councillors to be elected by these minority peoples should be fixed according to the proportion they occupy in their respective provinces or districts.

7. All national administrative matters which have to be carried out in the territory of a district which has attained complete self-government must be carried out under the supervision and control of the National Government.

8. The powers of the Central and local Governments should be regulated on the basis of the principle of "a fair distribution of powers". The local Governments may take such measures as are adapted to the special circumstances of the localities concerned, but the regulations issued by the Provincial and District Governments must not contravene the laws and decrees of the Central Government.

IV. MILITARY AFFAIRS

1. The army belongs to the State. It is the duty of the soldier to protect the country and love the people and to insure the unity both of military organization and of military command.

2. All military establishments should be adapted to the needs of national defense. The military system should be reformed in accordance with democratic institutions and the circumstances of the nation. The army and political parties should be separated from each other; military and civil authority should be vested in different hands; military education should be improved; equipment should be adequate; a sound personnel and finance system should be introduced. All these should be done in order to create a modernized national army.

3. The system of conscription should be improved and made to apply fairly and throughout the whole country. Some form of the volunteer system should be maintained and improved upon in order to meet the needs of a fully equipped army.

4. All troops of the country should be reorganized into a lesser number

of units in accordance with the provisions of the "Military Reorganization Plan".

5. Preparations for the rehabilitation and employment of disbanded and retired officers and men should be made. The livelihood of disabled officers and men should be guaranteed. The families of fallen officers and men should be provided for.

6. A time limit should be set for the repatriation of the Japanese troops who have surrendered. Adequate measures should be put into operation at an early date for the disbandment of puppet troops and the liquidation of roving armed bands.

V. FOREIGN RELATIONS

1. The Atlantic Charter, the Cairo Declaration, the Moscow Four-Power Declaration, and the United Nations Organization Charter should be observed. China will take an active part in the UNO in order to preserve world peace.

2. All remnants of Japanese influence in China should be extirpated according to the provisions of the Potsdam Declaration. The problem of Japan should be solved in cooperation with other Allied Nations in order to prevent the resurgence of Japanese Fascist-militarist forces and to guarantee the security of the Far East.

3. Friendly relations with the United States, the Soviet Union, the United Kingdom, France, and other democratic countries should be promoted; treaty obligations should be observed; and economic and cultural cooperation should be undertaken in order to work for the prosperity and progress of the world in conjunction with other countries.

4. Commercial treaties, based on the principles of equality and reciprocity, should be concluded at an early date with other nations when necessary, and the position of Chinese residents overseas should be ameliorated.

VI. ECONOMICS AND FINANCE

1. A plan of economic reconstruction should be formulated in accordance with the teachings of Dr. Sun Yat-sen's "Industrial Planning", and the cooperation of foreign capital and technique should be welcome.

2. Any enterprise which partakes of the nature of a monopoly or which cannot be undertaken by private initiative should be classified as a state enterprise; the people should be encouraged to undertake all other enterprises. Such should be the principles for the first stage of economic reconstruction, which must be effectively carried out. All existing measures should be examined and improved upon in the light of this principle.

3. In order to hasten the process of China's industrialization the Government should convene a National Economic Conference, to which will be invited social leaders interested in the problem of economic reconstruction. In this way the Government will be able to sound out popular opinion and decide upon the measures to be taken.

4. The development of "official capitalism" should be forestalled. Government officials should be strictly forbidden to take advantage of their official position to indulge in speculation and cornering, smuggle, evade taxes, embezzle public funds, and illegally make use of the means of transportation.

5. Active preparations must be made for the construction of additional railroads and highways, harbors and bays, irrigation and other projects. Subsidies should be granted to those who construct houses, schools, hospitals, and other public buildings.

6. Farm rents and interest rates must be effectively reduced. The rights of the lessee must be protected, and the payment of farm rents must be guaranteed. More and larger loans to farmers must be made available, and usury should be strictly prohibited. All these must be done in order to better the peasants' lot. The land law must be put into operation so as to attain the objective of "He who tills the soil also owns it."

7. Active measures should be taken to help the people increase their productive power by afforestation and the growth of grass, the conservation of water and soil, the development of animal husbandry, the reorganization and further development of agricultural cooperation, the expansion of agricultural experimentation and research, and the utilization of modern equipment and methods to kill locusts and other insects.

8. Labor laws must be put into operation. The conditions of labor must be improved; the bonus system should be put on trial; unemployment and disablement insurances should be started; child and female labor should be given adequate protection; more workers' schools should be established in order to raise the cultural level of the working population.

9. Laws governing industrial association should be made at an early date, so that those engaged in industrial undertakings may form their own associations. Laws concerning factory management should be examined and revised on the assumption that there prevails a spirit of conciliation between capital and labor.

10. Financial accounts should be made public. The budget system and annual accounts system should be strictly adopted. Public expenditure should be curtailed, and revenues and expenditures should be balanced. Central Government finance and local finance should be sharply differentiated. The currency should be deflated and the monetary system should be stabilized. The raising of both domestic and foreign loans and the use to which they will be put should be made public and subject to popular supervision.

11. The system of taxation should be reformed. All illegal taxes and extortions should be completely abolished. The various offices for the collection of taxes should be amalgamated, and the procedure of collection should be simplified. Progressive taxes should be imposed on assets and incomes. National banks should be entrusted with special economic tasks in order to help develop industry and agriculture. Assets which have escaped to foreign countries or have been frozen should be commandeered to be used for the balancing of the budget.

VII. EDUCATION AND CULTURE

1. The freedom of learning should be guaranteed. Religious beliefs and political ideologies should not be allowed to interfere with school and college administration.

2. Scientific research and artistic creation should be encouraged in order to raise the national cultural level.

3. Compulsory education and social education should be made nationwide; illiteracy should be actively wiped out. Professional education should be expanded in order to increase the professional ability of the people; normal education should be further developed in order to educate more qualified teachers for compulsory education. The contents of the teaching material in the various grades of schools should be revised in the light of the democratic and scientific spirit.

4. The proportion of the national budget to be devoted to education and cultural enterprises should be increased. The salaries and retirement annuities of teachers in the various grades of schools should be reasonably increased.

Poor students should be subsidized, so that they can go to school and continue their studies. Endowments should be made for scientific research and creative literary and artistic work.

5. Privately endowed schools and cultural work among the people should be encouraged and subsidized.

6. In order to promote national health encouragement and assistance should be given to all forms of child welfare, public health installations should be made nation-wide, and physical exercise should be actively encouraged.

7. The wartime censorships of the press, motion pictures, the drama, letters, and telegrams should be abolished. Assistance should be given to the development of businesses in connection with publications, newspapers, news agencies, the drama, and motion pictures. All news agents and cultural enterprises operated by the Government should serve the interests of the entire nation.

VIII. REHABILITATION AND RELIEF

1. Social order in the liberated areas should be restored at an early date. The people must be relieved of all oppressions and sufferings which were heaped on them in the period of enemy occupation. The tendency for prices to rise in the liberated areas must be curbed. All corrupt practices of officials who were sent to the occupied territories to take over from the enemy should be severely punished.

2. Railroads and highways should be quickly repaired. Inland and coastal shipping should be quickly restored. Those people who have migrated to the interior in wartime must be helped by the government to return to their native districts. Homes and jobs should be found for them, if necessary.

3. Good use must be made of the UNRRA supplies in order to relieve the war refugees; medical supplies must be distributed to them in order to cure and prevent diseases; seeds and fertilizers must be given them in order to restore farming. The authorities in charge of this work will be assisted by popular agencies and organizations in the discharge of their duties.

4. Factories and mines in the liberated areas must be quickly made operative; the property rights of the original owners must be protected; work must be resumed at an early date, so that employment may be found for those without useful occupations. Enemy and puppet property should be properly disposed of in order to enable those factories and individuals who have made significant contributions to the war of resistance in the interior to take part in its exploitation.

5. The Yellow River must be quickly put under control. Other irrigation projects which have been damaged or allowed to lapse in the course of the war must be made good at an early date.

6. The Government's decrees to stop conscription and exempt the people from the payment of agricultural taxes for one year must be carried out to the letter by the different grades of Government. No conscription or agricultural taxes under a different guise should be allowed.

IX. CHINESE RESIDENTS OVERSEAS

1. Chinese residents overseas who have become destitute as a result of enemy oppression will be helped by the Government to reestablish their former business; those members of their families who may be living in China will receive proper relief.

2. Assistance will be given to Chinese residents overseas who have returned

to China in the last few years in the course of the war, so that they may
go back to their former place of residence. Facilities will be provided for
hem for the recovery of their property and the reestablishment of their
-usiness.

3. All educational and cultural enterprises of Chinese residents overseas
will be restored and active assistance will be given them by the Government.
Encouragement and assistance will be given to the children of Chinese
residents overseas to come back to China for education.

ANNEX

1. In those recovered areas where the local government is under dispute
the status quo shall be maintained until a settlement is made according
to Articles 6, 7, and 8 of Chapter III on Political Problems in this program
by the National Government after its reorganization.

2. A Committee for the Protection of the People's Liberties will be formed,
composed of representatives of the local Council, the Lawyers' Association,
and popular organizations. Financial assistance will be given to it by the
Government.

3. Revisions will be made, in the light of the usual practices in democratic
countries, in the Citizen's Oath-Taking and the examination of candidates
for public offices.

4. Membership of the Supreme Economic Council of the Executive Yuan
should be increased by the addition of economic experts representing the
people at large and of experienced industrialists.

5. It is recommended that the Government put an end to the policy of
control over nitrate and sulphur.

6. (a) Those workers originally employed in factories which have been
removed to the interior in the course of the war, who now find themselves
unemployed due to the closing up of the factories as a result of the war,
should be granted a certain amount of financial assistance by the Government.

(b) Those factories which have made significant contributions to the
manufacture of military material in the course of the war should continue to
receive Government patronage by the latter's purchase of their ready-made
articles and as much of their material as possible.

7. The press law should be revised. The Regulations Governing the Regis-
tration and Control of Newspapers, Magazines, and News Services in Times
of Emergency; Provisional Regulations Governing Newspapers, News Agencies, Magazines, Motion Pictures, and Broadcasts in Liberated Areas; Regulations Governing the Censorship of the Drama and Motion Pictures;
Regulations Governing the Censorship of Letters and Telegrams, and other
regulations of a similar nature should be repealed. Amusement taxes and
stamp taxes on motion pictures, drama, and concert tickets should be
lightened.

3. Resolution on Military Problems Adopted by the Political Consultative Conference, January 1946

I. Fundamental principles for the creation of a national army.

1. The army belongs to the State. It is the duty of the soldier to protect
the country and love the people.

2. The army shall be established in response to the necessities of national defense. Its quality and equipment shall be improved in the light of the progress made in general education, science, and industry.

3. The military system shall be reformed in the light of the democratic institutions and actual conditions prevailing at the time.

4. The system of conscription shall be reformed and applied fairly and universally. Some form of the volunteer system shall be preserved and reforms shall be introduced in order to meet the requirements of a fully equipped army.

5. Military education shall be conducted in the light of the foregoing principles, and shall forever be dissociated from party affiliations and personal allegiance.

II. Fundamental principles for the reorganization of the army.

1. Separation of army and party.
A. All political parties shall be forbidden to carry on party activities, whether open or secret, in the army. So shall be all cliques based on personal relations or of a territorial nature.
B. All soldiers on active service who owe allegiance to any political party may not take part in the party activities of the district in which they are stationed, when they are on duty.
C. No party or individual may make use of the army as an instrument of political rivalry.
D. No illegal organizations and activities may be allowed in the army.
2. Separation of civil and military authorities.
A. No soldier on active service in the army may serve concurrently as civil officials.
B. The country shall be divided into military districts, which shall be made not to coincide with administrative districts as far as possible.
C. The army shall be strictly forbidden to interfere in political affairs.

III. Methods aiming at the civilian control of the army.

1. When the preliminary measures for the reorganization of the army have been completed, the National Military Council shall be reorganized into a Ministry of National Defense under the Executive Yuan.

2. The Minister of National Defense shall not necessarily be a soldier.

3. The number of troops and military expenditure shall be decided upon by the Executive Yuan and passed by the Legislative Yuan.

4. All troops shall be under the unified control of the Ministry of National Defense.

5. A Military Committee shall be established within the Ministry of National Defense to be charged with the double duty of drawing up schemes for the creation of a national army and of seeing to it that the schemes are faithfully carried out. Members of the Committee shall be drawn from various circles.

IV. Practical methods for the reorganization of the army.

1. The three-man military commission shall proceed according to schedule and agree upon practical methods for the reorganization of the Communist troops at an early date. The reorganization must be completed as soon as possible.

2. The Government troops should be reorganized, according to the plan laid down by the Ministry of War, into ninety (90) divisions. The reorganization should be completed within six (6) months.

3. When the reorganizations envisaged in paragraphs 1 and 2 have been

completed, all troops of the country should be again reorganized into fifty (50) or sixty (60) divisions.

4. A commission for the supervision of the reorganization plan shall be established within the National Military Council. Members of the commission shall be drawn from various circles.

4. Agreement on the National Assembly by Sub-Committee of the Political Consultative Conference

Based on the resolution on this subject introduced by the Government representatives, the following agreement on the National Assembly was reached in the PCC Sub-Committee dealing with this problem by the various delegations:

1. That the National Assembly shall be convened on May 5, 1946.
2. That the power of the National Assembly is to adopt the Constitution.
3. That the Constitution shall be adopted by a vote of three-fourths of the delegates present.
4. That the 1,200 geographical and vocational delegates, who have been or are going to be elected according to the electoral law of the National Assembly, shall be retained.
5. That the geographical and vocational delegates for the Northeast provinces and Taiwan shall be increased by 150.
6. That 700 seats shall be added to the National Assembly and they shall be apportioned among the various parties and social leaders. The ratio of apportionment shall be decided later.
7. That the total number of delegates to the National Assembly shall be 2,050.
8. That the organ to enforce the Constitution shall be elected six months after the Constitution is adopted.

5. Resolution on the Draft Constitution Adopted by the Political Consultative Conference, January 1946

I. Establishments of a Reviewing Committee.

1. *Name:* Committee for the Reviewing of the Draft Constitution.
2. *Organization:* The Committee will have a total membership of twenty-five (25), of whom five (5) will represent each of the five groups composing the Political Consultation Conference. In addition, ten (10) technical experts outside of the PCC will be invited to take part in the work of the Committee. In selecting the technical experts reference should be made to the membership lists of the Association for the Promotion of Constitutionalism and the Association to Assist the Inauguration of Constitutionalism.
3. *Functions:* The PCC will establish the Committee for the Reviewing of the Draft Constitution, which will draw up a comprehensive scheme for the revision of the 1936 Draft Constitution on the basis of the principles recommended by the PCC and in the light of the recommendations made by the Association for the Promotion of Constitutionalism and the Associa-

tion to Assist the Inauguration of Constitutionalism and opinions advanced by various other quarters. This scheme will be submitted to the National Assembly for adoption. It may also be laid before the PCC for discussion, if necessary.

4. *Duration:* Two months.

II. Principles to be applied in the revision of the Draft Constitution.

1. Concerning the National Assembly.

A. The entire electorate, when they exercise the rights of election, initiative, referendum, and recall, are called the National Assembly.

B. Pending the election of the President by universal suffrage, he shall be elected by an electoral body composed of the District, Provincial, and National Representative Assemblies.

C. The recall of the President is to be effected by the same means as that employed in his election.

D. The exercise of the rights of initiative and referendum will be defined by appropriate laws.

NOTE: The convocation of the first National Assembly will form the subject of discussion by the PCC.

2. Concerning the Legislative Yuan: The Legislative Yuan will be the supreme law-making body of the State and will be elected by the electorate. This function corresponds to those of a Parliament in a democratic country.

3. Concerning the Control Yuan: The Control Yuan will be the supreme organ of control of the State and will be elected by the Provincial Assemblies and the Assemblies of the Self-Governing Areas of Minority Peoples. It will exercise the functions of consent, impeachment, and control.

4. Concerning the Judicial Yuan: The Judicial Yuan will be the Supreme Court of the State, and will not be responsible for judicial administration. It will be composed of a specified number of justices, who will be appointed on the nomination of the President of the National Government and with the consent of the Control Yuan. The different grades of judges shall all be without party affiliations.

5. Concerning the Examination Yuan: The Examination Yuan will be in the form of a committee, whose members will be appointed on the nomination of the President of the National Government and with the consent of the Control Yuan. Its functions will be mainly to examine candidates for civil service and technical experts. Members of the Examination Yuan shall be without party affiliations.

6. Concerning the Executive Yuan.

A. The Executive Yuan is the Supreme executive organ of the State. The President of the Executive Yuan is to be appointed on the nomination of the President of the National Government and with the consent of the Legislative Yuan. The Executive Yuan is to be responsible to the Legislative Yuan.

B. If the Legislative Yuan has no confidence in the Executive Yuan as a whole, the latter may either resign or ask the President of the National Government to dissolve the former. But the same President of the Executive Yuan may not ask for the dissolution of the Legislative Yuan for a second time.

7. Concerning the Presidency of the National Government.

A. The President of the National Government may promulgate emergency decrees according to law when the Executive Yuan has so decided. But the action must be reported to the Legislative Yuan within one month.

B. The right of the President of the National Government to call the Presidents of the Executive, Legislative, Judicial, Examination, and Control Yuan into conference need not be written into the Constitution.

Appendix

8. Concerning the system of local government.

A. The Province is to be regarded as the highest unit of local self-government.

B. The powers of the Province and the Control Government will be divided according to the principle of "a fair distribution of power."

C. The Provincial Governor is to be elected by the people.

D. The Province may have a Provincial Constitution, which, however, must not contravene the provisions of the National Constitution.

9. Concerning the rights and duties of the people.

A. All freedoms and rights which are generally enjoyed by the peoples of democratic countries should be protected by the Constitution and should not be illegally encroached upon.

B. If the freedom of the people is to be defined by law, it must be done for its protection and not with a view to restricting it.

C. Labor service should be provided for in the Law on Local Self-Government, and not written into the National Constitution.

D. The right of self-government must be guaranteed to minority peoples who live together in one particular locality.

10. A separate chapter on elections should be provided in the Constitution. Only those twenty-three years of age or over have the right to be elected.

11. Concerning fundamental national policies: A separate chapter in the Constitution should be devoted to fundamental national policies, including items on national defense, foreign relations, national economy, culture, and education.

A. The aim of national defense is to guarantee the safety of the Nation and preserve the peace of the world. All members of the Army, Navy, and Air Forces should be loyal to the State, love the people, and rise above all personal, territorial, and party affiliations.

B. Foreign relations should be carried on in a spirit of independence. Friendly relations with foreign countries should be promoted, treaty obligations carried out, the Charter of the United Nations Organization observed, international cooperation fostered, and world peace guaranteed.

C. Dr. Sun Yat-sen's principle of economic democracy (the Min Sen Chu I) should serve as the basis of the national economy. The State must see to it that he who tills the soil also owns it; that workers have jobs; and that enterprisers have ample opportunity to carry on their business. These things must be done in order to attain the twin objective of fairness and sufficiency in the national economy and the people's livelihood.

D. It should be the aim of culture and education to foster the growth of the national spirit, the democratic attitude of mind, and scientific knowledge and technique. The general cultural level of the people should be universally raised; equality of educational opportunity should be made a reality; freedom of learning should be guaranteed; and scientific development should be pushed forth with vigor.

NOTE: The provisions in the Constitution relative to paragraphs (a), (b), (c), and (d) should not go too much into detail.

12. Concerning amendments to the Constitution: The right to amend the Constitution shall be vested in a joint conference of the Legislative and Control Yuan. The proposed amendments should be passed by that body in which is vested the right to elect the President of the National Government.

III. PERSONAL STATEMENT BY THE SPECIAL REPRESENTATIVE OF THE PRESIDENT (MARSHALL), JANUARY 7, 1947.

The President has recently given a summary of the developments in China during the past year and the position of the American Government toward China. Circumstances now dictate that I should supplement this with impressions gained at first hand.

In this intricate and confused situation, I shall merely endeavor here to touch on some of the more important considerations—as they appeared to me—during my connection with the negotiations to bring about peace in China and a stable democratic form of government.

In the first place, the greatest obstacle to peace has been the complete, almost overwhelming suspicion with which the Chinese Communist Party and the Kuomintang regard each other.

On the one hand, the leaders of the Government are strongly opposed to a communistic form of government. On the other, the Communists frankly state that they are Marxists and intend to work toward establishing a communistic form of government in China, though first advancing through the medium of a democratic form of government of the American or British type.

The leaders of the Government are convinced in their minds that the Communist-expressed desire to participate in a government of the type endorsed by the Political Consultative Conference last January had for its purpose only a destructive intention. The Communists felt, I believe, that the government was insincere in its apparent acceptance of the PCC resolutions for the formation of the new government and intended by coercion of military force and the action of secret police to obliterate the Communist Party. Combined with this mutual deep distrust was the conspicuous error by both parties of ignoring the effect of the fears and suspicions of the other party in estimating the reason for proposals or opposition regarding the settlement of various matters under negotiation. They each sought only to take counsel of their own fears. They both, therefore, to that extent took a rather lopsided view of each situation and were susceptible to every evil suggestion or possibility. This complication was exaggerated to an explosive degree by the confused reports of fighting on the distant and tremendous fronts of hostile military contact. Patrol clashes were deliberately magnified into large offensive actions. The distortion of the facts was utilized by both sides to heap condemnation on the other. It was only through the reports of American officers in the field teams from Executive Headquarters that I could get even a partial idea of what was actually happening and the incidents were too numerous and the distances too great for the American personnel to cover all of the ground. I must comment here on the superb courage of the officers of our Army and Marines in struggling against almost insurmountable and maddening obstacles to bring some measure of peace to China.

I think the most important factors involved in the recent breakdown of negotiations are these: On the side of the National Government, which is in effect the Kuomintang, there is a dominant group of reactionaries who have been opposed, in my opinion, to almost every effort I have made to influence the formation of a genuine coalition government. This has usually been under the cover of political or party action, but since the Party was the Government, this action, though subtle or indirect, has been devastating in its effect. They were quite frank in publicly stating their belief that cooperation by the Chinese Communist Party in the government was inconceivable and that only a policy of force could definitely settle the issue. This group includes military as well as political leaders.

On the side of the Chinese Communist Party there are, I believe, liberals as well as radicals, though this view is vigorously opposed by many who believe that the Chinese Communist Party discipline is too rigidly enforced to admit of such differences of viewpoint. Nevertheless, it has appeared to me that there is a definite liberal group among the Communists, especially of young men who have turned to the Communists in disgust at the corruption evident in the local governments—men who would put the interest of the Chinese people above ruthless measures to establish a Communist ideology in the immediate future. The dyed-in-the-wool Communists do not hesitate at the most drastic measures to gain their end as, for instance, the destruction of communications in order to wreck the economy of China and produce a situation that would facilitate the overthrow or collapse of the Government, without any regard to the immediate suffering of the people involved. They completely distrust the leaders of the Kuomintang and appear convinced that every Government proposal is designed to crush the Chinese Communist Party. I must say that the quite evidently inspired mob actions of last February and March, some within a few blocks of where I was then engaged in completing negotiations, gave the Communists good excuse for such suspicions.

However, a very harmful and immensely provocative phase of the Chinese Communist Party procedure has been in the character of its propaganda. I wish to state to the American people that in the deliberate misrepresentation and abuse of the action, policies and purposes of our Government this propaganda has been without regard for the truth, without any regard whatsoever for the facts, and has given plain evidence of a determined purpose to mislead the Chinese people and the world and to arouse a bitter hatred of Americans. It has been difficult to remain silent in the midst of such public abuse and wholesale disregard of facts, but a denial would merely lead to the necessity of daily denials; an intolerable course of action for an American official. In the interest of fairness, I must state that the Nationalist Government publicity agency has made numerous misrepresentations, though not of the vicious nature of the Communist propaganda. Incidentally, the Communist statements regarding the Anping incident which resulted in the death of three Marines and the wounding of twelve others were almost pure fabrication, deliberately representing a carefully arranged ambuscade of a Marine convoy with supplies for the maintenance of Executive Headquarters and some UNRRA supplies, as a defence against a Marine assault. The investigation of this incident was a tortuous procedure of delays and maneuvers to disguise the true and privately admitted facts of the case.

Sincere efforts to achieve settlement have been frustrated time and again by extremist elements of both sides. The agreements reached by the Political Consultative Conference a year ago were a liberal and forward-looking charter which then offered China a basis for peace and reconstruction. However, irreconcilable groups within the Kuomintang, interested in the preservation of their own feudal control of China, evidently had no real intention of implementing them. Though I speak as a soldier, I must here also deplore the dominating influence of the military. Their dominance accentuates the weakness of civil government in China. At the same time, in pondering the situation in China, one must have clearly in mind not the workings of small Communist groups or committees to which we are accustomed in America, but rather of millions of people and an army of more than a million men.

I have never been in a position to be certain of the development of attitudes in the innermost Chinese Communist circles. Most certainly, the course which the Chinese Communist Party has pursued in recent months indicated an unwillingness to make a fair compromise. It has been impossible even to get them to sit down at a conference table with Government representatives to discuss given issues. Now the Communists have broken off negotiations by their last offer which demanded the dissolution of the National Assembly and a return to the military positions of January 13th which the Government could not be expected to accept.

Between this dominant reactionary group in the Government and the irreconcilable Communists who, I must state, did not so appear last February, lies the problem of how peace and well-being are to be brought to the long-suffering and presently inarticulate mass of the people of China. The reactionaries in the Government have evidently counted on substantial American support regardless of their actions. The Communists by their unwillingness to compromise in the national interest are evidently counting on an economic collapse to bring about the fall of the Government, accelerated by extensive guerrilla action against the long lines of rail communications—regardless of the cost in suffering to the Chinese people.

The salvation of the situation, as I see it, would be the assumption of leadership by the liberals in the Government and in the minority parties, a splendid group of men, but who as yet lack the political power to exercise a controlling influence. Successful action on their part under the leadership of Generalissimo Chiang Kai-shek would, I believe, lead to unity through good government.

In fact, the National Assembly has adopted a democratic constitution which in all major respects is in accordance with the principles laid down by the all-party Political Consultative Conference of last January. It is unfortunate that the Communists did not see fit to participate in the Assembly since the constitution that has been adopted seems to include every major point that they wanted.

Soon the Government in China will undergo major reorganization pending the coming into force of the constitution following elections to be completed before Christmas Day 1947. Now that the form for a democratic China has been laid down by the newly adopted constitution, practical measures will be the test. It remains to be seen to what extent the Government will give substance to the form by a genuine welcome of all groups actively to share in the responsibility of government.

The first step will be the reorganization of the State Council and the executive branch of Government to carry on administration pending the enforcement of the constitution. The manner in which this is done and the amount of representation accorded to liberals and to non-Kuomintang members will be significant. It is also to be hoped that during this interim period the door will remain open for Communists or other groups to participate if they see fit to assume their share of responsibility for the future of China.

It has been stated officially and categorically that the period of political tutelage under the Kuomintang is at the end. If the termination of one-party rule is to be a reality, the Kuomintang should cease to receive financial support from the Government.

I have spoken very frankly because in no other way can I hope to bring the people of the United States to even a partial understanding of this complex problem. I have expressed all these views privately in the course of negotiations; they are well known, I think, to most of the individuals concerned. I express them now publicly, as it is my duty, to present my estimate of the situation and its possibilities to the American people who have a deep interest in the development of conditions in the Far East promising an enduring peace in the Pacific.

IV. STATEMENT BY PRESIDENT TRUMAN ON UNITED STATES POLICY TOWARD CHINA, DECEMBER 18, 1946.

Last December I made a statement of this Government's views regarding China. We believed then and do now that a united and democratic China is of the utmost importance to world peace, that a broadening of the base of the National Government to make it representative of the Chinese people will further China's progress toward this goal, and that China has a clear responsibility to the other United Nations to eliminate armed conflict within its territory as constituting a threat to world stability and peace. It was made clear at Moscow last year that these views are shared by our Allies, Great Britain and the Soviet Union. On December 27th, Mr. Byrnes, Mr. Molotov and Mr. Bevin issued a statement which said, in part:

"The three Foreign Secretaries exchanged views with regard to the situation in China. They were in agreement as to the need for a unified and democratic China under the National Government for broad participation by democratic elements in all branches of the National Government, and for a cessation of civil strife. They affirmed their adherence to the policy of non-interference in the internal affairs of China."

The policies of this Government were also made clear in my statement of last December. We recognized the National Government of the Republic of China as the legal government. We undertook to assist the Chinese Government in reoccupation of the liberated areas and in disarming and repatriating the Japanese invaders. And finally, as China moved toward peace and unity along the lines mentioned, we were prepared to assist the Chinese economically and in other ways.

I asked General Marshall to go to China as my representative. We had agreed upon my statement of the United States Government's views and policies regarding China as his directive. He knew full well in undertaking the mission that halting civil strife, broadening the base of the Chinese Government and bringing about a united, democratic China were tasks for the Chinese themselves. He went as a great American to make his outstanding abilities available to the Chinese.

During the war, the United States entered into an agreement with the Chinese Government regarding the training and equipment of a special force of 39 divisions. That training ended V-J Day and the transfer of the equipment had been largely completed when General Marshall arrived.

The United States, the United Kingdom and the Union of Soviet Socialist Republics all committed themselves to the liberation of China, including the return of Manchuria to Chinese control. Our Government had agreed to assist the Chinese Government in the reoccupation of areas liberated from the Japanese, including Manchuria, because of China's lack of shipping and transport planes. Three armies were moved by air and eleven by sea, to central China, Formosa, north China and Manchuria. Most of these moves had been made or started when General Marshall arrived.

The disarming and evacuation of Japanese progressed slowly—too slowly. We regarded our commitment to assist the Chinese in this program as of overwhelming importance to the future peace of China and the whole Far East. Surrendered but undefeated Japanese armies and hordes of administrators, technicians, and Japanese merchants, totalling about 3,000,000 persons, had to be removed under the most difficult conditions. At the request of the Chinese Government we had retained a considerable number of American troops in China, and immediately after V-J Day we landed a corps of Marines in north China. The principal task of these forces was to assist in the evacuation of Japanese. Only some 200,000 had been returned to Japan by the time General Marshall arrived.

General Marshall also faced a most unpropitious internal situation on his arrival in China. Communications throughout the country were badly disrupted due to destruction during the war and the civil conflicts which had broken out since. This disruption was preventing the restoration of Chinese economy, the distribution of relief supplies, and was rendering the evacuation of Japanese a slow and difficult process. The wartime destruction of factories and plants, the war-induced inflation in China, the Japanese action in shutting down the economy of occupied China immediately after V-J Day, and finally the destruction of communications combined to paralyze the economic life of the country, spreading untold hardship to millions, robbing the victory over the Japanese of significance to most Chinese and seriously aggravating all the tensions and discontents that existed in China.

Progress toward solution of China's internal difficulties by the Chinese themselves was essential to the rapid and effective completion of most of the programs in which we had already pledged our assistance to the Chinese Government. General Marshall's experience and wisdom were available to the Chinese in their efforts to reach such solutions.

Events moved rapidly upon General Marshall's arrival. With all parties availing themselves of his impartial advice, agreement for a country-wide truce was reached and announced on January 10th. A feature of this agreement was the establishment of a unique organization, the Executive Headquarters in Peiping. It was realized that due to poor communications and the bitter feelings on local fronts, generalized orders to cease fire and withdraw might have little chance of being carried out unless some authoritative executive agency, trusted by both sides, could function in any local situation.

The Headquarters operated under the leaders of three commissioners—one American who served as chairman, one Chinese Government representative, and one representative of the Chinese Communist Party. Mr. Walter S. Robertson, Charge d'Affaires of the American Embassy in China, served as chairman until his return to this country in the fall. In order to carry out its function in the field, Executive Headquarters formed a large number of truce teams, each headed by one American officer, one Chinese Government officer, and one Chinese Communist officer. They proceeded to all danger spots where fighting was going on or seemed impending and saw to the implementation of the truce terms, often under conditions imposing exceptional hardships and requiring courageous action. The degree of cooperation attained between Government and Communist officers in the Headquarters and on the truce teams was a welcome proof that despite two decades of fighting, these two Chinese groups could work together.

Events moved forward with equal promise on the political front. On January 10th, the Political Consultative Conference began its sessions with representatives of the Kuomintang or Government Party, the Communist Party and several minor political parties participating. Within three weeks of direct discussion these groups had come to a series of statesmanlike agreements on outstanding political and military problems. The agreements provided for an interim government of a coalition type with representation of all parties, for revision of the Draft Constitution along democratic lines prior to its discussion and adoption by a National Assembly and for reduction of the Government and Communist armies and their eventual amalgamation into a small modernized truly national army responsible to a civilian government.

In March, General Marshall returned to this country. He reported on the important step the Chinese had made toward peace and unity in arriving at these agreements. He also pointed out that these agreements could not be satisfactorily implemented and given substance unless China's economic disintegration were checked and particularly unless the transportation system could be put in working order. Political unity could not be built on economic chaos. This Government had already authorized certain minor credits to the Chinese Government in an effort to meet emergency rehabilitation needs as it was doing for other war devastated countries throughout the world. A total of approximately $66,000,000 was involved in six specific projects, chiefly for the purchase of raw cotton, and for ships and railroad repair material. But these emergency measures were inadequate. Following the important forward step made by the Chinese in the agreements as reported by General Marshall, the Export-Import Bank earmarked a total of $500,000,000 for possible additional credits on a project by project basis to Chinese Government agencies and private enterprises. Agreement to extend actual credits for such projects would obviously have to be based upon this Government's policy as announced December 15, 1945. So far, this $500,000,000 remains earmarked, but unexpended.

While comprehensive large scale aid has been delayed, this Government has completed its wartime lend-lease commitments to China. Lend-lease assistance was extended to China to assist her in fighting the Japanese, and later to fulfill our promise to assist in re-occupying the country from the Japanese. Assistance took the form of goods and equipment and of services. Almost half the total made available to China consisted of services, such as those involved in air and water transportation of troops. According to the latest figures reported, lend-lease assistance to China up to V-J Day totalled approximately $870,000,000. From V-J Day to the end of February, shortly after General Marshall's arrival, the total was approximately $600,000,000—mostly in transportation costs. Thereafter, the program was reduced to the fulfillment of outstanding commitments, much of which was later suspended.

A considerable quantity of civilian goods has also been made available by our agreement with China for the disposal of surplus property which enabled us to liquidate a sizable indebtedness and to dispose of large quantities of surplus material. During the war the Chinese Government furnished Chinese currency to the United States Army for use in building its installations, feeding the troops, and other expenses. By the end of the war this indebtedness amounted to something like 150,000,000,000 Chinese dollars. Progressive currency inflation in China rendered it impossible to determine the exact value of the sum in United States currency.

China agreed to buy all surplus property owned by the United States in China and on seventeen Pacific Islands and bases with certain exceptions. Six months of negotiations preceded the agreement finally signed in August. It was imperative that this matter be concluded in the Pacific as had already been done in Europe, especially in view of the rapid deterioration of the material in open storage under tropical conditions and the urgent need for the partial alleviation of the acute economic distress of the Chinese people which it was hoped this transaction would permit. Aircraft, all non-demilitarized combat material, and fixed installations outside of China were excluded. Thus, no weapons which could be used in fighting a civil war were made available through this agreement.

The Chinese Government cancelled all but 30,000,000 United States dollars of our indebtedness for the Chinese currency, and promised to make available the equivalent of 35,000,000 United States dollars for use in paying United States governmental expenses in China and acquiring and improving buildings and properties for our diplomatic and consular establishments. An additional sum of 20,000,000 United States dollars is also designated for the fulfillment of a cultural and educational program.

Before General Marshall arrived in China for the second time, in April, there was evidence that the truce agreement was being disregarded. The sincere and unflagging efforts of Executive Headquarters and its truce teams have succeeded in many instances in preventing or ending local engagements and thus saved thousands of lives. But fresh outbreaks of civil strife continued to occur, reaching a crisis of violence in Manchuria with the capture of Changchun by the Communists and where the presence of truce teams had not been fully agreed to by the National Government.

A change in the course of events in the political field was equally disappointing. Negotiations between the Government and the Communists have been resumed again and again, but they have as often broken down. Although hope for final success has never disappeared completely, the agreements made in January and February have not been implemented, and the various Chinese groups have not since that time been able to achieve the degree of agreement reached at the Political Consultative Conference.

There has been encouraging progress in other fields, particularly the elimination of Japanese from China. The Chinese Government was responsible under an Allied agreement for the disarmament of all Japanese military personnel and for the repatriation of all Japanese civilians and military personnel from China, Formosa and French Indo-China north of the sixteenth degree of latitude. Our Government agreed to assist the Chinese in this task. The scope of the job was tremendous. There were about 3,000,000 Japanese, nearly one-half of them Army or Navy personnel to be evacuated. Water and rail transportation had been destroyed or was immobilized. Port facilities were badly damaged and overcrowded with relief and other supplies. The Japanese had to be disarmed, concentrated and then transported to the nearest available port. In some instances this involved long distances. At the ports they had to be individually searched and put through a health inspection. All had to be inoculated. Segregation camps had to be established at the ports to cope with the incidence of epidemic diseases such as Asiatic cholera. Finally, 3,000,000 persons had to be moved by ship to Japan.

American forces helped in the disarmament of Japanese units. Executive Headquarters and its truce teams were able to make the complicated arrangements necessary to transfer Japanese across lines and through areas involved in civil conflict on their way to ports of embarkation. American units also participated in the inspections at the port, while American medical units supervised all inoculation and other medical work. Finally, American and Japanese ships under the control of General MacArthur in Japan, and a number of United States Navy ships under the Seventh Fleet transported this enormous number of persons to reception ports in Japan.

At the end of last year, approximately 200,000 Japanese had been repatriated. They were leaving Chinese ports at a rate of about 2,500 a day. By March of this year, rapidly increased efforts on the part of the American forces and the Chinese authorities involved had increased this rate to more than 20,000 a day. By November, 2,986,438 Japanese had been evacuated and the program was considered completed. Except for indeterminate numbers in certain parts of Manchuria, only war criminals and technicians retained on an emergency basis by the Chinese Government remain. That this tremendous undertaking has been accomplished despite conflict, disrupted communications and other difficulties will remain an outstanding example of successful American-Chinese cooperation toward a common goal.

Much has been said of the presence of United States armed forces in China during the past year. Last fall these forces were relatively large. They had to be. No one could prophesy in advance how well the Japanese forces in China would observe the surrender terms. We had to provide forces adequate to assist the Chinese in the event of trouble. When it became obvious that the armed Japanese would not be a problem beyond the capabilities of the Chinese Armies to handle, redeployment was begun at once.

The chief responsibility of our forces was that of assisting in evacuation of Japanese. This task was prolonged by local circumstances. Provision of American personnel for the Executive Headquarters and its truce teams has required a fairly large number of men, particularly since the all important network of radio and other communications was provided entirely by the United States. The Executive Headquarters is located at Peiping, a hundred miles from the sea and in an area where there was the possibility of local fighting. Hence, another responsibility was to protect the line of supply to and from Headquarters. Another duty our forces undertook immediately upon the Japanese surrender was to provide the necessary protection so that coal from the great mines northeast of Tientsin could reach the sea for shipment to supply the cities and railroads of central China. This coal was essential to prevent the collapse of this industrial area. Our Marines were withdrawn from this duty last September. Other units of our forces were engaged in searching for the bodies or graves of American soldiers who had died fighting the Japanese in China. Still others were required to guard United States installations and stores of equipment, and to process these for return to this country or sale as surplus property.

At peak strength a year ago we had some 113,000 soldiers, sailors and marines in China. Today this number is being reduced to less than 12,000, including some 2,000 directly concerned with the operations of Executive Headquarters and will be further reduced to the number required to supply and secure the American personnel of Executive Headquarters and the air field and stores at Tsingtao.

Thus during the past year we have successfully assisted in the repatriation of the Japanese and have subsequently been able to bring most of our own troops home. We have afforded appropriate assistance in the reoccupation of the country from the Japanese. We have undertaken some emergency measures of economic assistance to prevent the collapse of China's economy and have liquidated our own wartime financial account with China.

It is a matter of deep regret that China has not yet been able to achieve unity by peaceful methods. Because he knows how serious the problem is, and how important it is to reach a solution, General Marshall has remained at his post even though active negotiations have been broken off by the Communist Party. We are ready to help China as she moves toward peace and genuine democratic government.

The views expressed a year ago by this Government are valid today. The plan for political unification agreed to last February is sound. The plan for military unification of last February has been made difficult of implementation by the progress of the fighting since last April, but the general principles involved are fundamentally sound.

China is a sovereign nation. We recognize that fact and we recognize the National Government of China. We continue to hope that the Government will find a peaceful solution. We are pledged not to interfere in the internal affairs of China. Our position is clear. While avoiding involvement in their civil strife, we will persevere with our policy of helping the Chinese people to bring about peace and economic recovery in their country.

As ways and means are presented for constructive aid to China, we will give them careful and sympathetic consideration. An example of such aid is the recent agricultural mission to China under Dean Hutchison of the University of California sent at the request of the Chinese Government. A joint Chinese-American Agricultural Collaboration Commission was formed which included the Hutchison mission. It spent over four months studying rural problems. Its recommendations are now available to the Chinese Government, and so also is any feasible aid we can give in implementing those recommendations. When conditions in China improve, we are prepared to consider aid in carrying out other projects, unrelated to civil strife, which would encourage economic reconstruction and reform in China and which, in so doing, would promote a general revival of commercial relations between American and Chinese businessmen.

We believe that our hopes for China are identical with what the Chinese people themselves most earnestly desire. We shall therefore continue our positive and realistic policy toward China which is based on full respect for her national sovereignty and on our traditional friendship for the Chinese people and is designed to promote international peace.

Index

John Leighton Stuart was born in Hangchow, China, in 1876, the son of an American missionary. When he was eleven years old, he came to the United States and a few years later entered Pantops Academy at Charlottesville, Virginia. He graduated from Hampden-Sydney College in 1896 and returned to Pantops to teach Latin and Greek for three years. He then attended the Union Theological Seminary, Richmond, Virginia, graduating in 1902.

In 1904 he married Miss Aline Rodd of New Orleans, Louisiana, and in December of that year, he and Mrs. Stuart arrived in Hangchow, China, as missionaries of the Southern Presbyterian Church. Their son, J. L. Stuart, Jr., was born two years later. Dr. Stuart joined the faculty of the Nanking Theological Seminary in 1907, and while at Nanking published a Greek-Chinese-English Dictionary of the New Testament as well as a number of commentaries on books of the New Testament in Chinese.

He was elected the first President of Yenching University in 1919 and served in that position until 1946, when President Truman appointed him United States Ambassador to the Republic of China.

Dr. Stuart has received honorary degrees from Princeton University and from Austin College. He was awarded in 1946 the Special First Class Order of Merit, the highest honor awarded by the Republic of China.

He has traveled extensively in North America and Europe, and in every province of China. He has been an active sportsman, particularly enjoying swimming, hiking, mountain climbing.

Dr. Stuart now lives in Washington, D. C.

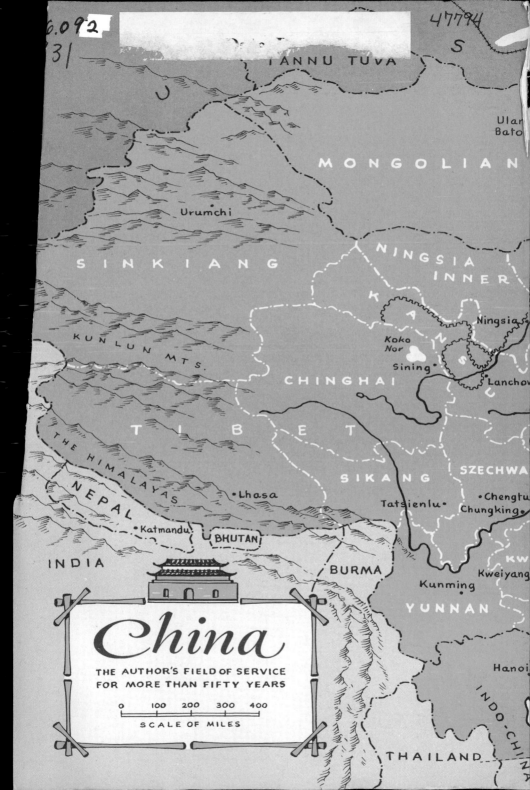

TANNU TUVA

Ular
Bato

MONGOLIAN

Urumchi

SINKIANG

NINGSIA

INNER

KUN LUN MTS.

Koko
Nor

Sining

Ningsia

Lanchow

CHINGHAI

T   I   B   E   T

THE HIMALAYAS

SIKANG

SZECHWA

NEPAL

Lhasa

Tatsienlu

Chengtu

Chungking

Katmandu

BHUTAN

INDIA

BURMA

KW

Kweiyang

Kunming

YUNNAN

China

**THE AUTHOR'S FIELD OF SERVICE
FOR MORE THAN FIFTY YEARS**

0   100   200   300   400

SCALE OF MILES

Hanoi

INDO-CH

THAILAND